The Ripple Effect

*The 7 Most Important
Decisions of Each Day*

Clay Waters

WestBow
PRESS
A DIVISION OF THOMAS NELSON

ISBN: 978-1-4497-6280-3 (sc)
ISBN: 978-1-4497-6281-0 (e)
ISBN: 978-1-4497-6279-7 (hc)

Library of Congress Control Number: 2012914376

WestBow Press books may be ordered through booksellers or by contacting:

WestBow Press
A Division of Thomas Nelson
1663 Liberty Drive
Bloomington, IN 47403
www.westbowpress.com
1-(866) 928-1240

Printed in the United States of America

WestBow Press rev. date: 10/16/2012

Acknowledgements

THIS BOOK CULMINATES A LONG process that has been a team effort. I wish to thank several individuals who have played a major part throughout this endeavor.

I am extremely thankful for my wife, Caryn. Had it not been for her support, *The Ripple Effect* would have only stayed an idea. She allowed me the time to turn the idea of the book into a reality. I am eternally grateful for my wife's encouragement and support.

I also owe a word of thanksgiving to my two sons, Graham and Lawson. They made at least two contributions to me as I worked on the book. First, they made sacrifices by sharing dad with his research and writing. Secondly, and most importantly, when I was stressed and strained by a blank screen or an evading thought, I knew I could spend time with Graham and Lawson to put this project in its proper perspective. Playing baseball in the yard, or going outside to swing helped me to remember that my family is my most valuable resource.

I wish to thank Bob and Emma Smart, who provided a place to write when I needed a quiet place to think. Their lake house proved to be a beautiful change of scenery. My parents have been a constant source of support and encouragement. Their quiet confidence in me and their unceasing prayers have under girded the completion of the book.

And what can I say about the congregation who has allowed me to partner with them in creating our own set of ripples. The people at Grey Stone are the greatest people in the world. Their love and support is something for which I thank God every single day.

Contents

Decision 1: How Will I Face My Challenges Today?

Chapter 1

When Life Isn't Blowing You Kisses

"DADDY, WILL IT HURT?" I can't tell you how many times I've had to answer this piercing question. I would give my classic answer, "I don't think so, son," and then, glancing up in my rear-view mirror, I could see crocodile tears trickling down his cheeks. Then, moments later, I could feel hot tears streaming down my own cheeks. In my mind, I knew I had just told a little white lie to try to comfort my son. "Daddy, will it hurt?" is a haunting question that has led me to grapple with a whole host of other questions, questions I thought I had already settled: "Is God really in control?"; "If God is all loving, why all the suffering?"; "Does God really answer prayer?"; "Can I fully trust God?" Like a Coke bottle rolling back and forth in the floorboard of my car, these questions were continually spinning around in my head. I thought I had already answered these questions academically, but now I had to wrestle with them personally. My test-tube theology was suddenly shattered by life.

Both of my sons, Graham and Lawson, have a genetic disease called tuberous sclerosis. This disease causes benign tumors to grow in the brain and on other vital organs such as the kidneys, heart, eyes, lungs, and skin. It creates a plethora of problems like seizures, mental retardation, developmental delay, behavioral problems, skin abnormalities, and kidney disease. Because the disease affects multiple organs, we are no strangers to doctor appointments. As we've managed the disease, we've consulted with geneticists, neurologists, neurosurgeons, cardiologists, nephrologists, ophthalmologists, pediatric psychiatrists, plastic surgeons, and general pediatricians. With virtually each doctor's appointment, I've had to face the same haunting question, "Daddy, will this hurt?"

The disease varies from individual to individual, with symptoms ranging from very mild to quite severe. Though both of my sons have their unique challenges with the disease, my older son, Graham, faces the greatest challenge with tuberous sclerosis. His frequent seizures have reduced his quality of life greatly. There are different kinds of seizures; Graham has tonic-clonic seizures. Basically, this means when Graham has a seizure, if he is standing, he will fall to the ground. Some people who have this kind of epilepsy will become aware of an oncoming seizure up to several minutes before the full seizure begins. This is called an "aura" and often gives the person time to sit down and to find safety before the full onslaught of the seizure begins. Unfortunately, Graham doesn't experience "auras," so he has no forewarning when a seizure will occur. At the height of Graham's grand mal seizures, he would have six to eight seizures a day. With these kinds of seizures, the mathematical odds for injury are stacked against him.

I recall eating in a cafeteria with the whole family. We had gone through the buffet line and had our trays full of food. Caryn, my wife, had a tray, and I was carrying a tray. Normally, we always hold Graham's hand just to be safe. Since we both had trays, we figured we could make it just a few steps to our table, without holding Graham's hand. Unfortunately, about half way to our table, Graham had a seizure. He fell straight back, hitting his head on the concrete floor. A seizure is like a terrorist attack on the brain; we never know when the next one will occur.

One day Graham was upstairs, playing on the computer. He decided he wanted to come downstairs to check on his younger brother. As he started down the stairs, without any warning, he had a seizure. For the rest of my life, I will have etched in my psyche the terrible sound of Graham falling down the entire flight of stairs. One morning, Graham was having breakfast, innocently eating a bowl of cereal. I prepared his cereal, sat him down, and then walked out of the room for a few minutes. When I returned, Graham's head was face down in his cereal. His nose was buried in his milk. Another seizure had attacked him. A few more minutes, and Graham could have easily drowned in his bowl of cereal. I could fill this whole book with non-stop stories about falls that have taken place at home, school, church, restaurants, and ballgames. Name a place, and we've most likely had a fall there. Falls are not pretty. Having to watch your son endure bloody noses, black eyes, swollen bruises, open cuts, and an endless stream of tears, eventually takes its toll. I'm not the only dad who could vouch for that.

Meet one of my good friends. I suppose I can identify with him more than any character in the Bible. In Mark 9, a desperate dad brings his son to Jesus. An evil spirit torments this man's son. The father tells Jesus the horrific details of what he has to watch his son go through every day. He says, "Whenever this evil spirit seizes him, it throws him violently to the ground and makes him foam at the mouth and grind his teeth and become rigid" (Mark 9:18). It's a textbook description of a seizure. He tells Jesus about watching his son fall into the fire and water. I've had the same front-row seat as this dad. It's a front-row seat I wish didn't exist. When you watch your child suffer each day, it's like a never-ending blow to the gut. Take it from someone who knows; by the time this dad gets to Jesus, he is desperate. In effect, he says, "Jesus, this is my son. Why do I have to watch him suffer like this?" "Why can't he be like the other kids who get to play little league baseball?" "Why can't he enjoy riding a bike without the fear of a crippling violent attack?" Then this dad makes a request that I've also made on many occasions, "Do something if you can" (Mark 9:22).

As we move toward handling the problems of each day, I want you to know I've had a few of my own. The disease that both of my sons have has forced me to examine my approach toward my own problems. Just for the record, I'm still on the journey. I don't always have the right perspective on my problems. I'm growing just like you, but out of my own struggles, I've gained some valuable insights I hope will be helpful to you.

Why Do Problems Exist?

Let's start with a basic question: Why do problems exist? If you don't get this right, typically you end up landing in a pile of mental poop somewhere. Problems exist because the world is broken. Genesis 3 paints the picture of a pivotal turn in history. Satan slithers his way onto the pages of human history and tempts Adam and Eve. Adam, our first ancestor, buckles under the pressure and disobeys God. Scripture teaches that when Adam sins, somehow his sins come to damage the whole human race, not to mention all of creation. When he sins, we all are plunged into a state of sin, brokenness, and selfishness. In theology, this teaching is known as "original sin." [1]

Before this tragic turning point, God looks at everything He had made and proclaims that it is good. It's hard for us to imagine a world only colored by goodness and perfection. But there was a time when everything was perfect and problem-free. No colds, no flus, no car accidents, no funerals, and no cancer existed. There was no need for Kleenex, morphine, or Tylenol. There were no seizures, no surgeries, no endless trips to the ER. But after the fall, all of human history was hurled from a state of goodness into a state of brokenness. The natural world went from a state of paradise and perfection to a state of decay and disappointment.

Romans 8:20-22 says, "Against its will, everything on earth was subjected to God's curse. All creation anticipates the day when it will join God's children in glorious freedom from death and decay. For we know that all creation has been groaning as in the pains of childbirth right up to the present time." There you have it. The world is not the way it's supposed to be because it's not in its original condition. It has been subjected to the effects of the fall. Now, decay, disease, and disappointment taint the whole world. All of creation has been "groaning as in the pains of childbirth" to be delivered from this broken condition. Scripture uses a striking and graphic image of childbirth to describe the pain and suffering of a damaged world.

I'm so glad God gave the "birthing children" assignment to ladies. When my older son was born, I missed the whole event. My wife had traveled to Knoxville, Tennessee, to spend a few days with her family before the baby was born. Before leaving, she had gone to the doctor to ask if the hour and a half plane ride would cause a problem. The doctor had assured her there should be no problem

---

1   See Romans 5:12 and 1 Corinthians 15:22

with such a short flight, but just to be safe, he had told her to take along her medical records. Those are now famous last words in our family! Caryn made it to Knoxville just fine, but after a couple of days, her water suddenly broke. This was six weeks earlier than when the "schedule" said it was supposed to break. Without any delay, Caryn's parents rushed her to the hospital.

En route to the hospital, Caryn's father had the presence of mind to call and tell me a baby was on its way and so was Dad. I rushed home, threw some clothes in the car, and was on my way to Knoxville to be there when my son was born. For seven hours, I drove like an insane maniac. The whole way I rehearsed my speech to the highway patrolman, just in case I got pulled over. Fortunately, I never saw those infamous blueberry and strawberry lights in my rearview mirror, but neither did I get to see my son's birth. I was 2 hours late. I was extremely disappointed I wasn't there, and for the longest time, missing my son's birth really bothered me. That is, until I witnessed the birth of my second child; then I was no longer bothered. Actually, witnessing the birth was a joy (well, not exactly, I put that in here to make my wife happy.) It was the "groanings of childbirth" that freaked me out.

I was at the hospital visiting someone in my church when my cell phone rang. It was my wife. She immediately said, "Clay, where are you?" I said, "I'm at the hospital." She said, "Get home as fast as you can; that's where I need to be!" Our house was 30 minutes away. Since I was used to driving like a maniac in situations like this, I made it back in record time. I helped my wife into the car and turned around for the 30 minute drive back to the hospital. I decided I was not going to scare my wife by driving in emergency mode, so I tried to be calm and collected. I did really good for a few minutes, until my wife screamed out with the loudest groan I've ever heard. I had flashbacks to my days as a youngster watching *The Incredible Hulk*.

Within seconds, I relapsed. I fell back to what I knew best—my insane maniac driving skills. "The groans" took me to a whole new level of driving ability I never knew I had. I turned on my blinkers and figured I could use the same speech I had memorized years earlier, should I have a vision of strawberries and blueberries in my rear view mirror. My wife shrilled, screamed, cried, and groaned the whole trip to the hospital. By the time we made it to the hospital, I was an emotional basket case. An hour and a half later, my wife gave birth to our second son. It was a stand still moment, one that will be planted in my memory for a lifetime. There's one other memory I will carry to my grave. I will never forget the sheer horror of hearing my wife groan and moan all the way to the hospital.

Scripture uses this picturesque language to describe the pain and suffering of our fallen world. Like a woman groaning because of severe labor pains, the world groans to be freed from its fallen condition. The world groans to be free from the disease, decay, and disappointment ultimately brought about by the consequences of Adam's sin. Remember, the world is not the way it's supposed to be. Because we live in a fallen world, we can expect a steady diet of hardships and problems. The human mind naturally craves an explanation for our human dilemmas. Why is it that we can barely make it 24 hours without having to grapple with a perplexing problem? Now you know. You are on earth, not in heaven. As long as you live on earth, you will experience the effects of a broken world.

Your Mental Reference Point

This truth becomes a mental frame of reference to help you filter your problems. If you don't frame your problems within the wider context of a fallen world, you are more likely to become bitter and frustrated by your circumstances. Without an understanding of how suffering came into the world, little in life will make sense, especially your problems.

Let's embrace the brutal facts. Living a problem-free life is not going to happen, even if you pay your taxes, are nice to your mother-in-law, and always eat your vegetables. Trust me, we lost our chance at a problem-free life the moment we breathed our first breath. James reminds us to "count it all joy when you fall into various trials" (James 1:2). Two of the most important words in this verse are "when" and "fall." James says it's not a matter of "if" you will face trials; it's just a matter of when. He also says we can expect to "fall" into trials. This is what makes a trial a trial. You fall into it. You're minding your own business, thinking it's going to be a normal, routine day. Then, without any warning, you fall into a trial. Problems are typically not planned. You don't wake up and find them scheduled in Outlook. You don't find them written down on your list of "Things to Do."

We seldom anticipate the problems we're going to experience in life. This is probably a good thing because if we could anticipate trials, we would be scared to death, simply by knowing we were going to have to face them. We would spend a lot of emotional energy worrying about the trial before it ever arrived. Therefore, in His infinite wisdom, God allows the vast majority of trials to be unplanned and unpredictable. We don't plan to have a child with an illness; we don't plan to get a pink slip when we show up for work on Monday; we don't plan for the car to break down on the way to our summer vacation. It just happens and it happens unexpectedly. Some trials are minor inconveniences. You get stuck in traffic. You have a runny nose. Your teenage daughter has the blues because her boyfriend broke up with her. Deadlines and demands at work are spiking your stress level.

Other trials come in the form of a major crisis. Your wife is diagnosed with cancer, and the odds are stacked against her. Your husband announces he's packing his bags and moving in with a younger woman. Your banker tells you that your business is probably going to go belly up. Whether they are minor or major, trials often catch us by surprise. Job 5:7 says, "Man is born for trouble just as the sparks fly upward." Light a fire and watch what naturally happens. The sparks fly upward. God says it's just as natural for us to have problems. If you're facing a trial, its proof positive you are a card carrying member of the human race. Interestingly, I've heard people try to sound super spiritual by saying, "God, I really want to grow in my faith so I ask you to send me some trials." Let me tell you what I've discovered. You don't have to pray for trials. They're coming whether you ask for them or not.

The apostle Paul was probably the greatest Christian who ever lived. Yet Paul's life was not all honey and no bees. Paul was well acquainted with suffering. In 2 Corinthians 12, he describes his suffering as a "thorn in his flesh." It wasn't a literal thorn, of course; otherwise he would have used a good pair of tweezers to take care of the problem. But tweezers couldn't remove this thorn. There has been a lot of speculation about what Paul was referring to when he mentions this thorn. Some have suggested it was poor eye sight, others have suggested it was epilepsy (I hope not), and others have really been creative by saying it was a bad wife. Interestingly, Paul never spells out in specific terms what this Achilles heel was in his life.

We do know that Paul repeatedly asked God to take it away. He kept going to God, and God kept giving him the same answer. "No, Paul, I know you want me to remove this, but I'm not going to remove it. Instead, I'm going to give you my grace." His exact words were, "My grace is sufficient for you" (2 Corin 12:9). God was promising to raise His level of grace to meet Paul's level of suffering. No matter how much Paul prayed for God to take away this thorn in his side, his circumstances were not changing. God didn't promise to change his circumstances; He promised to give Paul the grace to deal with his circumstances. God's sustaining grace gives us the strength to deal with things we can't change.

When our circumstances appear to be out of our control and we can't change them, they can begin to frustrate us and steal our peace. Go ahead and accept the fact that much of life is beyond your control. Worrying, becoming bitter, or having self-pity about what you can't change will never bring peace of mind. There is only one thing that will bring peace of mind, and it's accepting what can't be changed. Have you ever heard the Serenity Prayer? The first three lines are the most popular. It's something we should pray regularly: "God grant me the serenity to accept the things I cannot change, the courage to change the things I can, and the wisdom to know the difference."

When you go through an experience you don't like, do what you can to change the situation, but then accept what can't be changed. If you have a health problem, go to the best doctors you can find, and work to resolve your health problem. Yet, when you reach a certain point and nothing else can be done, accept what can't be changed. If you have a rebellious child, try to work with your child. Get the best advice you can from counselors. Some parents beat themselves up because their children are rebelling against them and God. As much as you would like to change your child's attitude, it's not something you can change. They are in control of their own attitudes.

If your spouse walks out on you, fight for your marriage, but understand you can't control their commitment to you. When you stood at the altar and said "till death do us part," you meant it, but that same enduring commitment is not something you can make for someone else. If you're spouse chooses to leave the marriage, at a certain point, you will have to accept what can't be changed.

One of the primary ways God uses to shape our character is through our circumstances—circumstances that are beyond our ability to change. God certainly uses His Word to make us more like Christ. He uses prayer and solitude to conform us into the image of Christ. God uses the impact of the local church and corporate worship to make us more like Christ, but God primarily works through our circumstances. Think about it. You can't read the Bible 12 hours a day, you can't pray 12 hours a day, and you can't stay at your church 12 hours a day, but God is working every hour of every day through your circumstances. God uses our circumstances more than anything else to make us more like Christ. Often the space and place in your life that is most difficult is where God does some of His greatest work.

For so many years now, I've been praying like Paul, "God, please take this away. Take my son's seizures away. I know you are powerful enough. Nothing is too difficult for you. Please take them away." Though I've pleaded with God, for whatever reason, God hasn't changed our circumstances by taking away Graham's seizures. He hasn't brought relief by removing the threat of the next seizure. But He has brought us relief. The relief has come in the form of His sustaining grace.

Don't get the impression grace means you no longer feel the full of weight of your problems. No, you feel the full weight of your problems; you're just not carrying the weight all by yourself. 2 Corinthians 12:9 is not just a nice, neat theological concept to me. This is not test tube theology for me; this is where I live each day. God's sustaining grace is one thing I know something about. When your circumstances are not changing the way you would like, God will raise His level of grace to meet your level of disappointment.

Don't get the idea I'm suggesting adversity is no big deal. It is a big deal. When we're tested, often the first emotion we experience is disappointment. If you apply for a job, but you don't get the job, you're disappointed. If you're child has rebelled and taken a major detour in life, you're disappointed. If you lost a big portion of your retirement when the stock market fell, you're disappointed. If you're starting to lose your health, you're disappointed. When a problem arises, be it small or great, disappointment is usually the first emotion we experience.

From Cautious Optimism To Shattered Dreams

After years of trying virtually every seizure medicine available, Graham has continued to have uncontrollable seizures, what is often called intractable epilepsy. Since the medicines were unsuccessful in controlling his seizures, we then embarked on a series of tests to evaluate whether or not surgery could eliminate his seizures. We spent 14 months of periodic testing to see what the data would reveal. The data from Duke University Medical Center and Detroit Children's Hospital seemed to indicate that Graham could benefit from brain surgery. Graham underwent two diagnostic brain surgeries where grids were placed over his brain. The diagnostic surgeries were supposed to help the doctors identify the major problem areas. Though Graham has multiple tubers on his brain, the data seemed to suggest the biggest offender was a dominate tuber on the right temporal region of his brain. The goal was clear; remove the tuber, along with a small section of the right temporal region of his brain, and eliminate the seizures.

Though no one likes to think about their child undergoing major brain surgery, my wife and I were extremely excited. We started dreaming about a whole new world of possibilities for Graham. We imagined him running and playing in the yard like he used to as a toddler, before his condition worsened. I caught myself daydreaming about taking him places and giving him the freedom to walk around on his own. I was excited about taking him to parks, arcades, ballgames, and not having to hold his hand the whole time and wondering in the back of my mind when the next seizure would strike. We were so excited about a greater quality of life for Graham and a greater sense of freedom for our family.

The prospect of surgery is something we had been praying about for well over a year. To hear Graham was a candidate for the surgery left us ecstatic. We also had tremendous confidence in the medical personnel who would be caring for Graham. We had one of the best neurological teams in the entire country. Because I pastor just a few blocks from Duke Medical Center where the surgery would occur, we felt as if we were right at home. Scores of people from my church work at the Medical Center so it was like we were surrounded by family. With faith in God, confidence in a world-renowned surgeon, and the prayer support of an incredible congregation, we were very much at peace with moving forward with the surgery.

I will always remember the drive to the hospital on the morning of Graham's surgery. On Monday morning, we got up at 5 a.m. so we could be at the hospital by 6 a.m. Graham and I made the trip together, and my wife was going to join us after she dropped our younger son off at school. As we got into the car, I reminded Graham where we were going. I said, "Graham, we're going to see the doctor today and he's going to do a procedure to keep you from having seizures." With sweating palms, I feared the haunting question I knew would be posed to me next. Sure enough, it came just as I expected, "Daddy, will it hurt?" With quivering lips, I told my classic white lie, "I don't think so, Son. I don't think so." As I drove to the hospital, I could feel my pulse pounding in my chest; I could also feel those same hot tears I had become so accustomed to feeling, streaming down my face.

His surgery was scheduled to begin at 8 a.m. The neurosurgeon would place a grid over Graham's brain to monitor where the seizures were coming from. The grid would stay in four days, and then the neurological team would go back in and remove the troubled part of his brain. The first surgery went well. Over the next five days, plenty of data was collected from the grid. After consulting with the neurosurgeon and the neurologist, there was enough evidence that indicated that Graham would benefit from the major brain surgery. With multiple tubers on his brain, they couldn't tell us for sure if the seizures would be eliminated entirely, but all arrows were pointing in the right direction.

Friday rolled around for the big day. After having prayer with the neurosurgeon, the medical team began the process of removing a portion of the right temporal region of Graham's brain. Though there was a measure of apprehension, it was swallowed up by a sense of excitement for Graham's future. Furthermore, a young man in our church had recently had brain surgery because of uncontrollable seizures, and we knew that since he had his surgery, he had been seizure free. Knowing his situation only added to our excitement.

The surgery went well, with no complications. Graham spent the first night in ICU, and then the next day he went to a regular room. During the first day in his regular room, I was sitting in Graham's room reading a book while he was sleeping. Out of the corner of my eye, I saw something that would send me into an emotional tailspin. It was an episode I had seen all too often—another seizure. To say I was disappointed would be the understatement of the century. I was devastated. I tried to recall the neurosurgeon's words before the surgery. He said, "Don't be alarmed if you see a few early seizures after surgery; it's common for that to happen." This gave me a little hope for the first few days; the only problem was, as the days passed, the seizures didn't stop. Graham continued to average four seizures a day with the same tonic-clonic response as before. The falling resumed, and with the falls, regular injuries continued to occur.

I was so disappointed with God. It didn't make sense to me. I found that familiar Coke bottle spinning around in my head again. This time, I was struggling with a new set of questions. "God, thousands of people have been praying for the success of this surgery; why didn't you answer?" "God, we're trying to live for you; is this what we get in return?" "God, you can't possibly take pleasure in seeing Graham suffer like this; why don't you turn the situation around?" These questions were like a little pebble caught in my shoe; they were irritating and annoying me at the deepest level.

I recall one trip home from the hospital. It was just days after Graham's surgery. Graham continued to have multiple seizures, and it was apparent the surgery didn't produce the outcome we were hoping for. As I was driving home, I became so overwhelmed and upset that I pulled my car under a bridge. I just sat in my car, with my face buried in the steering column, crying out to God. I felt so confused and so alone. After a few minutes, I reached over and decided to turn on the radio. At that very moment, when I felt so confused and so alone, I heard a song entitled, "You're Not Alone." It was a turning point for me. With His sustaining grace, God was reminding me I was not alone in my struggles. Even if Graham never improved, God would keep giving me the grace to deal with it. Though I still struggle watching Graham suffer, I also know our unaltered circumstances have had a profound impact on me. No one expressed this better than Philip Yancey, "Sometimes the only meaning we can offer a suffering person is the assurance that their suffering, which has no apparent meaning for them, has a meaning for us."[2]

Henri Nouwen was a renowned theologian. He taught theology at Yale and Harvard, and averaged writing a book every year. Amazingly, Henri Nouwen resigned his post at Harvard and went to serve at L'Arch, a home for the severely disabled. He worked at this special home outside of Toronto, Canada for the last 10 years of his life. At a certain point, Henri Nouwen was assigned to work with a young man named Adam. Adam was severely disabled. He couldn't talk. He couldn't walk. He was cognitively impaired. Yet every day, this giant theologian served this broken young man who could do nothing for him in return.

---

2   Philip Yancey, *Grace Notes* (Zondervan, 2009)195.

It took two hours in the morning just to get Adam ready for the day. Henri Nouwen spent time every day bathing him, shaving him, brushing his teeth, combing his hair, and feeding him his meals. Toward the end of his life, Henri Nouwen wrote a book entitled, *Adam*. It's a profound book about what it was like to serve Adam and how Adam had a gigantic impact on this world class theologian. Henri Nouwen said nothing impacted his spiritual life more and drew him closer to Christ like his time with Adam. No amount of time reading the Bible, no amount of time in prayer, and no amount of time studying or teaching theology in Ivy League schools impacted his life like his time with Adam.

In his book, Nouwen tells about a woman who was visiting L'Arch. When she saw Adam, she immediately walked up to him saying, "Poor man, poor man, why did this happen to you? Let me pray over you so that our dear Lord may heal you." She then signaled for one of the workers to make a circle around Adam for prayer. One of the other assistants gently spoke to her, "Adam doesn't need any healing; he is fine. He is just happy that you came for dinner. Please join us at the table." Nouwen commented that he had doubts as to whether this woman was ready to be touched by Adam or not. He wondered if she was ready to see his wholeness by his brokenness. She did quickly discover that everyone at L'Arch was very happy with Adam just the way he was. [3]

I am certainly no Henri Nouwen—that's for sure. However, I could certainly identify with him as he talked about Adam's impact on his life. In fact, while I was reading his book about Adam, I must confess I wasn't thinking about a young man named Adam. I was thinking about a little boy named Graham. I was thinking about my own son who is disabled, and how nothing has shaped my life more than having it intersect with Graham. Nothing has drawn me closer to Christ. Nothing has refined my values more. Nothing has clarified my vision for life more. More than any prayer retreat, theology book, or religion professor, nothing has led me to the person of Jesus like Graham. I'm convinced Graham was sent into

---

3   Henri Nouwen, *Adam* (Orbis Books, 1997) 68.

my life to witness to God's love and grace through his brokenness. Some children were sent into the world to be taught; others were sent into the world to teach. Graham happens to be in the second category. His unique mission is being fulfilled everyday in my life. One special little boy. One set of unchanged circumstances. One blessed dad.

CHAPTER 2

How to Live Through A Bad Day

WHAT DO YOU DO WHEN the odds are stacked against you? What do you do when the Law of Murphy is ruling the day (if something can go wrong, it will)? Have you ever had one of those days? Sometimes it seems as though the odds are 10 to 1 against you.

I will never forget taking a trip a handful of years ago. We were traveling from North Carolina to see my wife's parents who live in Tennessee. About half way there, my car broke down. I didn't hit the panic button because we were only about 45 minutes from my hometown. I called my dad, and he brought one of his cars so we could make the rest of the trip. The game plan was simple—while we were visiting in Tennessee, a mechanic would fix my car, and we could pick it up on our way back to North Carolina.

My dad brought me his car and we got back out on the interstate to finish our trip. After driving about an hour, just as we approached one of the steepest mountains in the state, smoke started billowing out of the engine. This was the car my dad brought me—two different cars, and two different break downs. By then, we were standing on the side of the Interstate. My wife was expecting our first child, and darkness was settling in for the night. Thankfully, a gentleman picked us up and took us to a convenient store.

While we were at the convenient store, I called a Christian conference center, which was located only two exits up from the store. I had been there on numerous occasions for different conferences. I told the lady at the conference center that I was in the ministry and I told her about our car breaking down. I also mentioned that my wife was pregnant and I needed to get her to a place where she could rest for the night. I graciously asked if we could stay in a room for the night while we worked out the details of our trip. Then I made a simple request, "Could you possibly send someone just two exits up from the conference center to pick us up?" She said, "No!" Our bad day became a miserable day.

The town where we were stranded wasn't exactly a metropolitan area. They didn't have taxis, so we spent several hours trying to find someone who would take us to get a rental car. The only person we could find was a man who worked for a local nursing home. He picked us up in his van and took us to get the rental car.

After he walked us in to rent a car, he came back out to his van, and his van wouldn't crank. At this point, we knew we were under a curse. After a while, we finally made it to Knoxville in our rental car and had a pleasant visit with my wife's parents. On our trip back to Durham, we stopped in my hometown to pick up my car—that is, the first car that broke down. We got in my car, which had been fixed by a mechanic, drove 45 minutes, and you'll never believe what happened. Then again by now maybe you will believe what happened—the car broke down again.

Another motorist stopped, hooked up his jumper cables, and had us back out on the Interstate in no time. But we weren't out there for long. You guessed it, we were enjoying our past time—standing on the side of the road. This time the car wouldn't even crank. By then, I was thinking, "Maybe we should just a take an airplane from here." Finally, we made it back home. Have you ever had a trip like that? I hope not.

Have you ever had a day where you felt like the whole world was ganging up on you? Have you ever had a day where you felt like everyone was conspiring to make it a terrible day? If you think you've had a bad day, let me introduce you to Job.

Job was from the land of Uz. Don't mistake that for the Land of Oz, for all you *Wizard of Oz* fans. As far as we can tell, the Land of Uz would be modern day Saudi Arabia. Saudi Arabia was and still is one of the wealthiest parts of the world. Some of the wealthiest people in the world reside in this Middle Eastern country. Job lived there, and we know he was very wealthy. Basically, Job was Bill Gates, Donald

Trump, and Warren Buffet wrapped up in one person; he was pretty prosperous to say the least.

It appeared that Job had it all. That's why he was an ideal man for a test. Suddenly, a dialogue took place between God and the devil:

> *"Then the Lord asked Satan, "Have you noticed my servant Job? He is the finest man in all the earth—a man of complete integrity. He fears God and will have nothing to do with evil." Satan replied to the Lord, "Yes, Job fears God, but not without good reason! You have always protected him and his home and his property from harm. You have made him prosperous in everything he does. Look how rich he is! But take away everything he has, and he will surely curse you to your face!" "All right, you may test him," the Lord said to Satan. "Do whatever you want with everything he possesses, but don't harm him physically." So Satan left the Lord's presence.* (Job 1:8-12)

When The Hammer Blows Don't Stop

The devil was suspicious of Job. He was suggesting the only reason Job was good to God was because God was good to Job. Essentially, Satan was saying the only reason Job loved God was "because." The devil said in no uncertain terms, "God, if you'll just take away the 'because,' Job will stop serving you; take away his blessings and Job will spit in your face."

Job didn't know about this conversation. The discussion took place in the unseen world, behind closed doors. Job had no idea that God and the devil are having a chat about him. That brings up an interesting thought. I wonder how many times Satan has called your name out before God. I wonder how many times the devil has called my name out before God, "God, if you will allow this to happen to Clay, he'll lay down his devotion to you and crumble." Job had no idea Satan was making this accusation against him. He had no idea that heaven and hell were about to collide in his life.

Suddenly, Job hears a loud banging at his door. When Job answered the door, his life was never the same. Talk about a defining moment. Job answered the door, and one of his workers was standing there, wide-eyed and white as a sheep. In a state of panic, he said, "Mr. Job, Mr. Job, while the oxen were plowing, and the donkeys were grazing, a band of robbers came and stole the animals." That was bad news because the oxen and donkeys were responsible for all the plowing on the farm. Job lost his entire labor force in one day.

No doubt, Job thought, "I have so much to be thankful for, I still have all my sheep and all my camels." Then another knock came at his door. "Mr. Job, Mr. Job, a terrible wildfire broke out in the fields and all your sheep, along with the shepherds were killed."

I'm sure Job thought, "Well, at least I still have the camels; after all, they're worth more than all the other animals." Just as Job sat down at the kitchen table, he heard the infamous knock at his door. By this time, I don't think I would have answered the door. He opened the door and it was another employee, "Mr. Job," he said, "we've been attacked by some bandits; they raided the land and have driven off all of your camels." Job knew what this meant. All his wealth had suddenly disappeared. In a matter of a few hours, Job went from burgeoning prosperity to complete bankruptcy. In one day, his savings and checking accounts went to double zero.

Job shut the door. He walked into his living room, turned out the lights, and sat down to try to absorb all he had lost. He thought to himself, "At least I still have my kids. I've lost everything, but at least I have my children. My kids will care for me while I get back on my feet." He remembered the words of his mother, "No man is poor when he has a great family." Job was holding back his tears, when without any warning, there was another bang at his door. Before Job ever got up, he anticipated more bad news. He barely pushed the door open, and saw another employee standing there, wiping tears from his eyes. "Mr. Job, Mr. Job, I'm so sorry I have to be the one to deliver the news. A terrible tornado has just swept through a nearby neighborhood, and all your children were killed in the storm."

This was the news that would bring Job to his knees. Job fell to the ground as though his life had been shattered into a million pieces. In one day, Job lost all 10 of his children. I can't imagine losing one child, not to mention ten. But the nightmare was not over. Satan decided to change the rules of the game.

> *"Satan replied to the Lord, "Skin for skin— he blesses you only because you bless him. A man will give up everything he has to save his life. But take away his health, and he will surely curse you to your face!" "All right, do with him as you please," the Lord said to Satan. "But spare his life." So Satan left the Lord's presence, and he struck Job with a terrible case of boils from head to foot"* (**Job 2:4-7**).

While Job was standing beside 10 fresh graves, his body started to tingle with a fever. At first, he thought that it was his body reacting to his grief. As time elapsed, though, his body felt like it was on fire. Before long, sores started to pop up everywhere. The itching was unbearable. Looking for some relief, Job went to a garbage dump. Rummaging through the garbage dump, Job found pieces of broken pottery and used them to scrape his sores. If you've ever had chicken pox, magnify chicken pox 1000 times, then you will begin to identify with Job's excruciating pain.

Job had lost his wealth, his health, and his children, but at least he still had his wife, the one who said, "Job, why don't you curse God and die." He probably thought, "Thank you honey, that's just what I needed to hear right about now." I don't guess I should be too tough on Mrs. Job. After all, Mrs. Job just finished attending 10 back to back funerals for her children. Sometimes, people don't always say the right things when they're hurting. Let's give Mrs. Job some grace.

The story of Job is not a fictional story. When we read the book of Job, we're not reading a make believe, imaginary tale. The book of Job is probably the oldest book in the Bible, and it's not a story God included in the Old Testament simply to teach us a history lesson. God has far more in mind than just teaching us a lesson about history. 1 Corinthians 10:11 says, "Now all these things were written (referring to Old Testament stories), for our instruction." Job offers us more than history lessons. The book of Job offers us principles for life. God wants to teach us what to do when the odds are against us.

Lessons from Job

Nothing Touches Your Life Unless It First Passes Through The Hands Of God.

Satan is the one who was bringing this calamity upon Job, but he could only touch Job because God had given him permission. Martin Luther famously said, "Even the devil is God's devil." God is completely sovereign, and nothing happens to us unless it first passes through the permissive will of God. I like to refer to this as the "Father's Filter." Before anything can come to your life, it must first pass through our heavenly Father's hands. Behind every detail of our lives, both good and bad, is the purpose, plan, and will of a sovereign God.

Events on earth must always be interpreted in light of events in heaven. It would have been great if Job knew what was going on behind the scenes. It would have been enlightening for Job to know he was the topic of conversation between God and Satan, but Job knew nothing about this conversation.

When you're in a trial, remember that God and Satan may be having a conversation about you. Satan may be suggesting to God if enough doesn't go your way in life, you'll simply abandon your faith. Whatever it takes to bring you down is what Satan will attack. If it means ruining your marriage, he'll try to create chaos in your marriage. If it means tempting you to cut a few corners in the ethics of your business, Satan will go there. Whatever it takes to bring you down is the path he will pursue. Satan may be invisible, but it doesn't mean he's not real. The story of Job teaches us that he does a big portion of his work behind the scenes.

When You Don't Have Answers To Your Questions, You Can Still Worship.

In the middle of his suffering, Job does something that seems totally out of sync with his terrible circumstances. He worships.

> *"Job stood up and tore his robe in grief. Then he shaved his head and fell to the ground to worship. He said, "I came naked from my mother's womb, and I will be naked when I leave. The Lord gave me what I had, and the Lord has taken it away. Praise the name of the Lord!"* (Job 1:20-21).

Well-known author and pastor, Chuck Swindoll, tells the story of getting an emergency call to go to the hospital one night. When he arrived, he found a young couple who were members of his church. Unfortunately, just moments before he arrived, their three month old baby suddenly died. Chuck Swindoll and this young couple made their way to the little chapel tucked away in the corner of the hospital. When they came to the small chapel, this young couple turned to their pastor and said, "Chuck, let's worship." He said those were the last words he expected to hear. Instead, he expected to hear, "Chuck, why did God let this happen?" "Why did God not intervene?" He never expected to hear them say, "Let's worship." For thirty to forty minutes, they sat in the chapel, holding hands, singing praises to God. This is exactly what Job did.[4]

Praise comes easy when everything in life is going well. We do Okay with "the Lord has given"; it's the "Lord has taken it away" part that trips us up. It's harder to worship after the Lord has taken something away. When we have questions about our lingering pain, worship seems forced and even out of step with our circumstances. Yet, Job reminds us we don't have to have answers that fully satisfy the mind to be able to worship.

Speaking of questions, I've studied the book of Job backwards and forwards. For the longest time, I kept looking for answers to

---

4   Charles Swindoll, Message delivered on Insight for Living radio broadcast

all the questions Job raised before God. Do you know what I've discovered? God never answered Job's questions. God never offered Job explanations about his suffering. Sometimes God doesn't offer us explanations; instead, He offers us Himself. He offers His strength, His grace, and His presence.

Conference speaker Jerry Vines tells the story about a young man who dedicated his life to be a foreign missionary. You can imagine the mixed emotions his parents had. On the one hand, they were proud of their son. He would be involved in a worthwhile endeavor. On the other hand, his parents knew this special calling would limit the amount of time they would see their son.

The day came when he boarded a plane to travel to the foreign field. For his parents, it was a bitter-sweet event. As his plane took off, he decided to write a note to his parents whom he had just left behind. He didn't have any writing paper close by, so he tore a piece of newspaper and wrote his note in the margin of the paper. After he wrote his note, he put the note in an envelope and when he had a lay over at another airport, he mailed the letter to his parents. He jumped on another plane, but unfortunately, his plane never reached its destination.

Tragically, the plane crashed. This young man, along with the other passengers, lost their lives. In a matter of hours his parents were notified. They were heartbroken. Just a few short days later, the note that their son had written arrived at their home. After reading the note on one side, ironically, they turned the paper over to the other side. The newspaper had been torn in such a way that there was one word in bold face print-one three-letter word, WHY? It was the very question these parents were asking. Why?[5]

I suppose there is no other question that has been posed to God more than that question. Why? Today, that sobering question is being asked in every major hospital and every local funeral home. Why is it that sometimes those who are so young seem to die so early? Why do those who are so old and wish to die seem to keep holding on with very little quality of life? Why does the teenager who had his

5   Jerry Vines, 3rd message in series entitled, The Wonderful World of Uz

whole life in front of him have his life cut short by terminal cancer? Perhaps more perplexing than any of those questions is this one— why would a young man, traveling around the world to proclaim the love of Christ, suddenly be killed in a plane crash? We all ask our own version of these questions. At some point, questions wash over us like Niagara Falls.

When questions stand as tall as sky scrapers, what do we do? One option is do something that seems counterintuitive—worship. As we worship, we're deciding that the unanswered questions in our lives are not going to stand on center stage.

When You Can't Locate God, It Doesn't Mean He's Not There.

I have a confession to make. There are times in my life when God appears to be hiding. It sure is comforting to know I'm not the first person who has felt that way. Job felt the same way. Job was experiencing excruciating pain and wondered if God was still around.

> *"I go east, but He is not there. I go west, but I cannot find him. I do not see him in the north, for he is hidden. I turn to the south, but I cannot find him" (Job 23: 8-9).*

Job is searching for God. He has an "All Points Bulletin" out for God. God appears to be missing. Job says, "I go to the east, but God is not there; I go to the west, but God is not there; I go to the north but I can't locate God. I go south but I can't find God anywhere." Job has gone in every direction possible and can't locate God. Job is asking, "God, where are you?" For the better part of the book of Job, this is the case. Job is suffering, but He can't seem to find God in His suffering.

At some point in your life, if you haven't already experienced it, you're going to be able to identify with Job. There are times when we can't seem to locate God. There are other occasions when we feel like we are all alone. When we encounter these experiences, it's important to remember that just because we can't see God in our suffering, doesn't mean God is absent. Even though we may not feel the presence of God, it does not mean God is not present. At times, God appears to hide Himself, but just because He seems to be hidden, doesn't mean He is not there. You may not know where God is in your particular problem, but God knows where you are.

God Is In Control Even When Life Is Out of Control.

For 37 chapters, God has been stone silent. Finally, God speaks to Job out of a whirlwind, out of a violent storm. Job, no doubt, wanted to meet God in the sunshine, but instead God spoke to Job out of a storm. God doesn't always tiptoe into our world in a gentle manner. Sometimes, God speaks in a storm. If you'll blow the thick layer of dust off the book of Nahum in your Bible (it's not a book we go to very often), you will find a very interesting verse there. Nahum 1:3 says, "The way of the Lord is in the whirlwind and in the storm." Job was about to hear from God in a way he hadn't anticipated. William Cowper wrote: "God moves in a mysterious way, His wonders to perform; He plants His footsteps in the sea, and He rides upon the storm." Job had been asking God to speak, but it didn't come the way he expected. God spoke to him out of a ferocious storm.

When God finally speaks to Job, it's as if God is saying, "Job, pull yourself together and be a man because I'm about to ask you some serious questions." In fact, this is the longest recorded speech God makes in the entire Bible, and it's loaded with rhetorical questions. In four chapters, God poses 77 questions to Job. All these questions are designed to stop Job dead in his tracks, to reorient his thinking. Basically when you size all these questions down, God is basically asking Job one primary question. "Job, are you controlling this universe?"

Here's a sampling of some of the questions:
- Job 38:4 says, "Where were you when I established the earth?"
- Job 38:8, "Who enclosed the sea behind doors when it burst from the womb?"
- Job 38:16, "Have you walked in the depths of the ocean?"

- Job 38:22, "Have you entered the place where the snow is stored?"

God speaks to Job from the only book Job had—the book of creation. Job didn't have a Bible. Job probably heard the oral stories about God, which were handed down to him, but they hadn't been compiled into book form yet. Therefore, God speaks to Job from a world Job could understand—the world of nature.

In essence, God says, "Job, where were you when I created the ocean? Where were you when I said to the ocean, you can only come this far? Job, have you been to the bottom of the ocean? Have you searched out the depth of the sea?"

Scientists tell us there are places in the ocean almost seven miles deep. God says, "Job, have you been down there to check things out?" I don't think so. God says, "Job, if you know all the answers, tell me about the snow." Researchers say they have never found two snowflakes alike. God says, "Job, if you know so much, tell me about each one of those snowflakes."

Don't miss the fine print here. God is teaching Job a lesson from nature. He is saying "Job, I'm God, and you're not. I'm running this show; I'm in control of this universe, and you're not."

When Rabbi Harold Kushner wrote his book, *When Bad Things Happen to Good People*, it resonated with lots of people. It became a best seller. Rabbi Kushner wrote the book after watching his son, Aaron, battle a cruel disease called Progeria. Progeria is an unusual disease in which the aging process drastically accelerates at an unprecedented speed. An eight year old boy may look like an eighty-year old man. He has the mind of a child, but the body of an elderly person. After battling the disease, Kushner's son, Aaron, died when he was 14.

As he watched his son suffer from the disease, Kushner struggled with doubts about God's goodness. This led the Rabbi to look for answers in the Book of Job. In Kushner's view, Job, who underwent terrifying suffering, was forced to rethink his own preconceived ideas about God. Either God is one who is all powerful but not totally good, or He's one who is good but not completely powerful. Kushner landed on the side of believing the story of Job is about a God who is good but less than all powerful. Rabbi Kushner suggested that bad things happen in the world because God is not controlling the whole world. Certain tragedies, calamities, and diseases occur because they are not directly under God's control.[6]

I must admit as a young theological student in seminary, I found Kushner's ideas troubling. As a young seminarian, when I referred to Rabbi Kushner, I made him sound like an off the wall Jewish theologian who had abandoned orthodoxy. This, of course, was long before I started to watch my own son struggle with a disease. Like Kushner, watching my son suffer has forced me to grapple with my own presuppositions about God. Watching your child suffer each day, with little apparent divine intervention, sends you back to the drawing board. The reason Kushner's book resonated so well is because he struck a common denominator in all of humanity. When we appeal to God (who by nature should be all powerful) and our suffering doesn't change, we're left wondering why.

Kushner entitled his book, *When Bad Things Happen To Good People*, but perhaps a better question is, "Why do bad things happen to everybody?" Whether you are good or bad, believer or unbeliever, you can anticipate some tough times in your life. If you've ever spent one hour of your life struggling with a question that has no apparent answer, you can identify with Rabbi Kushner's struggles.

Though I can identify with Rabbi Kushner's struggles, I don't reach his same conclusions. If God was all good but not all powerful, when God finally stepped on the platform to speak to Job, He would have said, "Job, I'm sorry about all of this suffering. I was powerless to do anything about it. Job, I wanted to help, but there was nothing I could do." God never apologized for His lack

---

6   Harold Kushner, *When Bad Things Happen to Good People* (Schocken Books, 1981).

of power. Instead, what you find in God's response to Job is an unparalleled description of God's power.

When God finally spoke, did God answer the question why Job suffered? No. God offered no point-by-point explanation. God basically took him on a nature trail. He said, "Job, I'm running this physical universe, which you don't understand, and I'm running the moral universe-which you don't understand."

I believe the Bible teaches God is a God who is all good and all powerful. Because God is all powerful, a logical conclusion is that God is in full control of the universe, including our circumstances. God does not cause evil. We know God has chosen to create human beings with the gift of freedom. This freedom often expresses itself as the source of moral evil when we make wrong and unwise choices. At other times, tragedies and hardships can't be easily traced back to our human choices. In the end, the Bible doesn't give a full, inexhaustible explanation of evil and suffering.

Tragedies and hardships raise perplexing questions in our minds. Like a pinball, we often bounce back and forth between faith and doubt. Doubt is often present because our finite minds are incapable of comprehending all of life's experiences. Trying to understand God's infinite plan is like a kindergartener trying to understand advanced calculus. We simply don't have the brain power.

I don't completely understand God's sovereignty (His control), but that doesn't mean I shouldn't believe it. I don't understand how cell phones work. I don't understand how a signal can bounce off of a tower and allow me to talk to someone on the other side of the globe. I don't understand the finer points of cell phone technology, but just because I don't understand how it works, doesn't mean I can't enjoy it. Chances are very good you'll never fully understand the depths of God's sovereignty. However, just because you can't fully understand it with your finite mind, doesn't mean you can't enjoy it. I say "enjoy" because when you believe God is in control, you don't have to be in control.

If you could travel to heaven today and were able to watch what was taking place around the throne of God, you would be amazed. One thing you wouldn't find in heaven would be any shred of evidence God was in a state of panic. You would never hear God saying, "Oops!" You would never hear God say, "Oh no! I wonder what we're going to do about that."

You would be stunned by how calm things are around the throne of God. God is in heaven, and He is in absolute control. When I find myself being anxious about something, it's usually because momentarily I have lost sight of who is still on the throne. God is on the throne, and He is ruling this universe, and He's in control of your life.

If God is God, He will have the last word over your circumstances. Our hope ultimately is found in eternity, where everything in our broken world is restored. Tuberous sclerosis, the genetic disease both my sons have, is the result of flawed DNA. Chromosome 9 or Chromosome 16 is the culprit for anyone who has the disease. However, the good news is that Chromosome 9 and Chromosome 16 will not have the final word. God will have the final word. All chromosomes will be perfect in heaven. Faulty DNA will be transformed. Hope finds its ultimate crescendo and climax in the life to come.

CHAPTER 3

What To Tell Yourself When
You Have A Problem

IT's A TALK THAT WILL be memorialized forever. When Bill McCartney was the head football coach for the University of Colorado, he gave a pre-game talk that created a ripple effect in its own right. Colorado was on their way to contend for a national championship, but they had a huge obstacle to face, namely the Nebraska Cornhuskers. Going into the game, they didn't exactly have history on their side. Colorado had lost to Nebraska the last 23 straight times. Coach McCartney knew he had to do more than simply execute a game plan; he had to figure out a way to motivate his players to play at a whole new level.

Coach McCartney devised one of the greatest pep talks recorded in football history. Just before the team was scheduled to leave for Nebraska, he called a team meeting. With the players gathered around him, he told them that after the game, everyone would get a brand new leather football with the final score printed on it. Depending on the score, the football would either be a prize to enjoy or a haunted memory that would stay with them for a lifetime.

The next part of his plan proves he was a coaching genius. He told all of his players, "Gentlemen, before we leave tomorrow, I want you to call somebody close to you and tell them you're going to play every down for them. Call them and tell them you want them to watch every play because you're dedicating your game to them. Tell them every tackle you make, every block you make, every run you make, every pass you throw will be for them. Make sure you tell them every time they see your jersey to remember you're playing for them."

The rest is in the archives of football history. Though Colorado was behind Nebraska by 12 points in the fourth quarter, Colorado came back to defeat the Cornhuskers 28-12. Coach McCartney attributes this win to how his players played selflessly when they were losing. The fact that they knew someone special was watching every play allowed them to muster up every ounce of strength to come back and win the big game. Coaches who win national championships know the power of a good pep talk.[7]

Pep talks aren't just relegated to coaches, parents, and school teachers. If you hope to win at life, you'll have to master the art of the personal pep talk. This is especially true when you're facing a time of adversity. By giving yourself a biblical, rational pep talk, you'll reduce the amount of time you stay paralyzed by your circumstances. Our problem is usually not the biggest problem; the biggest problem is what we tell ourselves about the problem. Researcher and well-known psychologist, Martin Seligman says overcoming suffering comes down to telling ourselves the right things when we're suffering. What we say to ourselves when we're facing adversity determines whether we endure the trial, or whether we slip into state of helplessness and depression. Dr. Seligman calls it explanatory style. We each have a style of explaining suffering to ourselves. It can be optimistic or pessimistic. It can be based on faith or based on fear.

Emotions come directly from what we think. If we think pessimistic thoughts during times of adversity, we tend to experience feelings of hopelessness. Basically, we need to learn how to talk to ourselves when we're suffering. Seligman's research demonstrates that the internal conversation we have with ourselves is the critical factor in how well we persevere through our problems. In his book, *Learned Optimism*, Seligman encourages us to change our internal dialogue, "What you think when things go wrong, what you say to yourself when you come to the wall, will determine what happens next: whether you give up or whether you start to make things go right." [8]

Most of us would agree how important thoughts are in almost every arena of life. In fact, one whole discipline within the field of psychology is called cognitive therapy. Cognitive therapy tries to change the way people think about their failures, losses, and setbacks. Scripture certainly affirms how important thoughts are in each of our lives. Proverbs reminds us we are what we think. "As a man thinks in his heart, so is he." Paul says, " ...to take every thought captive and make it obedient to Christ" (2 Corin. 10:5). As a result of the fall, our thoughts are often distorted. When you face some form of adversity, pay close attention to your own internal dialogue with yourself. Most likely, if you are like me, you'll have to dispute some of your initial thoughts. Self-talk is not simply a psychological coping mechanism, which has recently been discovered by the field of psychology. In fact, this is a classic case of science just now catching up with Scripture.

The psalmist routinely calls his thoughts into question. The psalmist says to himself, "Why are you cast down, O my soul? And why are you disquieted within me? Hope in God ..." (Ps. 42:11; Ps. 43:5). Call it what you will ... self-talk, explanatory style, or internal dialogue. David is talking to himself. He is actively disputing his distorted thoughts. He is arguing with his own thinking. I believe it's one of the key spiritual disciplines every believer has to learn to be spiritually mature.

Most of us are quite adept at arguing. We argue with our spouses. We argue with our kids. We argue with co-workers who have an opinion we feel is way off base. However, the most important argument you have in the course of the day is not the one you have at home, or at work, it's the one you have in your mind. Learning to argue with impulsive thoughts can yield big dividends in your personal life. Many of the thoughts we have are not based on the truth, but come from our propensity to distort reality. Since our thoughts tend to be distorted when adversity arrives, learning to second guess our

---

8   Martin Seligman, *Learned Optimism* (Vintage Books, 2006) 259.

negative thoughts is crucial to stay emotionally well. This is exactly what David is doing as he expresses himself in the Psalms. David is trying to prevent a state of helplessness and depression by calling his soul back to reality. Toxic thoughts lead to toxic emotions. We are more likely to experience depression and hopelessness when we allow toxic thoughts to rule our minds.

Thoughts like, "I'm never going to make it through this," or "If this doesn't change, I'll never be happy," or "Why does all this bad stuff happen to me?" are thoughts we have to detoxify. If we accept these thoughts and ruminate over them, they paralyze us emotionally. Each of these thoughts is distorted. The goal is to catch these thoughts as near to their beginning as possible. I recommend using a statement to offset these negative thoughts. You might call it your own Christian mantra. You can say it out loud, or you can purposely think the specific thought in the privacy of your own mind. We need a few "thought stoppers" we can use to combat distorted thinking. This is especially true when we're facing adversity. Let me give you a few of my favorites...

Christian Mantras...

"I am not a quitter!"

When we face adversity, regardless of the form it takes, we are inclined to battle distorted thinking. One of the most toxic thoughts we can have is one that says, "I'm never going to make it through this." If we accept this thought and reflect on it for an extended period of time, it will poison our perspective on the problem. Furthermore, it's impossible to buy into this type of toxic thinking without being emotionally paralyzed by it. We have to offset the negative thought with a statement that keeps us from throwing in the towel. When you're trial is fresh and you're stunned with disappointment, you may have to tell yourself, "I will not give up" no less than fifty times a day. You can say it out loud, or you can think the specific thought in the privacy of your own mind.

James 1:3 says, "*...the testing of your faith produces endurance.*" Trials have a way of teaching us how to persevere. God wants us to cultivate "staying power" in our personal character. This is the ability to keep on keeping on. All through the New Testament, the Christian life is compared to a race. Hebrews tells us to run the race that is set before us. In 1 Corinthians, we're challenged to run the race in such a way as to win the prize.

Have you ever entered a marathon before? You could call the first phase of the race the enjoyment phase. At the beginning of the race, running is fun. Your body feels great. Your blood is flowing, your head is clear, and your lungs are doing well. Everything seems to be running at peak performance. Then, without any warning, things begin to change. Your feet start to tingle, it feels like someone is stabbing you with knives in both of your sides, and your lungs start to feel like they've been set on fire. Runners often refer to this as, "hitting the wall!" If you keep running long enough, you will reach a point when everything inside of you screams, "Stop!" The ultimate test of a runner is what happens to them when they hit the wall. If the first phase of the race could be called the enjoyment phase, the last part could be called the endurance phase.

When I was a young boy, I competed in a "fun run." When I heard about the one mile fun run, I asked my dad if I could run in the race. He assured me that I could, but he told me if I expected to do well, I needed to train. Therefore, about a week before the race, I went out every night in the driveway, and ran some sprints. Did I mention that my driveway was only about 40 yards long?

The night before the race, I went to bed really early. I didn't sleep too much though; I couldn't get the race off my mind, especially the part when I crossed the finish line to receive my gold medallion. I woke up early the next morning, and my mother told me she would be cheering for me the whole way. Off I went to the race!

I was one of the smallest people in the race, so when it came time to take our position at the starting line, I made sure I wiggled my way to the very front. As I stood at the starting line, my stomach was fluttering with butterflies. When I heard the firing gun sound off, I came off the starting line like a rocket off a launching pad. I was running with all of my might. After about 40 yards, the very distance I had perfected in my driveway, I noticed no one was in front of me.

I looked behind me and remarkably everyone was far behind me. I thought, "I'm destined to win this race." I was running as a hard as I could, but when I came to the 100 yard marker, something changed dramatically. Without any warning, my legs started to feel like they weighed 1000 lbs each. My heart felt like it was going to explode out of my chest. For the first time in my life, I was introduced to "hitting the wall." I think it would be more accurate to say the wall hit me. Suddenly, it was like I was standing still. The other runners flew by me like a stampede of race-horses. For me, the enjoyment phase of the race was over in minutes. When I came to the endurance phase, the bottom line is, I choked!

Winning At The Wall

Races are won and lost at the wall. That's also where life is won or lost. The true test of our character is not how we're doing when we're in the enjoyment phase of life; it's how we respond when we're in the endurance phase that counts. Life is a mixture of both phases. Sometimes we enjoy the will of God, and other times we endure the will of God. The capacity to finish well is what the Bible calls endurance. When you are in a trial, there will probably come a time when you hit the wall. Everything inside of you will scream: quit, give up, stop, moan, groan, and complain. The true test of your faith is how you respond once you hit the wall. Refuse to give up. Refuse to throw in the towel. Endurance is when we decide that quitting is not an option.

When I was in high school, I had to take geometry. I still have nightmares and flashbacks about geometry. I have never excelled in math. I could breeze through English, history, and other subjects, but math always tripped me up. When I started taking geometry, I experienced a huge academic nose dive. My first semester of geometry, I made a big, fat, whopping F. I didn't even come close to passing. My parents helped me get a tutor, but even with the tutor, I still struggled in the class.

Finally, I got so exasperated, I remember telling my dad, "Daddy, I just want to quit. Forget this stuff. I can't do it. I want to quit." To this very day, I'll never forget what my dad said. He said, "Clay, if you quit on geometry, then you'll start to reinforce one of worst character traits anyone can possess." He said, "If you quit on geometry, my fear is you'll learn to quit in other areas of your life that will be infinitely more important than geometry." My dad said, "Son, if you quit now, you'll find it easier and easier to quit later on." My dad may not have been fully aware of it, but he wasn't giving me a lesson about geometry. He taught me a priceless lesson about life. Quitters never win and winners never quit. I didn't quit on geometry, I went on to make a B in the class. In fact, I have a geometry book displayed in a prominent place in my office. When life gets tough and I start contemplating quitting, a quick glance at my geometry book puts everything in perspective.

Well known writer, Gordon McDonald, tells about what happened to him when his mother died. Just shortly after his mother died, he was talking to one of his cousins on the phone. During the conversation, his cousin reminded him that his mother had seven other siblings. His cousin proceeded to tell him story after story about his mother and her brothers and sisters. At the end of the conversation, she said, "Gordon your mother and her family were a bunch of quitters." She said, "When life got tough, they would just quit." At first, Gordon McDonald says he was offended and taken back by what she said.

After he got off the phone, he started to reflect about his mother's life. As he thought about it, he had to acknowledge what his cousin said was a fair assessment of her life. He thought about all the times his mother had taken a new job, but in a short period of time, she would always quit. He thought about all the projects around the house she started, but rarely ever finished. He remembered all the times she announced that they were going to do family life in a new way, and have new priorities, but the commitment to change would never last.

Gordon McDonald said it suddenly dawned on him what he inherited from his mother. He calls it "a quitter's gene." It's the tendency to just give up and quit when things get tough. When he realized this tendency he inherited from his mom, he decided he was going to break the chain. He drew a line in the sand. The quitter's gene would stop with his mother.[9]

---

9   Gordon McDonald, *A Resilient Life* (Thomas Nelson, 2004) 1-2.

Perhaps you grew up in a family who modeled quitting. When work became difficult, mom and dad simply quit. When mom and dad hit the wall in their marriage, they decided to bail. When a friend disappointed them, instead of extending forgiveness, they chose to sever the friendship. When God didn't come through exactly like they were asking Him to, your parents didn't take their questions to God; they made the unfortunate decision of abandoning their faith.

Much like Gordon McDonald, you have an important decision to make. It's one of the most important decisions you will ever make. You must stare in the face of your heritage and boldly declare, "I will not develop a quitter's gene." "I'm breaking the chain." "The endless cycle of quitting will stop with me."

"God Has A Purpose For My Problems"

God's number one purpose in your life is to make you into the image of His Son-Jesus Christ. God's long range plan for your life is for you to be Christ-like. There are some Christians who always look for something "specific" God is trying to teach them when they face adversity. Out of good intentions, they ask, "God, what do you want me to learn from this?" Though I believe there are times when we can learn specific lessons from trials, more times than not, I'm convinced the trials are used to forge our character. If God wants to make us like Christ, He will take us through some of the same things Jesus went through. This means each one of us will log in some time in Gethsemane. This will mean traveling down the Via Delarosa. We may have our own six hours on a cross. The trials are not designed to destroy us but to develop us.

Regardless of the pain in your life, Romans 8:28 is still in your Bible: "We know that God causes all things to work together for good to those who love God and are called according to His purpose." The verse doesn't say that all our circumstances are good. Let's be honest—all our circumstances are not good. Fatal car accidents are not good. Broken marriages are not good. Leukemia and Muscular Dystrophy are not good. He doesn't say every circumstance is good, but He does say that God is taking our circumstances and He is working them together for good. The specific "good" may never become clear and apparent to us. It can be dangerous to assume you will find out God's specific message through your suffering. More times than not, we never know the specific lesson God is teaching us in our pain. We have to settle for knowing God's general purpose for our suffering— making us like Christ.

Life is a lot like a play. You may not understand Act 1, Act 2, or Act 3, but if we wait until the end of the storyline, then it will all make sense. At the moment, your problems may not make a lot of sense. But once you get to the other side of eternity, you'll be able to say, "Oh, now my circumstances finally make sense. God, you had a higher purpose in mind the whole time."

James reminds us that "the testing of our faith produces endurance" (James 1:3). Job makes a similar statement when he says, "When He (God) has tested me, I will come forth as gold" (Job 23:10). "Testing" is a term often used in Hebrew and Greek to describe the process of testing gold. In the ancient Jewish world, the goldsmith would take the gold and put it in a portable furnace; the goldsmith would then heat up the gold. The intense heat would turn the gold to a liquid form. All the impurities would separate from the gold and would rise to the top. The goldsmith would then take a skimmer and he would scrape off all the impurities. The goldsmith put the gold in the furnace, not to damage the gold, but to purify the gold. The Bible teaches that God does exactly the same thing in our lives. God places us in trials and difficulties to purify our faith. Proverbs 17:3 says, "The refining pot is for silver and the furnace for gold, but God tests the heart." The goldsmith gets the impurities out of the gold, and God wants the impurities out of our character.

Nothing reveals the true nature of our character like how we respond to sin and how we respond to suffering. Interestingly, in Christian theology, suffering isn't viewed as the ultimate thing to be avoided. This is what makes the Christian faith unique. Many other faith systems teach that suffering is either an illusion, an expression of evil, or a sign that the gods are ticked off at you. Christian theology teaches that suffering can be redemptive. Most of us have heard the well-worn adage, "no pain, no gain." Interestingly, a football coach is not the one who coined the phrase. The phrase was actually coined by

Ignatius of Antioch, one of the early Church fathers. His exact words were, "The greater the pain, the greater the gain." We shortened his words to, "no pain, no gain." From the earliest time, Christians have believed that God can redeem our pain for constructive purposes.

"Tough Times Don't Last Forever"

When you face adversity, remember it's important to pay close attention to your internal dialogue with yourself. Most likely, you'll have to dispute some of your initial thoughts by countering them with the truth. One of the most debilitating, toxic thoughts we have when we face a problem is, "This is never going to change." The weight of psychological research is undeniable. When we think our circumstances are permanent and will never change for the better, we emotionally curl up in a fetal position. Inevitability, we end up waving the white flag of surrender, and we give up our will to endure.

Keeping a "faith perspective" during times of trouble allows us to see beyond our immediate, temporary circumstances. We interpret our circumstances with a very limited perspective. We're confined by time, but God interprets everything that happens in time in light of eternity. Ecclesiastes 3:11 reminds us that "people cannot see the whole scope of God's work from beginning to end." Like a Polaroid picture, we only get snapshots of a situation, but God has a panoramic view of the whole situation. He sees the big picture. Let Paul's words sink in:

> *"That is why we never give up. Though our bodies are dying, our spirits are being renewed every day. For our present troubles are small and won't last very long. Yet they produce for us a glory that vastly outweighs them and will last forever. So we don't look at troubles we can see now; rather, we fix our gaze on things that cannot be seen"* (**2 Corin. 4: 16-18**).

Paul described his troubles as "small." He was beaten three times, but from his perspective, it was small. He was thrown in prison; he went day after day without food and clothes, but if you asked him, he would say, it's just a small problem, a light affliction that wouldn't last forever. How could he say that? It's all a matter of perspective. Paul measured his problems in light of eternity. Paul wasn't going to give up because he knew whatever adversity he faced was like a millisecond compared to eternity.

When you measure your suffering in light of eternity, it makes it more bearable. The adversity is only for a moment when you compare it to eternity. It's like staying one night in a bad hotel. When I was in my twenties, a friend and I drove across the country from Raleigh, North Carolina to Las Vegas, Nevada. On the first day, we made it to Memphis, Tennessee. We arrived in the city in the wee hours of the morning.

When we arrived, we couldn't find a vacant hotel anywhere. Memphis was hosting a country music festival, and all the hotels were fully booked, with the exception of one roach motel. The walls in our room were yellow from smoke stains. The toilet seat in the bathroom was broken into jagged edges. The bed I slept on had duct tape all over the sheets. The sheets were torn, but with some creative work, they were taped back together with duct tape. The motel was terrible, but we were either going to sleep at this motel, or we would have nowhere to sleep. We decided to stay with the roaches, but it was only for one night. We knew we could make it in the bad hotel for one night. We knew we were just passing through.

Our suffering on this earth, when we compare it to eternity, is like staying one night in a bad hotel. We're not going to stay there forever. It's just one night. A better day is right around the corner.

Joni Erikson Tada has spent her whole adult life as a quadriplegic. As a teenager, she had terrible diving accident, which left her crippled. Though she has spent her life reminding people that God has a purpose for their suffering, she also recognizes that suffering was an intruder that resulted from the fall. Joni says when she arrives in heaven, she has two specific things she wants to say to God: "God, thank you for this wheelchair. It was through this wheel chair that I learned to trust you." Then she has a second word for Him, "God, throw this wheelchair into hell where it belongs." God has a redemptive purpose for our suffering, but ultimately, there will be a day when we once and for all kiss suffering good-bye.[10]

"It's Okay to have Questions!"

When we suffer, we naturally raise questions. Some believers develop a false sense of guilt because they're questioning God about their circumstances. This can lead to additional anguish which complicates our perspectives on our problems. Our questions don't threaten God. His shoulders are broad enough to handle your questions. Our questions and even our honest doubts can be expressions of faith.

If you think your questions are offensive to God, I would suggest you review some of the prayers recorded in the Bible. You may be startled by what you find. Jeremiah complains about God's unfairness; Job concludes that maybe God is not listening when he prays; Habakkuk sarcastically accuses God of being deaf. You'll find no shortage of brutal honesty as you review these prayers. Neither do you ever get the impression God is offended by their raw prayers.

We simply don't have the mental capacity to understand God's infinite mind and plan. Paul writes in his letter to the Romans, "How unsearchable are His judgments, and His ways are past finding out" (Romans 11:33). God says through the prophet Isaiah, "For my thoughts are not your thoughts, neither are your ways, my ways, says the Lord. As the heavens are higher than the earth, so are my ways higher than your ways and my thoughts higher than your thoughts" (Isaiah 55:8-9). What this means in practical terms is that some of our questions may not be answered on earth.

Sometimes, as Christians, when a tragedy or a catastrophe occurs, we feel the pressure to always have an answer. The truth is there are certain things we don't know, and we dare not make the mistake of offering explanations when God has chosen to remain silent. We don't have access to God's private diary. We don't always have an answer.

---

10   Joni Eareckson Tada, *A Place of Healing* (David C. Cook, 2010) 191-208.

This happened when 9-11 took place. Many Christians felt the pressure to serve up explanations as to why the tragedy occurred. Some well-meaning Christians said, "Even in the tragedy, God displayed his grace and goodness." They pointed out that 3,000 people died when 50,000 people could have easily died if they had been in the towers. On the surface, this explanation makes perfect sense unless you were married to one of the 3,000. It makes perfect sense unless it was your father, mother, or child who died in the senseless tragedy.

Some well-meaning Christians offered another explanation. They said, "Yes, it was a tragedy, but think of all the people who will come to faith in Christ through this tragedy." It sounds good at first until you realize what you're arguing is that terror is a tool God uses for evangelism. I don't know that I'm willing to make that argument.

Then there were the folks that came out and said 9-11 was the judgment of God. However, it's always a mistake to presume we know exactly what God had in mind when an event takes place. Simply put—we don't know. This was the mistake Job's friends made. His friends saw all the bad things happening to him, and they made the assumption Job was suffering because God was judging him. Was God judging him? No. God allowed Job to suffer, but the Bible couldn't be clearer— his suffering wasn't the result of God's judgment.

I'm not suggesting that rational explanations can't be helpful. Rational explanations for why suffering happens can be useful, but typically rational explanations are not sufficient. Our human formulas and systems of theology are incomplete. Often, it bothers us when we can't give exhaustive answers, but we need to remember our faith is in a person, not a system of theology. Truth is a person. Jesus said, "I am the way, the truth, and the life." Eventually, you'll run into some circumstances in life that won't fit into your neatly packaged theology. Logic will fail you. Knowledge will fail you. Resources will fail you.

I can unroll a lot of rational arguments for suffering, but I've discovered, if you're the one who is suffering, those arguments aren't going to bring you relief for one nano second. Ask John

Feinberg. As an acclaimed Christian theologian and philosopher, his life changed dramatically when his wife was diagnosed with an incurable, genetically transmitted disease. In a book called, *Deceived by God*, Feinberg tells about his struggle to find peace through his painful circumstances. Though he had plenty of pat answers for the problem of suffering, Feinberg found very little comfort in these answers while watching his wife suffer from this debilitating disease.[11]

Like Feinberg, even if we have answers, they often don't satisfy the deepest part of our souls. When you're suffering, what you need is a person—one who is willing to weep with you in your pain, just like Jesus did when Mary and Martha lost their brother. You need a God who can do more than offer you answers. You need a God who cares. When we don't have complete answers, there is a person who cares. Jesus cares.

---

11   John Feinberg, *Deceived by God: A Journey Through The Experience of Suffering* (Good News Publishing, 1997)

Decision 2: What Kind of Attitude Will I Have Today?

CHAPTER 4

No Such Thing As A Bad Mood

IF I TOLD YOU THAT you could do one thing in the next 90 days to improve your personal life, family life, business life, sex life, and your spiritual life, would you be interested? If your heart is beating, you're probably interested. The one thing you can do to improve every part of your life is to adopt the right kind of attitudes. With the right kind of attitudes, you will improve every day, and also every facet of your life.

I love crawling into bed. One Friday night, I slipped into bed at 11:30 p.m. and snuggled up with my two jumbo pillows. While I was lying in bed, I couldn't remember if I locked the front door of the house. I finally convinced myself to get out of bed, go downstairs, and make sure I had locked the door. Sure enough, I had. Before I went back to bed, I just happened to flip on a light switch that turns on some flood lights outside. Since I've always wanted to be an FBI agent, I'm always doing a little detective work on my own. When the lights came on, I looked out the window to take a quick peek. The very moment I glanced toward the driveway, I happened to see a snake slithering along the pavement. I watched the snake curl up right beside the steps we use to enter the house.

I knew I couldn't let the snake stay there. My boys come in and out of the house, sometimes barefooted, right beside where he was curled up. I was going to have to try to do something that was as counterintuitive as you can imagine—kill the snake. For you to appreciate how counterintuitive this was, understand that in the dictionary, right beside the word, aphidiophobia-the fear of snakes, there's a picture of me. I am terrified of snakes. When I was growing up, we would find snakes in our yard occasionally, and my mother would say, "Don't kill that snake; it's a good snake." I would say, "Momma, there's no such thing as a good snake!" I'm older, but that's still my philosophy.

Given the location of the snake, I knew I was going to have to try to go for the jugular. The first thing I did was go upstairs and put on my boots. I mean my big boots--the kind of boots that come all the way up to my hips. I picked up my flashlight because it was already after midnight. Then, I went to our utility building and got a shovel. I had my flashlight in one hand, pointing its light right at the snake. In my other hand, I had the shovel. Both were shaking. At this point, sweat was pouring off my face. I hadn't even gone for the kill yet, and sweat was dripping off my chin. After a personal pep talk, I mustered up enough courage to go for it. When I lunged for the snake, I missed it completely. I knew I had scared it pretty good though, because he reared back and struck out at me.

By then, my whole t-shirt was soaking wet. After a few minutes, I mustered up enough courage to give it another try. This time, I didn't miss. With one thrash, I beheaded the snake and pronounced him dead. To say I was feeling relieved would be quite an understatement. I went inside and changed my t-shirt, my underwear, my socks, and climbed into bed. The next morning, I went out to take a better look at the snake. I noticed some unique markings on it, and I decided to find out what kind of snake I had killed. After a little research, it was super clear—I killed a copperhead.

I didn't know much about copperheads, other than the fact that they were poisonous. I continued to read and discovered that copperheads are one of the most aggressive snakes in North America. I stumbled over several research projects which investigated why copperheads are more aggressive than other snakes. My first thought when reading this was, "Thank God I didn't know this last night!" Well, I went on to read a little more about snakes. I found out a very interesting fact about snake bites. Did you know more people are bitten trying to let go of a snake than when they are grabbing it? I guess you could call it the secret of the snake. It's easier to grab, but it's harder to let go.

What is true of snakes is also true of our attitudes. Attitudes are much easier to grab a hold of than they are to let go of. Once we take hold of a wrong attitude, it's much harder to let it go. Taking the next 90 days to replace destructive attitudes with the right ones is one of the most practical ways you can improve every day. Research suggests it takes about three months to establish a new habit. It's also easier to form a good habit than it is to get rid of a bad one. Focusing your attention on developing a new attitude is much better than focusing on removing the old one.

I've Got An Attitude

What is an attitude? It's a habit of thinking. You are what you think. Think of it as the great domino effect; your thoughts control your emotions, your emotions control your actions, and your actions determine your character. The best way to change your life is by changing the way you think. Your thoughts determine your life. Your thoughts are more important than your heredity, family background, environment, or educational opportunities. Nothing has a greater influence on your life than your thoughts. The writer of Proverbs says, "As a man thinks in his heart, so is he."

Romans 12: 2 says, "Do not be conformed to the world, but be transformed by the renewing of your mind." Don't race by the word transformed. In Greek, it's "metamorphoomai." You're probably more familiar with one of its kin folks, "metamorphosis." Metamorphosis describes a change. It's what happens when a caterpillar is transformed into a beautiful butterfly. Scripture teaches that each one of us should go through a metamorphosis-a deep change. Specifically, our minds and thoughts should change. Today, in our American culture, the emphasis is on changing the body. Yet, just a cursory reading of the Scriptures reminds us that God is far more interested in changing our minds than He is of changing our bodies.

One of the most often repeated commands Jesus gave was "Repent." I realize we don't use this word very often in our English vocabulary. When was the last time you went to work and said, "Repent!" Though we don't use it often, it's a very significant word. If Jesus gave this as a frequent commandment, it must be important.

The word Jesus used literally means "to change your mind." When we repent, we change the way we think. Did Jesus ever give us a command that is impossible to keep? Not a chance. According to Jesus, changing the way we think is possible.

God created the mind with breathtaking power. The mind can process 800 memories a second, yet God has placed this extraordinary asset under our control. Though God is the creator of our minds, we are the managers of our minds. We choose what we will think about. Our thoughts become the tracks that our lives run on.

Imagine a well-worn path in the forest. Through the never-ending pounding of footprints at exactly the same spot, over time, a clearly worn path emerges. In the same way, when we perpetually think the same thoughts, we establish clearly worn paths in our minds. Neuroscience research has established that our minds develop something like hardwiring so that we begin to think and behave automatically. When we develop patterns of thinking, we're establishing deep rooted attitudes which become our default mode for life. Our attitudes become the framework by which we process relationships, decisions, priorities, and setbacks.

Psychological and neurological research confirms that what we think about shapes who we become. Persistent and focused thinking can actually change the way the brain works, establishing mental maps which direct our thoughts and feelings. Every thought we have comes with a little emotional charge attached to it. An angry person thinks a lot of angry thoughts. A joyful person thinks a lot of joyful thoughts. Our emotional state follows our thinking. The best way to shift the way we feel is by shifting the way we think. It's critically important that our internal maps are developed on the solid foundation of God's truth. Changing our mental maps will improve life at the deepest level.

The Myth of the Bad Mood

"I'm in a bad mood." I've said it, and so have you. I've heard people describe a bad mood as if it's something that jumps out of the closet, sort of like a boogeyman. They appear to have no control of the sudden take over. Like a bank robber, the bad mood moves in to take them hostage.

I want to dismantle the myth of a bad mood. There is no such thing as a bad mood. It's possible to have a chemical problem in your body that causes you to be irritable. A good medical doctor can help you sort this out. However, most of the time, it's not a chemical problem. The problem is our attitude. You and I may choose to have a bad attitude, but let's do not sugarcoat it by calling it a bad mood. There was a time when I thought I couldn't change my attitude. By default, I saw myself as a victim of mysterious forces that controlled by emotional temperature. Years ago, I stopped telling myself and other people that I was in a bad mood. I started to be brutally honest with myself, telling myself, "You are choosing to have a selfish, narcissistic attitude." Until we take ownership of our attitudes, we will never improve them.

In our house, it's not uncommon for my youngest son, Lawson, to wake up with a bad attitude. In fact, sometimes when he first wakes up, he resembles the Tasmanian devil. It's still a work in progress, but we're trying to teach Lawson that he's in control of his attitude. When he comes into the kitchen barking out orders, I simply take him by the arm and lead him back to his room. I then say, "Lawson, whenever you decide to have a good attitude, you can come out of your room." We want Lawson to know attitude is a choice. He is responsible for his attitude. His father is responsible for his attitude. That's why, occasionally, my wife has to send me to my room. It's much healthier to own up to our bad attitude than let it operate under the guise of a bad mood. When we take responsibility for our attitudes, we take a huge step in improving them. Consider the wise words of best-selling author, Chuck Swindoll:

> *"Words can never adequately convey the incredible impact of our attitude toward life. The longer I live the more convinced I become that life is 10% what happens to us and 90% how we respond to it. I believe the single most significant decision I can make on a day to day basis is my choice of attitude. It is more important than my past, my education, my bankroll, my successes or failures, it's more important than fame or*

pain, what other people think of me or say about me, it's more
important than my circumstances, or my position. Attitude
keeps me going or it cripples my progress. It alone fuels my
fire or assaults my hope. When my attitude is right, there's no
barrier too high, no valley too deep, no dream too extreme,
no challenge too great for me."[12]

It's much easier to control your attitudes than your circumstances.
Many of your circumstances are completely out of your control, but
your attitudes are completely under your control. If you try to channel
all your energy to control your circumstances, before long, you'll be
an emotional wreck. After all the time you log in on your emotional
treadmill, you'll have very little to show for all your sweat and tears.
Instead, focus your energy on maintaining the right set of attitudes.
You'll find that this is far more productive than focusing on your
difficult circumstances.

This is why it's so important to surround yourself with the right
kind of people when you are facing problems. Our attitudes tend to
be shaped by our closest companions. When you're facing a tough
situation, the last thing you need is to be surrounded by people who
keep telling you about how bad your circumstances are. You need
people around you saying, "You will make it through," and "God
will see you through." When people continue to remind you about
how bad your circumstances are, over the course of time, they will
turn you into a victim. Get the right people around you, and it will
protect you from developing the attitude of a victim.

I only knew her by one name—MommyCile. When I was dating
my wife, she often talked about her grandmother, MommyCile, with
a sparkle in her eye. When I finally met her, I wasn't disappointed.
MommyCile lived to be 96 years old and had a contagious enthusiasm
for life. In her nineties, she was still working out at a gym. She
took trips to Canada and Montana to fish. It's pretty amazing for
someone in her nineties, but even more amazing when you realize
she was legally blind. Though she had her vision for many years,

---

12   Charles Swindoll, *Day by Day with Charles Swindoll* (Nashville: W
Publishing Group, 2000).

MommyCile became legally blind in her sixties. When she lost her sight, she made a choice. She decided that though she might not have her sight, she would still have her life. She decided that blindness would not highjack her life. MommyCile knew she couldn't control her circumstances, but she could control her attitude. Instead of wallowing in self-pity, she lived full throttle. Through her attitude, she made the last part of her life the best part of her life. Clement Stone wrote, "There is little difference in people, but that little difference makes a big difference. The little difference is attitude."[13]

Keep in mind we're talking about improving your personal life, family life, business life, sex life, and your spiritual life. The key to increasing your level of happiness in these areas is by developing the right kind of attitudes. However, there are two specific attitudes that tend to be the mother of all attitudes. By taking the next 90 days to work on these two "mother attitudes," you'll improve your life exponentially.

Shifting from An Attitude of Fear to An Attitude of Faith

It's hard to be fulfilled and happy when you're living in fear. In the most influential sermon ever delivered, Jesus taught us to live in faith, rather than in fear. Jesus goes to the world of nature to teach us a lesson about faith.

> "So why do you worry about clothing? Consider the lilies of the field, how they grow: they neither toil nor spin; and yet I say to you that even Solomon in all his glory was not arrayed like one of these. Now if God so clothes the grass of the field, which today is, and tomorrow is thrown into the oven, will He not much more clothe you, O you of little faith?" (**NKJV**, **Matt 6:28-30**).

It's obvious what the disciples feared. They feared they were not going to have enough food to eat, enough water to drink, and enough

---

13   W. Clement Stone, *Success Through a Positive Mental Attitude* (Pocket, 1991).

clothes to wear. Periodically, I hear people say they wished they could have lived during the 1st century … when life was simpler, and people didn't have as much to worry about. Anyone who says he wishes he could live back in those simpler days doesn't understand the conditions of 1st century Palestine. Most people in 1st century Palestine lived like third world countries live today. Work was scarce, government was dictatorial, and taxes were unbearable. Times may be hard today, but it pales in comparison to what the first disciples endured. Yet, Jesus challenged the disciples not to live in fear. With a velvet glove, he gingerly slaps the disciples and says, "O you of little faith."

If you are a follower of Christ, you have every reason to have a positive attitude. A positive attitude will allow you to do everything better than a negative attitude will, but I'm not simply talking about thinking warm, fuzzy, happy thoughts about yourself. I'm not talking about propping yourself with pop psychology. I'm talking about a positive attitude which is based on biblical faith. I realize life is not a giant bowl of cherries, but when I maintain a faith based attitude, it translates into the right perspective on life. Faith says, "God can!" God can heal my diseased body. God can save my troubled marriage. God can straighten out my wayward child. God can mend my broken heart.

Because Jesus really died for my sins; He really walked out of the grave alive; and my past is forgiven; my circumstances are under His control; I have every reason to have a positive outlook on life. Refuse to be someone who has a sour outlook on life. Some Christians go to church, and they seem to be more excited about bad news than good news. The vast majority of prayer time in churches often revolves around the sick. We should certainly pray for the sick, but how about carving out some time to thank God for what's going right.

Do you know the most frequent commandment given in Scripture? It's not to be more loving, even though that's certainly repeated in the Bible. It's not the commandment to be holy and have integrity, even though Scripture is replete with the call to be holy and have integrity.

The commandment which occurs more than any other commandment in Scripture is made up of 2 words, "Fear Not."

Why does God tell us repeatedly not to be afraid? I think it's because fear is the number one reason people fail to do what God wants them to do. It's the number one reason people disobey God. I believe that most followers of Christ actually want to obey God. They don't set out to live rebelliously, actively resisting God's plan in their lives. Yet, fear cripples them from reaching their redemptive potential in life.

God continues to use simple "play times" with my sons to teach me valuable lessons about life. Several years ago, Lawson and I were outside playing while we were visiting out of town family. I put Lawson up on a cement block that covered up a well. The cement block was elevated about 4 feet from the ground. After I put him on top of the block, he thought he was the king of the hill. Eventually, I said something to Lawson that caught his attention. I held out my hands and said, "Lawson, jump." He looked up at me, and I could see fear was in his eyes. But there was also a little glitter that I caught in the corner of his eye. I said it again, "Lawson, jump " then I added an important phrase, "Don't be afraid; I'll catch you."

Internally, there were two forces at work in his mind right about then—fear and faith. On the one hand, everything inside of his little mind was screaming, "Don't budge. If you move, things could go south in a hurry." On the other hand, he heard Daddy say "Jump." In his mind, he was reviewing daddy's track record. "What kind of batting average does Daddy have?" "Is he trustworthy?" "Will he really catch me?" Lawson stepped back, put his little legs in overdrive, and went running as fast as he could, leaping into my arms. "Ah, Daddy caught me," he seemed to be thinking. He looked up at me with his big eyes, and said, "Daddy, do it again." And so we did it again, and again, and again The battle was between fear and faith. But on this day, faith won the day.

Every day we wake up, we decide if fear will win, or faith will win. Fear says, "No," "Stay Put," "Don't Budge." Faith says, "Jump!" With a faith driven attitude, you stay focused on the opportunities of the day, and not the potential for disaster.

Shifting from An Attitude of Worry
To An Attitude of Trust

Mark Twain said, "I'm an old man and I've known a great many troubles, and most of them never happened." Have you ever noticed most of what we worry about never even comes to pass? We waste too much emotional energy worrying about something that hasn't even happened. Jesus pulls another illustration from the world of nature.

> *"Look at the birds of the air, for they neither sow nor reap nor gather into barns; yet your heavenly Father feeds them. Are you not of more value than they?"* (**NKJV, Matthew 6:26**)

In our modern vernacular, Jesus is saying, "Go watch the birds." I'm not a bird watcher per se, but after reflecting on these words, I decided to take Jesus up on the challenge. I took my binoculars and for the first time, I went bird-watching. I must say I made sure no one else was watching. I felt like my masculinity was being assaulted; nevertheless, I took the challenge seriously. I was amazed as I watched the birds. They seemed to be so relaxed and carefree as they flew from one tree to another tree without any thought.

As I thought about their behavior, one word kept coming to mind, "happy." The birds seemed genuinely happy. I'm sure they may not always feel happy. It appeared that some of them had indigestion. My binoculars had a perfect view of bombs dropping from their missile launchers. Nevertheless, I didn't see any taking Prilosec or Zantac. Neither did I did see the first bird lying down on a little birdie couch, talking to a bird psychiatrist. There's a reason—birds don't worry about anything. God's point is clear. If the birds don't worry, then why should we? If the birds are trusting God to take care of them, then why can't we? God cares about you far more than He cares about the next little tweety bird.

Jesus connected worry with tomorrow. He said, "Do not worry about tomorrow" (Matt. 6:34). This is what makes worrying such a vicious cycle. We try to control things in the future that are completely beyond our control. In some cases, we think we're controlling the situations simply by thinking about them. Interestingly, no matter how much "thinking time" we give to the problem, it doesn't affect the future one iota.

Worry begins as a thought, and most of the time it is a "what if" thought. What if this happens? What if that happens? When we worry, we have the tendency to play out the worst-case scenario. I call them "deadly hypotheticals." When we imagine negative hypotheticals, it's a guarantee for misery. The possibilities for negative hypotheticals are endless.

What if my children grow up to disappoint me? What if they become addicted to drugs? What if my business fails? What if this cancer treatment doesn't work? What if I never get married? What if I get sick? The "what if" game breeds stress and anxiety. When you mentally focus on all kinds of negative hypotheticals, it's like placing your mind on death row.

What if David played this game when he went out to fight Goliath, the overgrown Philistine? He could have easily thought, "Now, what if I happen to choke under pressure?" "What if I throw a ball instead of a strike?" "What if my sling shot goes on the blink?" He could have played out the "what if's" and "could be's." But I don't read that anywhere in the story. In quiet confidence, David picked up His stones and trusted that God would control them.

Several years ago, a cancer patient in my church came to see me. I happened to share how our minds naturally drift toward the worst-case scenario. He was worried the chemotherapy may not work. The next week, he came back to see me. He said, "Clay, for so many weeks I've been thinking, what if my chemo doesn't work? What if my radiation doesn't work?" He said, "Now, I've decided to trust God it will work, and then if it doesn't, I'll cross that river when I get there." He described how this was a turning point in his cancer treatment. He refused to allow tomorrow to rob him of today.

Jesus Said Worry Is A Killer

Jesus reminds us, "Which of you by worrying can add one cubit to his stature?" (Matt 6:27). It's better translated, "Which of you by worrying can add a single hour to his life?" Jesus is saying, "Do you think by worrying that you're going to add length to your life?" The opposite is true. Worrying will shorten your life. Medical science has proven that unmanaged stress kills. If you never learn to manage what you worry about, you're more likely to have high blood pressure, heart disease, cancer, diabetes, and depression. Dr. Charles Mayo, founder of the famed Mayo Clinic, said, "Worry effects the circulation, the heart, the glands, and the whole nervous system, I have never met a man, or known a man to die of over work, but I've known a lot to die from doubt."[14] Doubting and failing to trust God is what generates most of our worry.

Being a follower of Christ doesn't mean your list of worries is automatically shortened. The number of things we can worry about is just about the same as an unbeliever. Christians get sick just like non-Christians. Christians lose their jobs just like someone who doesn't believe. Christians have kids that get pregnant. The difference, though, is that we have an alternative to worrying. We can give the situation over to the Lord.

It's not that we become passive observers of our circumstances. We do our part to be responsible in the situation, but we don't worry about the outcome. Instead, we commit it to God. Sometimes we live like Christian atheists; we worry about the same things unbelievers do, and we're just as stressed about the situations as they are.

I'm convinced when we're at work and something goes wrong, our response should be different from an unbeliever. Coming unglued in hysteria is not exactly an expression that we're trusting God in life. Sure, we have emotions as well. We're not stoic philosophers with plastic feelings, but even in the midst of our sadness, disappointment, and frustration, we have the quiet assurance that God is in control.

The peace I experience on a daily basis is in direct relationship to how much I am trusting God. What is the basis of our trust in God? Why can we trust Him? We can trust Him because of His faithfulness. Scripture calls us to "feed on His faithfulness" (Ps 37:3). If you've been a follower of Christ very long, you know something about the faithfulness of God. Do you have any reason to

---

14   http://quoteworld.org/quotes/8804

believe that the God who has been faithful to you in the past is not going to be faithful to you in the future? Think about His faithful track record. The more we trust in God, the easier it gets.

When Graham was younger, one of his favorite things to do was play in the sand box. One day, Graham and I were outside taking in a beautiful summer day, and Graham was playing in his sand box. After a few minutes of playing with his fire truck, suddenly he got sand in his eye. The first time it happened, he went ballistic. He started crying, hollering, and immediately ran over to where I was sitting. When Graham came over to me, I took my t-shirt and wiped his eye. The sand came out, and he was once again a happy camper.

Several days later, he was back in his sand box, and it wasn't too long before he had sand in his eye again. It was the same story. He went wild, with his arms flailing, teeth chattering, and voice screaming for his dad. I took my t-shirt and wiped out his eye, and he was fine.

About a week later, Graham was back in his sandbox. As you can imagine, he got sand in his eye again. By now, you're probably thinking, "Why don't you put some goggles on that dude?" This time, the reaction was different though. Graham quietly crawled out of the sandbox, walked calmly over to where I was sitting, and said, "Daddy, I've got sand in my eye." You know my next step. I reached down and with my t-shirt, I removed the sand.

What happened there? Why didn't Graham go ballistic this time? Why didn't he panic? Why didn't he start to cry and scream? Because He started trusting that Daddy was going to take care of the sand in his eyes. Once he had come to me three times, and received help, he started to believe that Dad was more than capable of taking care of the problem. Every other time Graham got sand in his eye that summer (and it was a lot), he never once got upset. Each time, he calmly walked over to me and said, "Daddy, I've got sand in my eye."

The truth is we all get sand in our eyes. Life will arrange circumstances where we can easily worry about how things are going to turn out. It could come in the form of a health challenge, financial crisis, job layoff, or a relational letdown. When the sand appears, we don't have to panic, experience a cataclysmic meltdown, or come emotionally unglued. We can calmly and confidently go back to our heavenly Father and say, "Daddy, it's me again. I've got sand in my eye. I've been here many times before. You've taken care of many raw situations in the past, and I'm trusting you will take care of it once again."

CHAPTER 5

Squeeze The Moment

TWO PRISONERS WERE IN THE same small cell. The cell was depressingly dark-pitch black. The only light came through a small window in the corner of the cell. Both prisoners spent a great deal of time looking out that window. One of the prisoners focused on the bars that covered the window. It was a reminder to him that he would probably never experience freedom again. Day by day, as the prisoner focused on those bars, he became bitter and hopeless.

The other prisoner looked out the same window. Instead of focusing on the bars, he focused on the stars. He looked beyond the bars, and he saw light of the stars that twinkled in the night. The stars gave him a glimmer of hope; it reminded him that maybe there was a possibility he would be free one day. These two prisoners were looking out the same window; one saw bars and the other saw stars. In life, what we choose to focus on makes all the difference in the world.

Did you know one whole section of the New Testament is called prison letters? They're often called prison letters because Paul wrote these letters from behind bars; one of those letters Paul wrote from prison is called Philippians. When you read his letter, you find that Paul, the prisoner, wasn't focused on the bars. Instead Paul was focused on the stars.

In fact, the theme of the book of Philippians is joy! Here's a man who knows excruciating hardship. Paul was arrested and thrown in prison for preaching the gospel. He was under house arrest and was chained to a Roman soldier for two solid years. Yet, joy is the thread that holds the book of Philippians together.

What Paul says in the 104 verses of the book is remarkable. He had every reason to be down and out; he was in prison and isolated from everyone he loved, yet Paul deliberately chose to have an attitude of joy. In the repertoire of attitudes we select daily, one of the most important is an attitude of joy. It's wise for us to learn from a man like Paul who has gone through debilitating hardship, but he did it all with a smile on his face.

The Attitude of Joy

Attitudes are not connected to our circumstances. Remember, they're connected to our choices. Joy is a choice. Blaise Pascal said, "If you're waiting to be happy, you will never be happy." If I went to a Wal-Mart shopping center and asked 1000 people, "What are you waiting on to be happy?" the answers would be surprisingly predictable. Most likely, we would hear a variation of three different answers. Some would answer, "I'm waiting on a few things and when I get them, then I'll be happy." If you were to press and probe a little further about the "few things," you would find out it translates into a new car, a new house, or maybe a new job. They're connecting their happiness with what they have.

This outlook cuts against the grain of what Jesus taught. Jesus said, "A man's life (his quality of life) doesn't consist of the abundance of things possessed" (Lk 12:15). In other words, things will never make you happy. If this philosophy actually worked, Americans should be the happiest people in the world. We live in the most prosperous nation on the globe. Though we are numbered among the most materially elite in the world, ironically, we are also numbered among the most dissatisfied.

I'm convinced some people would answer by saying, "I'm waiting on the right person, and then I'll be happy." You name the person… my future marriage partner, my first baby, my new boss, my soul mate, and then I'll enjoy the rest of my life. It's not uncommon for singles to think that if they were only married, they would be happy and fulfilled. However, if you're unhappy and unfilled as a single person, you'll be the same way as a married person. No human being can make you happy. Every human being on this planet will eventually disappoint you. But there's a prevailing thought that Mr. Right or Mrs. Right will be your ticket to a life of happiness.

If you're waiting for a person to make you happy, you're going to be waiting for a lifetime.

Here's a third answer I would get if I conducted a random interview. If I asked, "What are you waiting on to be happy?" some people would say, "I'm waiting until I accomplish my goals, then I'll be happy." There's nothing wrong with goals. I would encourage you to develop personal goals, but your level of happiness isn't going to change when you reach your goals. You'll feel the exhilaration of achieving a goal, and that's exciting, but eventually the exhilaration wears off. What do we do then? We add another goal. It's usually a bigger and better one, but even when we reach the skies, we always have to come back to earth. Reaching a goal will never satisfy the deepest part of the soul.

Don't wait for "someday" before you're happy. Someday will probably never occur. Decide to be joyful today. Joy starts with the simple things. Find joy in this moment. You don't have to wait until all your circumstances are aligned perfectly before you decide to be joyful. If there's one man who proves that very point it's the apostle Paul. Paul was the classic example of a victim. He was illegally arrested in Jerusalem; he was misrepresented in court; as he was sailing to Rome, he suffered a terrible shipwreck. When Paul finally got to Rome, he was placed under house arrest. He was chained to a Roman soldier 24 hours a day. Yet, when Paul picked up his pen to write Philippians, he wrote a letter about joy. Knowing his circumstances, you would think the theme would possibly be grief, anger, or maybe vengeance, but out comes a beautiful letter about joy. How could Paul maintain an attitude of joy under such circumstances? The secret behind his joyful attitude was his mindset.

Joyful People Focus On Others

Let's be honest; most of us have been demanding our own way since we were infants. Because of our fallen nature, we have a default drive that's set on selfishness. God is fully committed to bump us off our self-centeredness. God knows we will never be full of joy as long as we are full of ourselves. The happiest people

I've ever known are not focused on themselves. When Paul wrote from prison, he wasn't focused on himself; he was focused on the Philippians.

> *"I thank my God in all my remembrance of you, always in every prayer of mine for you all making my prayer with joy, because of your partnership in the gospel from the first day until now"* (**ESV, Philippians 1:3-4**).

Don't miss an obvious truth here. While Paul is writing, he's thinking about the Philippians. He says, "Every time I think of you, I thank God for you." Paul could have easily focused on his own circumstances. Right out of the shoot, his opening line could have been, "Can you believe this? I didn't deserve this? Why am I in prison? Why me? Life is nothing but a raw deal." Had he opened his letter this way, I don't think as many people then or now would have read his letter. We're usually not drawn to whiners.

There's a subtle little phrase in this passage that reveals Paul's mindset. It's the little phrase, "you all." Paul uses the phrase frequently throughout Philippians. Why did Paul use this phrase? Was he Southern? I'm convinced this subtle phrase speaks volumes about Paul's mindset. Paul wasn't focused on himself. It was always about "you all." It could have easily been written as an epitaph. His focus in life was "you all."

If we were experiencing the hardships Paul was facing, most of us would have probably been thinking about ourselves. If I were writing the book of Philippians, I might have told you about the narrow quarters of my jail cell; I would have told you about how the mice kept me up each night and how terrible the food was, but when you read what Paul writes, he's focused more on the Philippians than himself.

This is one of the secrets of establishing a joyful attitude. Joy eludes us as long as we build the world around ourselves. We have to establish a mindset that puts others before ourselves. Paul wanted the Philippians to experience his same level of joy. Further into his letter, he gives them some specific instructions.

"Do nothing from rivalry or conceit, but in humility count others more significant than yourselves. Let each of you look not only to his own interests, but also to the interests of others" (**NEV, Philippians 2:3-4**).

Paul tells everyone not to simply look out for themselves, but to look out for others. "Look out" is a fascinating word in the original language. It's "scopeneo," where we get the English word "scope" from. I like to hunt, and I have a scope on several of my guns. There's nothing like getting up at 5:00 a.m. in the morning and getting frostbite, just to be able to see a North American whitetail deer. I've been hunting for years, but I still love to get the adrenaline rush that comes when a whitetail deer comes out in open view.

I enjoy putting my scope up to my eye and getting the crosshairs positioned squarely on the target. I also enjoy pulling the trigger, and most of the time, having something to show for it. I'm not a marksman. I will be the first to admit that apart from the scope I have on my guns, my aim would be hopeless. The scope takes something far away and brings it up close. Paul is saying, "I want you to put your scope, not on your own interests, but on the interests of others." In other words, don't zoom in on your interests, but zoom in and focus on the needs of others. Admittedly, it's hard to do.

When we focus on others, inevitably it improves every relationship we have. Zig Ziglar puts it in perspective with the following scenario... A husband has been gone all week. He comes home at dinner time carrying a heavy suitcase and a bulging briefcase. He doesn't want to set it down and ring the doorbell so he just kicks the door. "Bang! Bang! Bang!" He practically knocks the door off the hinges.

His wife comes to the door, and he says, "Now, the reason I'm late is I've been at a meeting, and boy am I glad I went to the meeting. I learned there are some rights around this house I haven't been getting. As a matter of fact, I've made a list of them." He says, "The first thing you and I are going to do is sit down and we're going to talk about this list, because there are going to be some changes around here."

Can't you just imagine his wife's response? She says, "Buster, I didn't go to a meeting because I didn't have to. I didn't need to write down a list because I've got one burned indelibly on my mind. Come on in here big boy, I'll be happy to talk to you. I agree there need to be changes around here, and you're not going to like most of them."

Let your imagination run wild. Think it was a star spangled night of ecstasy? Think their conversation was a romantic one? Think they had a splendid weekend?

But what if we change the scenario slightly? What if it's the same husband, with the same basic set of circumstances, but he has a different attitude. What if he comes to the front porch, carrying his heavy suitcase, but instead of banging on the door, he gently taps on it. His wife comes to the door and he says, "Honey, the reason I'm late is I've been at a meeting, and I'm so grateful I was able to attend the meeting. While I was there, I learned about some things that really disturbed me. I learned that in all probability, as a husband, I haven't been meeting your needs." He says, "Before I unpack, I want us to sit down and talk. I want you to tell me what I can do to be the husband you thought you were getting when you married me."

I can just imagine her response. She says, "Actually, here lately I've been very happy being your wife, but from time to time, I've often wondered if I'm meeting all your needs." Let your imagination run wild for a second time. Which couple do you think will have the happiest, healthiest marriage? Which couple do you think will raise positive, well-adjusted kids? Which couple do you think will have a better shot at reflecting the love of Christ to the world? It doesn't take a Phi Betta Kappa to get the right answer. When we put the other person first, everybody wins.[15]

---

15   Audio recording entitled, *A View From the Top* by Zig Ziglar

Joyful People Believe God is Sovereign

Paul believed God was in absolute control of his life. Though he was in prison, Paul knew God was at work, and he believed God would take use his circumstances to accomplish His divine purposes. Paul encourages the Philippians to place their complete confidence in God.

> *"And I am sure of this, that He who began a good work in you will bring it to completion at the day of Jesus Christ"* **(ESV, Philippians 1:6).**

The one who started a good work in you will complete it. God finishes what He starts. This is why we can resign from trying to be the Master of the Universe. There is no opening to fill a vacancy in the Trinity. God hasn't abdicated His rule over the universe. He is in complete control. Nothing that happens to you will ever come to your life unless it first passes through the permissive will of God.

Behind every microscopic detail of our life, both good and bad, is the purpose, plan, and will of a sovereign God. I hope you believe that. Job believed that. Jesus believed that, and Paul believed that. Sixty six books of the Bible teach it; when you understand God is in control of your life, it keeps you from feeling like you have to micromanage every detail of your life. The God who started a good work in you will complete it! Joyful people have learned to trust the details of their lives into hands of a sovereign God.

Paul's positive outlook was rooted in his conviction that God was in control of his life. Paul was even convinced that the negative, difficult parts of his life would be redeemed to accomplish God's sovereign purpose. Paul speaks about this confidence:

> *"I want you to know, brothers, that what has happened to me has really served to advance the gospel, so that it has become known throughout the whole imperial guard and to all the rest that my imprisonment is for Christ"* **(ESV, Philippians 1:12).**

Paul says his adverse circumstances are actually helping to advance the gospel. One of the reasons I believe the Holy Spirit used the Greek language is because the Greek language is so picturesque. God knew our minds think best in terms of pictures. This word, "advance" is such colorful word. In the original language, it was a military term. It describes a group of engineers that would travel ahead of the army. The engineers would prepare the road by removing obstacles and trees. Even today, in our world, military strategy is very similar. The military often sends a group of engineers ahead of the army. They build bridges and get the roads ready for the army.

Paul is saying his circumstances are just like those engineers. God is using his circumstances to prepare the way for the gospel. Most likely, at this very moment, there is a cascade of different problems, hardships, and trials in your life which God will use to advance His purposes.

I'm thinking about the man born blind in John 9. The disciples asked Jesus, "Why is the man blind? Did he sin, or his parents?" Jesus said, "Neither one." In other words, these bad circumstances didn't happen to him as punishment for sin. "No," Jesus said, "This has happened so the glory of God can be displayed in his life." Blindness would be the platform God would use to showcase His glory. Your circumstances might be the very thing God uses to showcase the gospel. Your adversity could parade God's glory down Main Street.

Your adversity can take the form of many different circumstances. It could take the form of sickness. This is when the doctor walks in and says, "The results are not good." Adversity can take the form of a spouse walking out. Adversity can show up when the boss comes in with a pink slip. Adversity can show up in the empty nest syndrome when your last child leaves for college. The family atmosphere is about to change; it's frightening, and it leaves you with an empty ache in the bottom of your stomach. Adversity can show up in the form of a long waiting period. You're waiting for a spouse. You're waiting for a new job opportunity. The resumes are out, the contacts have been made, but no one has called for the first interview.

Adverse circumstances can leave us reeling with questions, but all of our circumstances are being guided by the Providence of God. Happenstance isn't ruling the day; Providence is ruling the day. God is using your circumstances to advance His purposes.

How were Paul's specific circumstances advancing the gospel? For two long years, Paul was chained to Roman soldiers. These were elite soldiers—the Rambos of the first century. Caesar would use these elite soldiers to guard prisoners. They would actually chain themselves to the prisoner. Paul was chained to a Roman guard 24 hours a day. Historians tell us the guards would change shifts every six hours; therefore, every day Paul had at least four new people He could talk to about Christ. Isn't that great?! Paul looked beyond his chains, and saw the person at the end of his chains. He looked beyond his obstacle and saw an opportunity. While he was in chains, he took the opportunity to tell each soldier about the love of Christ.

You know what Paul could have done when he was chained to the praetorian guards? He could have filled their ears with a sob story. He could have told every soldier the same sad story, "This is a bunch of baloney; I'm nothing but a victim; I've gotten one raw deal after another; I've been mistreated, abused, and taken advantage of." He could have filled their ears with a multitude of complaints. But Paul understood a basic principle of human nature—whining never attracts anyone.

Whining typically becomes the incubator for self-pity, and inevitably carves out a bigger sink hole for us to fall into. I don't think Paul cut cartwheels because he was in prison, but neither do I believe he spent his time sucking his thumb in self-pity. In the 104 verses of this book, I can't find one time when Paul is licking his wounds, or throwing a temper tantrum. Paul retained an attitude of joy because of his confidence in God's control.

Squeeze The Moment

There's a catechism used in the Presbyterian Church to teach people how to think correctly about God. It starts like this: "What is the chief end of man?" Then, the answer is given, "The chief end of man is to love God and enjoy Him forever."[16] You mean God can be enjoyed? We're not simply called to serve Him, sacrifice for Him, obey Him, but we're also called to enjoy Him.

For some strange reason, so many Christians turn God into a cosmic kill joy. Do you know the one attribute of God we talk less about than any other attribute? His joy. We talk frequently about His love, righteousness, compassion, holiness, and mercy, but how about His joy? Nehemiah 8:10 says, "The joy of the Lord is my strength." Joy is one of the attributes God possesses. The Lord is full of joy. Until you believe God is full of joy, you'll never give yourself permission to enjoy life. Perhaps you grew up in a legalistic home. For you, God was viewed as a grim, angry, vindictive God. The sooner you can get rid of that warped perception of God, the happier you'll be.

We lose our joy over the simplest things in life. Someone seems aloof and doesn't speak to us at work, and we allow them to steal our joy. We encounter a problem at home, and instead of trusting God to help us deal with it, we allow the problem to steal our joy.

Don't wait for "someday" before you start enjoying life. Decide to be happy and joyful this day. We have the tendency to divide life into two categories: Living and Existing. We throw a lot of our minutes into the "Existing" category. We spend a lot of our time in transition: we're waiting in the doctor's office, trying to get somewhere in the car, we're trying to complete a task, but we wouldn't say those activities are truly living. We dump them into the Existing category. We're trying to get these things over with so we can really start living. From God's perspective, there is no such thing as an Existing category. We're never waiting to live because each second is a gift from God. God wants you to enjoy the journey. Don't think that when you finally get to your destination you're going to truly start living. Those small, mundane, routine tasks are not getting in the way of your life. They are your life.

Joy starts with the simple things. Some of us are goal driven; we struggle with enjoying the moment because we're thinking about

---

16   Westminster Shorter Catechism. See creeds.net

the next big goal to accomplish. I've been learning a profound truth lately. Joy is not out there somewhere. Joy is in the middle of this moment. Joy is not in the next big event or the next big promotion; joy is in the next sacred moment. To get the most out of life, squeeze the joy out of this moment.

CHAPTER 6

When Candy Is In Your Socks

STEEL BARS AND FIBERGLASS SEPARATED us. Wearing an orange jumpsuit and a fearful look, he picked up the phone and said, "Thanks for coming to see me." I'm sure as a young child playing on the seesaw and monkey bars, he never dreamed that he would be here. When he was asked what he wanted to be when he grew up, he answered like all the other children: a police officer, a firefighter, a doctor, a teacher. What child ever says, "I want to grow up and go to prison"? I told him I came to see him because I cared about him. Since the visit was restricted to twenty minutes, we talked rapidly and to the point. Then, as if I caught him off guard, I asked a question, "Do you have any dreams?" There was a long pause and then his answer, "No!" I asked a follow-up question, "Do you have any goals in life?" With the same stoic dryness, he simply said, "No!" I asked one more question before I left. "Do you have any purpose in life?" His answer seemed to emerge from the deepest part of his psyche, "No!"

I left, but for a few moments, I just stood in the hallway and thought about what had just happened. I had just been an eyewitness to the greatest tragedy on earth: life without purpose. I glanced back as the jailor came in to return him to his designated cell. As I looked into his eyes, I had a conspicuous flashback of someone else who was once in the same dire condition. This man I was intimately acquainted, unlike the prisoner with whom I had just spoken. I knew him like I knew no other person; the man was me.

Though I have never spent one single night behind literal prison bars, I have spent plenty of other days and nights in a far worse prison. For many years, I was incarcerated by my own lack of purpose. I had tasted the bitter herbs of self-consumption, but then after years of searching, I laid my pinstripes aside. I was no longer a prisoner; I found the greatest commodity known to man: purpose.

My search for purpose began as a quest to achieve happiness. Isn't everyone looking for happiness? Happiness is a quality of life that everyone is entitled to experience. It is stated that way in the Declaration of Independence. We say that everyone has the right to life, liberty, and the pursuit of happiness. My pursuit of happiness led me to embrace the myth of more. I spent more time filling up my bank account, filling up my garage, and filling up my closet. The bitter irony was that the very thing I had clung to so tenaciously was keeping me from being fulfilled. In almost paradoxical form, while I was filling up, I seemed to be growing empty. Spiritual bulimia had stricken me, always wanting more, but never being satisfied.

When I bought a new car or a new suit, I seemed happy, but after the newness wore off, so did my happiness. My pursuit of happiness led me down the golden streets of pleasure. Yet, every form of pleasure seemed so short-lived. I felt like a teenager who stands in line at an amusement park for five hours to take a thrill ride that lasts two minutes. I could agree with Solomon, the Jewish sage, who pursued pleasure for a lifetime. After his pursuit of pleasure, he exclaimed, "Vanity, vanity, all is vanity!" Of course, there is nothing inherently wrong with pleasure. Pleasure is good, but it is not the deepest good.

I believe that it is a futile attempt to find happiness by pursuing happiness. Happiness is the result of seeking something else: purpose. My search for happiness came to a close when I found purpose. Happiness will remain elusive until we find purpose. Ultimately, purpose finds its origin in God. Bertrand Russell, the famed atheistic philosopher said, "Unless you assume the existence of God, the question of life's purpose is meaningless."[17] Russell was probably more of a prophet than he realized.

Until I became acquainted with the God who created me, my purpose was irrelevant. When I embraced the truth that God created

17   Rick Warren, *The Purpose Driven Life* (Grand Rapids: Zondervan, 2002), 17.

me in His image, suddenly purpose sprang to life. I no longer saw myself as a composite of flesh and bones. I now understood myself to be a special creation made in the image of God. This meant that I was a spiritual being. God created me to love me. It would be accurate to say that God created me so I could love Him, yet I believe it is more accurate to say that God created me so He could love me. In one of the most well known passages in the Bible, we are reminded, "God is love." I am alive because God wants to express His love to me.

An Unforgettable Encounter

As a pastor, I now spend a significant amount of my time helping others get acquainted with the God who loves them so passionately. Meet Junior, for instance. I first met Junior, an eight-year old boy, on a rainy night. I was driving home from an evening meeting when I saw Junior walking home in the rain. He had been at our church playing basketball in our gym. Though I had never met him before, I pulled up beside him and said, "It's pretty messy to be walking in the rain tonight; let me give you a lift." He knew that I was the pastor up the street, so he climbed in wringing wet. I said, "Where are you going?" In a gruff voice, he said, "I'm going home to get something to drink, then I'm going back to the church to play some more basketball." I said, "Okay, I'll take you home and wait for you to get a glass of Coke, and then I'll take you back to the church."

Junior helped to navigate me to what was his tiny house. But before he got out, I said, "Junior, after you're done playing basketball, how are you going to get home?" With little concern, he said, "I'll walk home, it's not too far." He was right; it wasn't too far for him to walk home, just several blocks. I said, "You probably want to grab an umbrella so you won't get wet when you walk home." What he said next was something I wasn't prepared for. He said, "We don't have an umbrella. We're too poor!" I sort of took a hard swallow and said, "That's Okay, go ahead and get your drink and we'll figure something out."

From what I could see by looking at his house, I knew his remark was probably true. After he went in to his house, I looked in the back of my car and found a small black umbrella under my seat. He dashed in and out and was back to the car in record time. I drove him back to the church, but before he got out of the car, I handed him the umbrella and said, "Junior, this is your umbrella. You keep it." His eyes started to sparkle; he couldn't believe it. You would have thought I had given him the most expensive video game on the market. I'll never forget how excited he was. I drove off and looked in my rear-view mirror there was Junior, standing in the rain holding his new umbrella. I circled the block a few times thinking about what had transpired. I decided to drive back by the church, and guess who was still out in the rain? Junior. He was grinning from ear to ear, relishing his time with his new toy.

Thus, my friendship with Junior began. I would learn so much about the story behind his story. His father died several years earlier; his mother was unemployed and a drug user. Junior and his older sister, Charlie, were left to take care of themselves. But what eight-year-old child could possibly care for himself? What eight-year-old boy, left to himself, would bathe, brush his teeth, and comb his hair? This would explain Junior's body odor. In fact, on many occasions I would take Junior around town in my car. The next morning I would get in my car to go to work, and the odor from Junior's ride was there to greet me. This would also explain his dirty clothes, his poor manners, and his foul language. As you might imagine, Junior resembled a mangled piece of prey after the kids at school were done with him. With his clothes reeking of fecal smells, the kids took no mercy on him. Junior was a walking target for jokes, jeers, and fits of laughter.

But I saw in Junior someone who was a special creation of God. Junior didn't believe it, but I was determined to show him that he was a special boy. I started by sharing Junior's story with my congregation. They refused to stay on the sidelines. Before long, several men were taking him on fishing trips. Some of the ladies were making certain that he had clean clothes to wear. Junior played on one of our basketball teams, his first chance at playing on a recreational team. I'll never forget awards night. Junior received his very first trophy. I could tell that something positive was happening to Junior, and yet, I knew something greater was happening to me.

I will never forget the days I heard a soft knock on my office door. Junior knew how to by-pass the secretary. Honestly, on many of those occasions, I would catch myself thinking, "I have so many things to do; I have messages to prepare, hospitals to visit, counseling appointments, leadership meetings to prepare for." But every time I started to let those thoughts distract me, God reminded me very tenderly that spending time with Junior was exactly what He wanted me to do. After his knock on the door, I would often walk to the kitchen, where I would serve up two cups of Dr. Pepper, Junior's favorite drink. We would sit in my office and talk.

Did I accomplish my goal? Did Junior ever start to believe that God had a purpose for him? I'm not sure. I certainly saw glimpses of hope. I saw him smile when he got his basketball trophy; I saw him bubbling with joy when the church bought him a red bike for Christmas; his demeanor and self-esteem seemed to be on its way up. We taught him that God loved him and had a special plan for his life. Perhaps I will never know if Junior truly believed he had a special purpose in life. After two years of building a friendship with him, his mother decided to take the kids and move several states away. Our friendship came to a close. I often find myself daydreaming about Junior. Will he remember what we taught him? Will he remember how we spent time with him to demonstrate his worth? Will he pursue excellence in school and in his profession? Will he grow up to raise a healthy and stable family? Then, there are other thoughts a little more troubling. Will Junior be another statistic? Will he be another juvenile delinquent who began an early life of crime? Worse still, will Junior grow so tired of the jokes and teasing that he will decide to make someone pay for it?

Did I help Junior find purpose in life? Honestly, I do not know. But I do know that Junior helped me find purpose. Human beings who make a passionate commitment to the well-being of others live purposeful lives. Purpose is tied inextricably to relationships. I am here to do more than amuse myself; my life is to be given to something bigger than myself. It is, in a word, "other-centeredness."

Purpose and fulfillment coexist when we try to meet someone else's need rather than our own.

Finding Purpose By Finding A Leper

I have found purpose by learning to "touch the leper." Leprosy, especially in the ancient world, was a horrible disease. The modern day medical term is Hansen's disease. Leprosy begins with little specks on the eyelids and palms of the hands. Then it spreads all over the body. It covers the skin with oozing sores, but that is just what happens on the surface. Under the skin, leprosy eats all the way to the nerves. And before long, the victim loses all sense of touch. Dr. Paul Brand, a world-renowned expert on leprosy did much of his pioneer research in India. While he was working in India, Dr. Brand observed that many of the lepers were missing their fingers and toes. He also observed that many of his patients seemed to lose their fingers and toes during the night. Dr. Brand made a startling discovery. During the night, rats were coming in to where his patients were sleeping, and the rats were literally chewing off their fingers and toes. The lepers never woke up because they had no sense of feeling or pain. Dr. Brand also noticed that young children with leprosy were gnawing off their fingers, because they had no sense of pain.[18]

No wonder this disease had such a social stigmatism attached to it. Imagine what leprosy patients often looked like before the advent of modern medical treatment. According to experts, when leprosy progresses, the skin around the eyes and ears begin to sag. This is why a leper was said to resemble a lion. In an advanced case of leprosy, people thought the victims looked more like animals than human beings. Is it any wonder why they were ostracized? In the ancient Middle East, when you discovered you had leprosy, you were obligated to tear your clothes and shout, "Unclean, Unclean, Unclean!" This public declaration was made so no one would get too close to you. According to rabbinical tradition, if you were Jewish, you could come no closer than six feet to a leper. If the wind was

---

18   Dr. Paul Brand & Philip Yancey, *Pain: The Gift Nobody Wants* (New York: HarperCollins Publishers, Inc., 1993), 126-127.

blowing, the distance had to be a 150 feet. The leper was the epitome of a social outcast.

Understanding this social stigmatism may explain why thousands of people have sat mesmerized while reading an ancient story in the Bible. The story has two central figures: Jesus and a leper. The book of Mark says that this particular leper heard that Jesus was in town, and decided to approach him. There is no record of him shouting, "Unclean, Unclean, Unclean!" He didn't need to. It wasn't necessary since he knew that this man would accept him just like he was. No pretense. No striking a pose. No attention to proper etiquette. The fact that he was willing to approach Jesus is extremely significant. Lepers didn't approach anyone. They were forbidden to come close to anyone. But this leper knew that Jesus was different. The most remarkable turn in the story takes place when Jesus does the unthinkable. Jesus reaches out and touches the leper.[19]

How long had it been since someone last touched this man? Years and years! It was against the law to touch a leper. The law was even applied to his closest family members. Can you imagine how long it had been since he held his wife's hand? Imagine how long it had been since his little daughter took his hand and said, "Daddy, let's go for a walk." The law of the day restricted her from touching Daddy. The absence of touch was the worst part about leprosy. The result was complete isolation and loneliness.

In one well-known study, research showed that infants who are not held and touched, even if they have caregivers who feed them and clothe them, suffer from lack of neurological development. Other psychological research confirms the significance of touch. Children who are hugged, held, and caressed develop a healthier emotional life than those who go without any physical contact.[20] No wonder the biblical account says the leper was healed when Jesus touched him.

---

19   Mark 1:40-45.

20   John Ortberg, *Everybody's Normal Till You Get to Know Them* (Grand Rapids: Zondervan, 2003), 21.

One other detail from the narrative is striking and arresting. In other biblical accounts, Jesus simply healed others by speaking to them. So we beg an important question, "Did Jesus have to touch the leper for him to be healed?" Undoubtedly, He did not. Breaking all rules and traditions, Jesus reaches out and does the unimaginable. He touches a leper. The significance, of course, lies in the fact that He was willing to touch someone that no one else would touch. In other words, He was willing to touch Junior. Jesus seemed to gravitate toward the ostracized and outcast. Mother Teresa said that loneliness is the leprosy of our modern world. Lepers are in every corner of our lives waiting for us to touch them.

People with purpose seem to share something in common. The common denominator could be called a Copernican approach to life. It's the realization that purpose comes when we don't demand that the universe revolve around us. People with purpose have a healthy degree of "self-forgetfulness." They are focused on others and not on themselves. Jesus calls this attitude the "servant."

Jesus said, "Love your neighbor as yourself." Who is your neighbor? Is it the person who has a similar address as you? Is it the person who has a mailbox close to yours? No, your neighbor is anyone who has a need that you could something about. Whenever someone stands before us with a need and we can do something about the need, we are looking at our neighbor. God is giving us a golden opportunity to serve.

When people question whether or not God exists, I want to say, "Look, are you some kind of fruitcake?" That's my paraphrase of Ps. 14: 1, "The fool has said in His heart there is no god." The universe is full of evidence that God is exists. It takes far more faith not to believe in God than to believe in Him. The complex design of the universe screams that there is a designer. The logical question is not, "Does God exist?" The question we should be asking is, "What is God like?" What we can see through the microscope and telescope points to a God; we simply need to know what He is like.

If you want to know what God is like, take a long hard look at Jesus. If you want to know how God reacts to people, look at how Jesus reacted to people. If you want to know how God deals with hurting people, examine how Jesus dealt with hurting people. If you want to know what God thinks about something, don't get a bunch your friends together and take a poll. Truth isn't discovered by human opinion. If you want to know what God is like, don't get a theology book to figure it out. Don't go to a preacher. For God's sake (and I mean that), go to Jesus. Jesus is God in human flesh. When He came to earth, he was Emmanuel—God with us.

We find out about the nature and character of God from Jesus. Christ is the standard for everything we think about God. If something we think about God violates and contradicts what we know about Jesus, then what we're thinking about God is wrong.

By looking at Jesus (God clothed in human flesh), it's quite apparent that God Himself is a servant.

The Towel and Basin Mentality

One evening, Jesus was having dinner with His disciples, but for some reason, the foot washer didn't show up. In first century Palestine, people walked up and down the dusty roads in sandals. When it came time to eat, they reclined at tables that were built low to the ground. Much like Oriental cultures, their feet usually ended up being close to someone's face. It was customary that a common servant washed your dirty feet before you ate. But something went wrong at the dinner party. The foot washer didn't show up. Can't you just imagine watching the scene through a glass window? The first disciple enters the room, and he discovers there's no foot-washer. Does he decide to wash His own feet? No! Does he take off his outer garment and start washing the other disciple's feet? Not a chance. In his mind, he's thinking *"Oh no, not me, that's not my job. I'm not a common servant. That's below me. I'm not a foot washer."* As each disciple entered the room, they all reacted the same way, "No way, there's not a chance I'm washing dirty feet. I'm not a foot washer."

Then Jesus enters. He too notices there's no foot-washer. Jesus looks at the filthy feet of the disciples. Suddenly He gets up from the table, and begins to pour water into a basin. He slips the towel into His belt, just like a common servant would. Then, one by one, He begins to wash the feet of the disciples. This was God in human flesh washing dirty feet. After He finished washing the feet, Jesus said, "I came not to be served, but to serve." This is the second person of the Trinity saying, "I didn't come to get all the service to come my way. I came to serve others." Jesus uses this as a teachable moment for the disciples, and all who would follow Him in the future. He said, "I have given you an example that you should do as I have done to you." Jesus said I want you to spend the rest of your life following my example. Live with a towel and basin attitude. Spend your life being a foot washer, giving your life away in service to others.[21]

The primary reason to embrace the attitude of a servant is not just because other people need our service. It's because of what happens to us when we serve. We begin to focus on others rather than ourselves, and the byproduct is a life of fulfillment and purpose. I must admit, even though I long to maintain this "servant's attitude," I often find myself unwilling to move out of my La-Z-Boy recliner. Being a servant means I must focus on others, but sometimes a touch of narcissism stills plagues me.

Sometimes I want to revert back to my days as a freshman football player. When I was a freshman in high school, I played on the junior varsity football team. I was one of the youngest players on the team, not to mention one of the smallest. As you might imagine, I didn't see much action on the field. I pretty much found a permanent spot on the sidelines. Half way through the season, I thought, "You know if I'm never going to play, I'm at least going to have a good time on the sidelines." So before each game, I stuffed my socks with candy. I loaded up with jolly ranchers, jaw breakers, and snickers bars. I stuffed bubblegum and blow pops in my shoulder pads, and the whole time the game was going on, I ate candy on the sidelines. The next year's football season, I had to forego my candy. I was the starting quarterback for the team. It would have been a little difficult running the triple option with jolly ranchers and jaw breakers in my socks.

I'm so glad I had those sideline experiences now. You know what I learned? I learned that being in the game is infinitely more exciting than eating candy on the sidelines. Being a spectator doesn't begin

---

21   John 13:1-17.

to compare with the thrills of being in the game. I know people who pursue comfort at all cost. Each day they go to work, come home, eat supper, watch TV, and go to bed. They never do anything to serve other people. They might as well stuff their socks with candy each day.

God has something far better in store for our lives. We weren't designed to make comfort our number one goal. God engineered us to make a difference with our lives. The world should be different because we spent some time on planet earth. The way we truly make a difference is by serving other people. Some people think they have to be perfect before God can use them. If God only used perfect people, nothing would ever get done. God isn't looking for perfect people because there aren't any. God is looking for people who are more confident in His strength than their own strength.

My great grandfather grew up on a farm. He was also textile worker. Because he had very little education, he was illiterate. He couldn't read or write a single word. However, my grandmother has passed down to me the amazing story of how things started to change for my great grandfather. One day, he came in from the fields, knelt down on his knees, just in front of his wife. He took an open Bible and placed it on her lap. He said, "Honey, God is calling me to preach the gospel of Christ. I can't read a single word in this book, but I know God wants me to preach the good news." For several years, my great grandmother would travel with him to churches throughout several counties. She would read his Scripture for him, and then my great grandfather would preach God's Word.

Slowly but surely, my great grandmother taught him how to read. The day came when he could take his own Bible, read his own Scripture, and then preach. I'm sure my great grandfather didn't pronounce all his nouns and verbs correctly. He didn't know Hebrew or Greek. He probably didn't split infinitives, he probably mutilated infinitives. No, he wasn't a Phi Betta Kappa, but God used my great grandfather in powerful way to expand His kingdom. In his weakness, God became strong. God goes looking for the weak because the weak rely less on themselves and more on God.

Albert Schweitzer, the famous medical missionary in Africa, found purpose in serving others. One of his biographers, Norman Cousins, spent a considerable amount of time with Dr. Schweitzer in a little hospital at Lambarene. He left an indelible mark on his associate: "The biggest impression I had in leaving Lambarene was of the enormous reach of a single human being. Yet such a life was not without punishment of fatigue. Albert Schweitzer was supposed to be severe in his demands on the people who worked with him. Yet any demands he made on others were as nothing compared to the demands he made on himself. History is willing to overlook almost anything: errors, paradoxes, personal weaknesses or faults, if only a man will give enough of himself to others."[22]

Therein lies the secret of a life of purpose— giving enough of ourselves to others!

22   Norman Cousins, *Albert Schweitzer's Mission: Healing and Peace* (W.W. Norton & Company, 1985).

Decision 3: How Can I Make Good Choices Today?

Chapter 7

How to Be A Champion Decision Maker

A THREE YEAR OLD BOY was playing in his father's workshop. Pushing the envelope as most unsupervised boys do, he picked up his father's knife and started to play with it. Somehow he poked himself in the eye with the sharp knife. Since he didn't have access to medical care, his parents tried using herbs and natural remedies. Unfortunately, their attempts to save his eye didn't work. Because of the spreading infection, or perhaps a weakened immune system, his other eye was also damaged. Now, he was blind in both eyes. But this little boy made a decision, "Even though I may not have my eyesight, I still have my life." He went on to become a fine student and an accomplished musician.

His greatest achievement came when he was only fifteen years old. He developed a dot-dash reading method that was punched into thin cardboard. He worked out a complete alphabet, punctuation marks, and numbers. Now, thousands of people can take their index finger and translate two to three thousand little dots into 120 words per minute. This reading method could have never been developed by someone who had 20/20 vision. It took someone who knew the personal challenges of being blind to establish the system. His name, as you probably guessed by now, was Louis Braille. When his eyesight was taken from him, Louis Braille made the life-defining decision not to give up. Instead, he decided to make his mark on history by creating a reading system for the blind. Now, thousands of people read Braille and enjoy a greater quality of life. It all started with a heart-felt decision.[23]

23   A.J. Dunning, *Extremes: Reflections on Human Behavior* (Harcourt Brace Jovanovich, 1992) 180-190.

He's called "Bill," or "Bill W." Call him what you may, but as a hopeless alcoholic, one day Bill Wilson made a decision. He said, "I will not take another drink. No matter what, I will not." He had made similar promises before, but this time he meant business. Bill made that decision on December 11, 1934 and he made the same decision for the next 36 years. He decided he would rearrange his life without alcohol.

Bill had been sober for six months until he made a trip out of town, where a business opportunity fell through. Feeling dejected in the hotel lobby, he heard the familiar sounds of his past—ice rattling in a bottom of a glass, laughter, and conversations buzzing with life. He took a few steps in the direction of the bar thinking, "I need a drink." Thankfully, his second thought was saner than his first one. "No, I don't need a drink," he thought, "What I need is another alcoholic."

Instead of picking up a beer, he picked up a telephone in the lobby of the bar. The phone call began a pattern of calls that would put him in touch with Dr. Bob Smith, the very man who would become his foxhole friend against alcohol. That one decision led to the birth of Alcoholics Anonymous, which, in turn, has changed the lives of millions of alcoholics. Bill Wilson has been lauded as one of the top 20 Heroes and Icons of the 20th century. His heroism, though, started with one decision.

On another day, an unassuming Sunday school teacher who worked as a seamstress made a decision. She said, "No, I will not move to the back of the bus. I'm tired of the injustice. I'm tired of the mistreatment. I'm tired of being treated like a second class citizen. Do whatever you will. Arrest me. Throw me in jail. I'm not going to give my seat up simply because I'm black. I have made my decision." That one decision from Rosa Parks forever changed the conscience of our nation. It sparked the Montgomery, Alabama Bus Boycott which in turn created a public symbol for the Civil Rights Movement. Rosa Parks made one decision which changed the course of our entire country.

Decisions matter. One decision you make can literally change the world. Just ask Louis Braille, Bill Wilson, and Rosa Parks. Outside of God himself, one of the most remarkable forces at work in the universe is the power of a human being to make a decision. Every day, we make decisions that set in motion the ripple effect.

Scripture teaches that, "God made man in His image." It would take several entire books to adequately explain what is wrapped up in this one phrase. However, one of the most important aspects of being made in the image of God involves our freedom to make decisions. You can call it "free will," "personal autonomy," or "partial sovereignty." What you call it isn't nearly as important as recognizing that you have it.

God created us as free creatures with the capacity to make our own decisions. This is the pinnacle of personal stewardship. Some people think stewardship is only relegated to money, but it's far more than that. Stewardship is the Old English word for "management." Actually, our present day managers used to be called stewards. When we talk about stewardship, we're talking about how you manage your life. How do you manage your relationships, time, talents, intelligence, and especially your decisions?

Everything you have is a gift from God—your health, wealth, friends, family, business, and your personal freedom. God has given us the power of personal decision making as a sacred trust. Ultimately, how you manage your decisions is how you manage your life. You are the sum total of your decisions. What is your life? It is a series of decisions. We make our decisions, and then our decisions make us.

Did you know God put a book in the Bible to help us make wise decisions? Proverbs is in the Bible to help us navigate through the wide world of decision making. What is a proverb? Simply put, it's a wise saying. So the entire book of Proverbs is a collection of wise sayings designed specifically to help you make good decisions.

Ever met a wise person? It's not necessarily someone who is articulate or has distinguishing looks. Someone who is wise has the unique ability to make good and right decisions. In Scripture, wisdom has very little to do with IQ. Instead, wisdom has more to do with the ability to make good decisions. Nothing will improve your life more than making smart decisions. Proverbs paints us a beautiful picture of the champion decision maker.

Get Guidance from the Right People

Let's start with the man who wrote many of the Proverbs. Solomon wrote the vast majority of these pithy, wise statements. God came to Solomon and made him a unique offer. God said, "Solomon, ask for anything you want and I'll give it to you!" Can you imagine God making you the same deal? What if God came to you and said, "Here's a blank check. Go ahead fill in what you want. I'll give you whatever you ask for, with no questions asked." What would you ask for? Lamborghini? Billion Dollars? Beautiful Runway Model? Solomon had somewhat of a surprising request. He didn't ask for a long life without illness. Neither did he ask God for riches. Solomon's request was on the solemn side; he asked for wisdom and discernment. Because Solomon asked for wisdom and discernment, God also promised him a long life and riches. Of all the things Solomon could have requested, he asked for wisdom-the ability to make good and right decisions. Because of the divine wisdom granted to him, Solomon is described as the wisest man who ever lived. Look what this wise man tells us.

> *(Since we're supposed to pay attention to the proverbs, notice the next few.)*

> *"Let those who are wise listen to these proverbs and become even wiser. And let those who understand receive guidance by exploring the depth of meaning in these proverbs, parables, wise sayings, and riddles."* **Proverbs 1:5-6**

> *"Where there is no counsel, the people fall; But in the multitude of counselors there is safety." (NKJV)* **Proverbs 11:14**

> *"Fools think they need no advice, but the wise listen to others."* **Proverbs 12:15**

The wisest man who ever lived says we should put a high premium on getting advice from other people. No one ever rises above the need for wise counsel. Regardless of our age, educational background, or experience level, we never reach a point when we don't need counsel from other people. Psalm 1:1 says, "Blessed is the man who does not walk in the counsel of the ungodly." Great decision makers get their advice from great people. If there's a question mark about someone's character, we don't have to write the person off or exclude them out of our lives, but neither should we make them a part of our personal cabinet. Imagine where the president of the United States would be without capable advisors that sit on his cabinet. He has to rely on his cabinet to give him pertinent advice as he makes decisions. The wrong people giving you advice can spell disaster. The reason some people make idiotic decisions is because they get their advice from the wrong people.

I have a good friend who is a clinical psychologist. Recently, we were having lunch together and he brought up how many people in his field indiscriminately tell people to get a divorce. He said many counselors don't encourage the couples to do the hard work that's required to have a good marriage; the counselors simply suggest they take the easy way out by getting a divorce. What a shame. Most of the couples I know who have great marriages paid a price to get there. It's very common in our day for people to see counselors. If you do, make sure you see one who isn't going to give you unbiblical advice.

Most of us, however, get the vast majority of our advice from people who are not professional counselors. Family, friends, co-workers, and acquaintances from the PTA all chip in to give us their "two cents worth." In some cases, they try to offer us their "million dollars worth" of advice. Sometimes their "million dollars worth" of advice isn't worth the price of a bowl of rice. Who you listen to in life shapes the way you make decisions. Great decisions are the result of getting guidance from the right people.

Think About Where Your Decisions Are Taking You

Ever made a really dumb decision? When I started thinking about it, I realized I had plenty of viable illustrations I could use in this chapter. My first year in seminary, I lived in a trailer. The trailer was old, and it ran on oil heat. From time to time, during the winter, I would go out and check the gauge on the oil tank. When the tank gauge read "low," I would call the oil company and they would come and fill up the tank.

One evening I was watching the news, and the meteorologist said to expect a cold snap for the next several days. To be honest, I didn't even think about checking my oil tank. I'm an optimist, so I simply thought, "I'm sure I have enough oil to last me a while." This is one time I wish I had been a pessimist.

About 7 o'clock that night, my heat kicked off. It ended up being 10 degrees that night, and in the trailer, it felt like I was inside an ice box. There was virtually no insulation in the trailer. Did I go to a hotel? No! I got the bright idea that I would tough it out in the trailer for the night.

By bedtime, I was freezing. I put on my long underwear, added a pair of sweatpants on top of my underwear, and threw on my hunting coveralls on top of that. I had on several sweatshirts, my winter jacket, gloves, and my toboggan. I had so many layers of clothes on I felt like a mummy; I could barely move. In Eskimo style, I then jumped into bed. I threw the covers over my head to try to trap all the heat from my breathing. As far as I can remember, I didn't get a single wink of sleep that night. About 4 o'clock in the morning, I happened to get another bright idea. I thought, "I know what I'll do to get warm. I'll go take a hot shower." Have you ever tried to take your clothes off when it's 10 degrees? Now that I've tried it, I would not recommend it.

After I took off all my clothes, which took me about 15 minutes, suddenly it dawned on me, "Wait a minute, I don't have any warm water because the oil heats the hot water heater." It took me another 15 minutes to get all my clothes back on. Finally, I had the most rational thought of the night, "If I don't get out of here, I'm going to freeze to death." I went outside, cranked up my car, and sat with the heat running for several hours. Then, I drove to a fast food restaurant, and waited until the restaurant opened. I went inside so I could start to thaw out. It all turned out OK, but it wasn't exactly a textbook case of wise decision making.

The book of Proverbs is classified as wisdom literature. Solomon wants us to see the opposite of someone who is wise, so he introduces us to the fool. The fool is not someone who has a low I.Q.; the fool is someone who makes poor decisions. A fool makes decisions without ever thinking about the repercussions of the decisions. Here's a brief sampling of what Proverbs says about the fool.

"Wise people don't make a show of their knowledge, but fools broadcast their folly." **Proverbs 12: 23**

"The wise person makes learning a joy; fools spout only foolishness." **Proverbs 15:2**

"A wise person is hungry for truth, while the fool feeds on trash." **Proverbs 15:14**

The Scriptures teach that a fool is notorious for his folly. Folly and foolishness carry the exact same meaning. Someone full of folly makes foolish decisions. They make poor decisions because they don't think ahead. Fools tend to make decisions without playing out the long term repercussions of the decisions. Nothing causes us to make unwise decisions like short term thinking. No one sets out to build a life that crumbles; people just drift through life without ever thinking about where their decisions are taking them.

Case in point: the man who built his house on the sand. Jesus told the famous story about the two men who were building houses. One man built his house on the rock; the other man built his house on the sand. The Bible says both houses faced the same exact storm. The rains fell, the flood waters rose, and the wind beat against both houses. Jesus said after the storm that only one house was left standing. The house built on the rock was the one that withstood the test of the storm. The house built on the sand crumbled into ashes.

Do you know what Jesus said about the man who built his house on the sand? Jesus didn't say he was a wicked man. He didn't say he was an immoral man with a twisted mind. What adjective did He use to describe the man who built on the sand? "Foolish!" Jesus said he was a foolish man. When Jesus calls you a fool, it's not exactly a compliment. The man who built his house on the sand was foolish because he never thought about where his decision would take him. Foolishness is not thinking about the long term impact of our decisions.

I've never met someone who intentionally sets out to build a life that crumbles. No kid says, "I think I'll grow up and become homeless." No one ever takes their first drink of alcohol hoping they'll become an alcoholic. They take the drink, and then the drink takes them. No one takes a puff on a joint hoping it will be a stepping stone to another drug. No one holds a grudge hoping the grudge will eventually hold them in a self-imposed prison. No one ever clicks on a pornographic website hoping they will become a sex addict. Nobody sits down at a desk and develops a strategic plan on how to wreck their lives; they just drift into it with a series of decisions. They drift through life without ever thinking about where their decisions are taking them.

I played baseball against the number one draft choice of Major League Baseball. Brien Taylor, who grew up in Beaufort, North Carolina was an amazing athlete. It was stunning to stand at home plate and watch Taylor throw a 99 mph fastball. Each pitch zoomed by almost every batter. After graduating high school, Taylor was drafted by the New York Yankees as the # 1 draft choice. He was signed for a 1.5 million dollar bonus. After spending 3 years getting ready in the minor leagues, Taylor was expected to start for the Yankees the following season. However, that day would never arrive. Brien Taylor would make one fateful decision that would forever change the course of his life. He is in the record books, but not as a successful pitcher. He's just the second player in baseball history to be picked first in the Major League Draft who never pitched one game in the majors.

While Taylor was back in his hometown, his younger brother, Brenden, was in a fistfight at a local trailer park. Brenden suffered some cuts in the fight. Brien Taylor was outraged that his brother had been beaten up. Taylor went to the trailer park to do his part in defending his younger brother. He screamed for the guy to come out of the house so they could fight. Once outside, Taylor balled up his left fist, aimed for his victim, and swung as hard as he could. He ended up missing everything. He was much better at throwing fastballs than punches. One second later, his million dollar pitching arm was dangling by his side. In the hours following the altercation, the Yankees had Taylor visit a doctor in California. The doctor performed surgery on Taylor and gave him a good prognosis. However, after the fight, Taylor was never the same. He lost 8 mph off his fastball, and he had major control problems. After struggling in the minor leagues for a few years, no Major League team had any interest in him. Taylor moved back home to work with his father as a bricklayer. This million dollar athlete now lives with his parents and brings home $909 per month. One decision, made in a split second, would change his life forever.[24]

When it comes to the high drama of decision making, champion decision makers often ask themselves one question: what is the wisest decision for the long term? This is a fog cutter. It's a question which has saved me time and time again. Think back over your life for a minute. Rehearse some of the worst decisions you've made. We all have decisions we're embarrassed about. If you had asked yourself the question, what's the wisest decision for the long term, do you think you would have still made those bad decisions? Probably not. As I think about the worst decisions I've made in life, the vast majority of them happened when I wasn't thinking about the long term impact of my decisions.

Short term thinking has long term consequences. Several years ago, I was invited to a special forum to address the problem of AIDS. Since our city has the largest AIDS population in North Carolina, medical professionals were reaching out to leaders of faith based institutions. Different churches and pastors were invited to participate in the discussion. The meeting started with a presentation of the facts. The doctors wanted us to know that there are individuals who have AIDS who got it through some other means other than sexual contact. However, they also made it clear that the research shows that the overwhelming majority of people who have acquired the disease got it through sexual conduct.

There was a lot of meaningful discussion about how churches could help remedy the problem of AIDS. Pastors and leaders agreed

---

24   Wayne Coffey, *"Tracking Down Brien Taylor"* (New York Daily News) July 14, 2006.

that God calls us to love, support, and show compassion to patients who are infected with AIDS. Being judgmental and condemning is the opposite of how Christ would respond. However, the medical community also wanted feedback as to how churches could partner with them in preventing the spread of the disease.

As the discussion progressed, a lady at my table made a statement that brought laser-like focus to the discussion. She said, "At the end of the day, this problem comes down to personal moral decision making." She said, "The greatest thing we can do as faith based communities is to teach people that the decisions they make in a moment can impact them for the rest of their lives." She was right on target. Some of the greatest social problems we have today can be traced back to short term thinking.

There's No Such Thing As A Private Decision

Ever heard this mantra, "The decisions I make in private are nobody else's business." When you think it through, the logic is fraught with peril. The logic doesn't work because we rarely can make a private decision without it impacting others. This is why the book of Proverbs places an emphasis on honesty and integrity.

> *"It is better to be poor and honest than to be a fool and dishonest."* **Proverbs 19:1**

> *"The godly walk with integrity; blessed are their children after them."* **Proverbs 20:7**

Integrity is who you are when nobody is looking. When you have integrity you are the same person privately as you are publicly. When you have integrity, you realize your private decisions don't just affect you; they also affect a lot other people around you. Your private decisions impact your family, friends, co-workers, and neighbors. Romans 14:7 says, "No man lives to himself." No man (or woman for that matter) can live to themselves and think that their decisions aren't going to trickle down. Decisions do trickle down; they create a ripple effect. They cascade onto a lot of other people.

The private decisions I make as a father and a husband impact my family. The private decisions I make at work affect my co-workers. Think about it; the news is littered with stories about thousands of employees who have been affected by one foolish decision made by a greedy executive. All of us know families who have been torn apart because of a private decision they thought would never go public.

George O'Leary was the head football coach for Notre Dame for 4 days. It was his lifelong dream to coach the Fighting Irish. After a successful career at Georgia Tech, his dream came to reality. Notre Dame hired him, but within several days, the University discovered their new coach lied on his resume. Coach O'Leary said he had a master's degree from a NYU-Stony Brook University. Upon further investigation, school officials discovered the school didn't exist. O'Leary also claimed he had earned three letters in football from his alma mater, the University of New Hampshire. The truth was O'Leary never played in a single game. In private, he made the drastic decision of fabricating his resume. When the story went public, Coach O'Leary sat in his hotel room asking a sobering question, "Oh, Jesus! Oh, Jesus! What will my mother say?"[25] The private decision he thought would never go public was no longer quarantined. It was a decision that would not only impact his mother; it would impact his wife, family, and his future.

A part of what makes sin so deceitful is the notion we can do it in private and get away with it. David most likely believed the same thing when he first laid eyes on Bathsheba. One day, David sees a woman taking a bath on the roof top; she is remarkably attractive, a show stopper. Sometimes people try to incriminate Bathsheba, saying she is partly to blame because she was taking a bath outside. Actually, it was the custom of the day, and there's no indication the Bible incriminates her for taking a bath on her rooftop.

When David sees Bathsheba, he is attracted to her. He sends a servant to find out who this beautiful woman is. The servant comes back and says, "King David, this is Bathsheba, the daughter of

---

25   Gary Smith, "Lying In Wait" (cnn.com, April 8, 2002).

Eliam, and the wife of Uriah the Hittite?" The servant was saying, "King, this is somebody's daughter. This is somebody's wife." By now, David's hormones were smoking. But if David would have been half way paying attention, he would have seen the yellow caution light flashing before his eyes. If David would have been spiritually sensitive, that one statement by his servant should have stopped him dead in his tracks. But when David saw the yellow caution light, he didn't hit the brakes. He did what a lot of drivers do, he hit his accelerator. He took one more step in the direction of sin.

David thought he could camouflage the whole thing. That is until the unforgettable day when Nathan, the prophet, knocked on his door. After telling him a story about a stolen lamb, Nathan put his boney finger in the chest of the king. He said, "David, you are the man. You have stolen someone else's wife, and you will pay fourfold for this sin." This is when David would learn a hard lesson: what happens in Vegas rarely ever stays in Vegas. Private decisions don't stay private. They go public when we least expect it.

Remember the Titanic? Experts said the ship was unsinkable. Supposedly, not even God could sink it. The reason they made such a claim was because the Titanic was compartmentalized. The idea was simple. If the compartments were ever flooded, the compartments could possibly break off, but experts believed it wouldn't sink the whole ship. Of course, history has proven the experts wrong. Many people take the same approach with their personal lives. They think, "I've got this one little area of private sin over here. It's no big deal. It's not going to bother anybody; it's not going to sink the whole ship. This compartment may be flooded but the boat can still float." Personal biographies show otherwise. That's not how life works. Sin can't be contained or compartmentalized. One little area of sin can sink our entire lives. One private lapse of integrity can change the course of life forever.

One day, I went out to get my mail at our mailbox. I thought it was going to be another routine, mundane trip to the mailbox. I was expecting the usual—some cards, bills, and advertisements. But let's just say I got a whole lot more than I bargained for. I pulled out the mail, and underneath the stack of mail was a Playboy magazine. Not exactly what you would expect to find in the Rev's mailbox. What made things even worse is that it had my name on it: David Clay Waters.

The first thing I did was tuck the magazine under my arm and walk straight into my house. I immediately found my wife and said, "Caryn, could you come in here, I want you to see something." I wanted her to see what had been delivered in the mail. The magazine was a complimentary issue to try to get me to order a subscription. I couldn't believe it. I was just minding my own business, thinking I was going to get my mail, and pronto—out came a Playboy magazine. Temptation often appears unexpectedly. You don't have to go looking for opportunities to do something wrong; opportunities will come looking for you. When those opportunities arrive (and they will), integrity is our frontline defense. Champion decision makers make the right decisions even when nobody else is looking.

CHAPTER 8

The Case of The Broken Decision Maker

"NEVER MAKE A DECISION WHEN your decision maker is broken." I'll always remember when my wife spoke these words to me. After having a difficult day at work, I came home and unloaded all the chaos of the day on my wife. I told her the next day, I was probably going to issue "walking papers" to a staff member who had caused so many problems for me. My wife could tell I was emotionally charged about the whole situation. My anger continued to escalate as I talked about how I was going fire the employee. She let the room get real quiet and then she spoke the show stopping words, "Clay, never make a decision when your decision maker is broken." Had I made a quick decision, it would have been the wrong decision. I didn't have a good frame of reference at the moment to be able to make a rational, solid decision. Thankfully, my wife spoke these quiet but thunderous words. Once I cooled down, I knew the right decision was not to fire the staff member.

Making a decision at the wrong time can breed disaster. Timing is everything when it comes to making wise decisions. Babe Ruth was right, "The only difference between a home run and strike out is timing." Timing often determines whether you hit a homerun, or strike out with your decisions. There are times in our lives when we are more susceptible to making poor choices. Being aware that we have the propensity to make wrong decisions when gripped by intense emotion is very important. When we encounter those times, it's important to deem our decision maker broken. Temporarily postponing the decision may save you a lifetime of consequences.

The High Drama of Decision Making

Did you know David is mentioned more than any other person in the Old Testament? David is mentioned over 600 times in the Old Testament. Sixty-six entire chapters from the Old Testament deal with David. Don't race by those important facts. Whenever God puts so much information in His Word about a particular person, it's not accidental. It's providential. God wants us to learn some valuable lessons from David's life. Perhaps one of the greatest lessons from David's life comes from the darkest part of his life. When most people think of David, the first thing that comes to mind is "Bathsheba."

Scripture sets the context for this fatal attraction. "It happened in the spring of the year, at the time when kings go out to battle." King David was supposed to be out on the battlefield. But instead of spending time on the battlefield, David was spending time in the bedroom. Had David been where he was supposed to be, in all probability, there would have never been a Bathsheba episode in our Bibles. If given the chance, this was one decision David would have taken a mulligan on. Think about it; no sin has gotten more press coverage than the sin of David and Bathsheba. Books have been written. Movies have been produced. Scores of sermons have recounted the details of David's blunder. None of us would want our biggest failure recorded so everybody could read about it. Yet, for generations and generations, David's sin has been dissected from every possible angle. Though his downfall was great, let's don't forget that his failure began with a simple decision. David failed to be where he was supposed to be.

Have you ever met someone who got into trouble because they were at the wrong place, at the wrong time, and didn't have the sense to leave? Being at the wrong place at the wrong time can lead to the wrong thing. Just ask David.

One of the most celebrated Old Testament events was when Elijah defeated the 450 prophets of Baal. After he was victorious, Jezebel sent a message telling Elijah that she was going to kill him. In no uncertain terms, she told Elijah that she was going to turn him into dog food. Elijah was afraid, and ran for his life. He finally settled in a cave at Mt. Horeb. While he was in the cave, God asked a pivotal question,

"What are you doing here?" He asked him a second time, "Elijah, what are you doing here?" The implication is, "I never told you to come here." God basically told Elijah to go back the way he came.

When we're in the wrong place at the wrong time, it's easier to make poor choices. If we're sensitive to God's voice, we will hear the same words God spoke to Elijah, "What are you doing here?" "What are you doing at this bar?" "What are you doing flirting with somebody you're not married to." "What are you doing at this hotel?"

Perhaps you feel confident about your spiritual life. You may consider yourself a strong believer. In reality, it doesn't matter how strong you think you are. If we're in the wrong place at the wrong time with the wrong person and the right set of circumstances, we are capable of anything.

When Hotter Is Not Smarter

David is probably about 50 years old when this fatal attraction occurs. He wasn't an old man, but neither was he a spring chicken. He could have been having a mid-life crisis. David probably started to notice that the women didn't pay attention to him like they used to. He knows he is losing some of his edge. When he opens the cabinet every morning, it's a reminder that he's not getting younger. Metamucil, Viagra, and B-12 shots are all a part of his daily regimen. One day, David walks out on his patio roof, and he sees Bathsheba taking a bath. She is drop dead gorgeous. When David sees her, there is no mistaking that he is attracted to her. David could have walked back inside and closed the window shade, but instead of reaching for the window shade, David reached for his binoculars.

Before we act on temptation, God promises to always give us a way out of the temptation. The Bible promises, "No temptation has overtaken you but such as is common to man. God is faithful who will not allow you to be tempted beyond what you are able to resist, but with the temptation, He will provide a way of escape" (1 Corin. 10:13). With every temptation, God provides an escape route. When David sees Bathsheba, he sends someone to find out about her. The servant returns and says, "King David, this is Bathsheba, the daughter of Eliam and the wife of Uriah the Hittite." This statement should have sent a chill down his spine. The servant was saying, "David, this is somebody's daughter. This is somebody's wife." This was his escape route. Unfortunately, David gave little thought to the escape route. David went full speed ahead in the direction of sin, and then he crashed. You know the rest of the story … David brings her to the palace, and he makes a decision that would cost him greatly.

When David saw Bathsheba, there was only thing on his mind. He completely forgot about God. He forgot about his commitment to be a man after God's own heart. He forgot about all those psalms he had written. And he forgot that if he stepped across the line and committed this sin, there would be consequences.

Dan Ariely is a social scientist who has studied how our decisions are affected by our emotional state. In his landmark book, *Predictably Irrational*, Ariely writes about his research findings. In one research project, he tried to understand how rational, intelligent people could predict how their decisions would change when they were in a sexually aroused state. The study had male students answer questions when they were in a cold state (non-aroused) and in a hot state (aroused).

In every case, the research participants answered the questions differently when they were in a hot state (aroused) than when they were in a cold state (non-aroused). The results showed that when the participants were in a cold state, they respected women; they were not attracted to odd sexual activities; they also tended to take the higher moral ground in decision making. However, when the participants were in an aroused state, they tended to throw moral restraint and caution to the wind. The participants had difficulty predicting just how much their passion would change them, but it did. Even the most rational person, in the heat of passion, was divorced from the person he thought he was. In the heat of passion, Professor Ariely's research shows that our thinking is often compromised and irrational. Emotions take control of our behavior, and we often make poor decisions.[26]

---

26   Dan Ariely, *Predictably Irrational* (Harper, 2008), pp. 89-102.

Ariely rightly points out that our human condition is much like Dr. Jekyll and Mr. Hyde. When Robert Louis Stevenson awakened from a nightmare one night, he told his wife he was going to work on a "fine bogey tale." The fine bogey tale was an instant blockbuster. In the story line, Dr. Jekyll and Mr. Hyde proved that "man is not truly one, but truly two." Dr. Jekyll thought he knew how to handle himself—that is, until Mr. Hyde took control.

Romans 13:14 says, "Make no provision for the flesh." The flesh is our fallen nature—Mr. Hyde if you will. Mr. Hyde lives in me and he also lives in you. Carl Sandburg captured our human condition quite well, "There is an eagle in me that wants to soar, and there is a hippopotamus in me that wants to wallow in the mud." The hippopotamus in me that wants to wallow in the mud is the "flesh." The flesh creates a gravitational pull away from God. Our fallen nature creates an undercurrent, pulling us away from what we know to be true and right. No wonder the Bible warns us, "Make no provision for the flesh." If we place ourselves in a vulnerable position, our flesh can easily take over.

When Caryn and I first married, we made a commitment that we would never eat out alone with someone of the opposite sex. We also decided we would never ride alone in a car with someone of the opposite sex. We didn't feel forced to make these decisions because we didn't trust each other. We trust each other deeply. We made these simple commitments, and still hold to them today, because we never want to place ourselves in a vulnerable situation. Being in the wrong place at the wrong time with the right set of circumstances can leave shrapnel flying everywhere.

Typically when we are emotionally charged, we are predictably irrational. This could involve sexual arousal, hunger, anger, or fear. Regardless, when we act on our impulses, we tend to make foolish decisions. Firing a staff member, firing off an irate email, or going to an extreme to fire a gun at someone is often the result of impulsivity gone wild. Postponing our immediate response usually allows us to be in a better condition to make smarter decisions. A short walk, a conversation with a friend, or a 911 prayer asking for God's help could have put everything in perspective for David.

The Life-Giving Quarter-Second

Interestingly, all of us have a part in the brain called the amygdala. It's the primary place in the brain that experiences strong emotions, like rage or fear. In certain animals, when researchers remove the amygdale, the animals are incapable of experiencing things like rage or fear. Normally, when input comes into your brain, it goes to a place called the neocortex, and it gets processed there. But occasionally, about 5% of the time, it goes directly to the amygdala, and the thinking part of your brain gets short-circuited. This is especially true when we have intense moments of anger. This explains why it is more difficult to exercise self-control when we are emotionally hyped. Our emotions are trying to hijack the amygdala. It's remarkable how God has wired us together.

Dr. Benjamin Libet is a neurosurgeon who made some remarkable discoveries while performing brain surgeries. Because the brain has no nerve endings and feels no pain, he could perform certain brain surgeries without using general anesthesia. Dr. Libet would perform these surgeries and communicate with his patients during the course of the surgery. He would often use a special clock that tracked time in the thousandths of a second. He would ask his patients to move their finger as he monitored the electrical activity in the brain that regulated that movement.

Through his experiment, Libet was able to identify the moment of intent to move the finger, the moment of awareness of that intent, and the moment the patient actually moved their finger. Libet discovered that when your brain has the impulse that says, "Move your hand," the impulse travels down to that part of your body, but it takes about a quarter of a second for it to get there.[27] In between the time when the brain activity happens and the hand moves is what Daniel Goleman calls "the life-giving quarter-second."[28] In other words,

27   *Behavioral and Brain Sciences*, volume 8, 1985, pp. 529-566.

28   Daniel Goleman, Emotional Intelligence (New York: Bantam Books, 1994).

once the patient was aware of the intent to move, there was another quarter second before the movement began.

Interestingly, that quarter of a second, although it doesn't seem very long, is plenty of time for the mind to reject or accept the impulse. We have a quarter of a second to "veto" our automatic responses to our emotions. This is the defining moment when we can yield to God. This is the moment of truth when we can allow the Holy Spirit to take control of our emotions. The "life-giving quarter-second" is my opportunity to say, "Okay God, I have this impulse right now. I'm really ticked off. I'm really afraid. I'm really aroused. God, Should I act on this impulse?"

What David did with his life-giving quarter-second is now in the history books. He blew it. Though we certainly can't defend or justify what David did, let's acknowledge that we all have had plenty of blown life-giving quarter-second opportunities. Thankfully, unlike David, our moments weren't recorded down in Scripture for everyone to read about. We can be thankful God is done writing Scripture. Instead of pointing the finger at David, we would be smarter by admitting that our flesh is no different from David's flesh. Our flesh and his flesh are equally weak. The Bible says, "Let him who thinks he stands take heed lest he fall."[29] If we don't take heed, we too will fall. With that in mind, I want us to glean several lessons from this tragic decision.

Decisions Create 'The Ripple Effect'

David's one decision would make waves for years to come. The consequences of his behavior proved costly. Decisions can't be contained. They create the ultimate ripple effect. Think back to a few decisions made in the Garden of Eden.

"If you eat from that tree, you will surely die." It's not exactly an ambiguous statement. Eve knew clearly what God meant by it. Satan comes slithering through the garden and says, "Eve, I know what God has said, but if you eat from the tree, you will not die."

---

29 1 Corinthians 10:12

Let's dissect this statement and put it under the microscope. Do you know what Satan was really saying? He was saying, "Eve, your wrong decisions won't have any consequences." "Eve, your sin won't have any negative repercussions. You won't die." The truth is our decisions do have consequences; it didn't take long for Adam and Eve to arrive at that conclusion. The ripple effect was now set in motion.

Did Adam and Eve really die? Yes, they died. They didn't drop dead immediately after ingesting the forbidden fruit. We know Adam went on to live 930 years, but Adam and Eve eventually died. Sometimes the consequences of our decisions don't show up immediately. 1 Tim.5:24 in The Message says, "The sins of some people are blatant and march them right into court. The sins of others don't show up until much later." Eating a banana split doesn't show up on the scales 5 minutes after we eat it, and the same is true for our sin. Sometimes the consequences of our sin can show up much later than when we first commit it.

It's important to note that Adam and Eve's decision affected their relationship with God. God said, "If you eat the fruit, you will die." Whenever death is used in the Bible, it doesn't always refer to physical death. Sometimes the term refers to spiritual death. Spiritual death is being separated from God. Before Adam and Eve sinned, they enjoyed perfect fellowship with God. However, when they fell into sin, their perfect fellowship was broken. Sin created a wall between them and God. Wrong decisions break our fellowship with God.

The ripple effect from this one decision also made waves between Adam and Eve. When God confronted Adam, he had a golden opportunity to take responsibility for his sin. God honors honesty. Adam could have said, "Okay God, I blew it," but Adam didn't. Instead, Adam blamed his actions on Eve. He said, "It was the woman that you gave me." Eve is no longer "bone of my bone and flesh of my flesh." Adam calls her "the woman." He is no longer calling her sweetie-pie, baby-darling, or honey-bun; now it's "the woman." For the first time in their relationship, Adam and Eve experience disharmony. Poor decisions certainly affect our relationship with God, but they also affect our relationships with other people. You can trace a lot of fractured marriages to a string of poor decisions. It could be the daily decision to use a harsh tone of voice toward your spouse. That one decision practiced on a routine basis can be a death sentence for your marriage. When we make wrong decisions, we not only hurt ourselves, we hurt the people closest to us.

Bad Decisions Require Truth Tellers

David could not undo what had been done. That's the bad news about bad decisions. Once we make one, we're left to deal with it. Unfortunately, instead of coming to grips with his wrong decision, David tried to cover his tracks. For one solid year, David lived a life of hypocrisy, trying to cover up his wrong doing. Then, one day, there was knock on the palace door. Thankfully, David had one friend who cared enough to tell him the truth.

2 Samuel 12:1 says, "Then the Lord sent Nathan to David." God designed a strategy to bring David to his knees. The strategy involved Nathan-a true friend. Think about how tough this must have been on Nathan. He was supposed to go stand before the most powerful man in the nation and tell him that he was way off base.

Nathan must have stayed up countless nights rehearsing how he would confront one of the most powerful men in the world. After reflecting for hours, Nathan came up with a story he thought would catch David in his proverbial pajamas. Nathan tells David about a poor man who had a little pet lamb. He and his family loved this little lamb; it was more than an animal, the lamb became a household pet. At night, the little lamb would snuggle up next to his children and keep them warm during the cold winter. As Nathan tells the major story line, he introduces a greedy rich man in the story. The rich man, who had all kinds of lambs, came by and stole the poor man's little lamb. The poor man only had this one little lamb, and the rich came by and stole it.

Nathan tells David the story, and he drops back to see how the king will respond. David walked right into the trap. After hearing the story, the Bible says David was outraged. He said, "As the Lord lives, the man who has done this will surely die." Then Nathan hit David with the punch line, "You are the man!" "You had all kinds of wives and concubines, but Uriah, the Hittite, only had one wife and you stole her. David, you are the man."

Thankfully, David had someone in his life who told him the truth about his sin. No one else would, but Nathan cared too much for David to watch him self destruct. The story has a happy ending. David listens to Nathan, and he regrets his wrong decision. David is broken over his poor choices, and says, "I have sinned against the Lord. Yes, Nathan, I am the man." But what if David didn't have a friend like Nathan? What would have happened to David if Nathan didn't care enough to confront him? There is a good possibility David would have lived the rest of his life trying to cover up his tracks.[30]

Question. Do you have anybody in your life who will tell you the truth? Do you have a Nathan who loves you too much to watch you self destruct? We all need accountability. We all need yellow and white lines to keep us out of the ditch. We all have blind spots, and we need people we trust who can point them out. We need some people who care enough to tell us when we're getting off track. What we really need are a few good truth tellers.

I've discovered that very few people intend on making a mess out of their lives. They drift toward disaster, decision after decision, without anyone close by to tell them the truth about their decisions. I don't know any couples who take a vow, fully intent on watching it go up in smoke. I don't know any dads who bring their children into the world for the purpose of getting so busy at work they no longer have time to play catch with their kids. No one sits down and plans these things, but every day, they happen—decision by decision. Do you know why? For the vast majority of us, we haven't given anyone permission to tell us if they see us making bad decisions. We think we can stay on course without any help, but if given enough time, we will prove we can't.

Let me get personal. Who is your Nathan? Have you invited anyone in your life to tell you when they see you making a bad decision? You could invite a close friend, someone from your small group Bible study, or perhaps your spouse. I've asked my wife to tell me if she sees

---

30   2 Samuel 12:1-15.

obvious signs of pride in me. I've asked her to tell me if she thinks I'm starting to get impressed with myself. I have invited her to speak the truth to me if she ever starts to feel like I'm leaving our family in the dust. I told her, "If I ever start to lie, I want you to tell me. If I ever start to develop a habit of complaining, I want you to tell me. If I seem to be enamored with material things, I want you to tell me." Guess what? There have been some times when she's had to tell me. Every one of us needs a trusted friend to tell us the truth.

A God Who Trumps Your Bad Decisions

Without question, David's rendezvous with Bathsheba was one of the worst moments in his life. However, David never allowed himself to be defined by his worst moment. Once confronted by his truth teller, David was broken over his sin. Shortly after coming clean, David picked up his pen and wrote Psalm 51, which is a heart-wrenching confession. David's ultimate desire was expressed in the psalm-to return to a clean heart. In spite of his terrible blunder, David would still be described as a man after God's own heart. Our worst decisions don't have to define us for the rest of our lives.

Ask Peter. He's known for his great confession, "You are the Christ, the Son of the living God." Yet, when the heat was on, Simon Peter caved under pressure. He denied that he even knew Christ. I imagine the critics of his day had a field day. But thankfully, God is a God of second chances. God didn't throw Simon Peter under the bus after his poor decision. The same Simon Peter who stumbled and crumbled would go on to become the Rock-Petros. Simon, the Rock, would become one of the leading apostles, preaching on the Day of Pentecost when 3000 people believed in Christ. Peter never allowed his worst moment to define who he would become.

Ask John Mark. He was the quintessential momma's boy. He was on a mission trip with the apostle Paul and Silas, but on the trip, John Mark grew homesick. He was frightened, tucked his tail between his legs, and went back home. Paul, the leader of the missionary campaign, lost all confidence in John Mark. When his team got ready to go on another mission trip, someone came up with a bright idea, "Let's take John Mark." Within a nanosecond, Paul rejected the idea, "No Sir Re ... he defected one time already. He's a quitter; he's not a team player." Paul excluded him from the trip. Barnabas extended grace to John Mark and decided to give him a place on his roster. In the end, John Mark was restored. Later on, he went on to write the gospel you have in your New Testament, the one that bears his name-the gospel according to Mark.

I remember speaking to a hundred and fifty juveniles one Christmas. The vast majority of the juveniles were teenagers who had been convicted of serious crimes. What do you tell a 12 year old girl who pulled the trigger of a 357 and murdered someone? I knew, more than likely, this would be my one and only chance to speak to these young people. I knew each one of them had a lifetime ahead of them. What do you say to a child who thinks life is hopeless? You say exactly what God said to David, "Don't let the worst moment of your life define the rest of your life. You can still be a man or woman after My own heart." I reminded each juvenile not to let their worst moment in life define them for the rest of life. Their failure didn't have to be final.

I feel sorry for David. I feel sorry for Simon Peter. I feel sorry for John Mark. I can't think of anything more embarrassing than having the unedited, uncensored truth about your life broadcast for everyone to see. Think about it. For centuries, preachers and teachers have exposed their failures repeatedly. People have been reading about their mishaps for generations and generations. How would you like it if all your failures were written down for people to talk about year after year? The proposition doesn't get me too excited. However, the emphasis in Scripture is not on their failure; the emphasis is on God's forgiveness. God is a God of second chances ... and third chances ... and fourth chances ... His grace triumphs your worst decisions.

CHAPTER 9

In the Zone

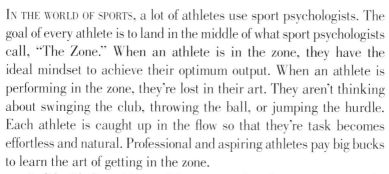

IN THE WORLD OF SPORTS, a lot of athletes use sport psychologists. The goal of every athlete is to land in the middle of what sport psychologists call, "The Zone." When an athlete is in the zone, they have the ideal mindset to achieve their optimum output. When an athlete is performing in the zone, they're lost in their art. They aren't thinking about swinging the club, throwing the ball, or jumping the hurdle. Each athlete is caught up in the flow so that they're task becomes effortless and natural. Professional and aspiring athletes pay big bucks to learn the art of getting in the zone.

In life, I believe it's possible to get in the ultimate zone—God's Will. There's not a better place to be than in the middle of God's Will. When you step into the ultimate zone, you experience God's best plan for your life. Finding and staying in the will of God is determined largely by your decisions. To determine that your decisions are in alignment with God's will, start by asking yourself six critical questions. How you answer these questions will dictate how much of your life is spent in the zone.

These questions serve like a bag of golf clubs. Different clubs are needed for different situations. An accomplished golfer will know when to use the sand wedge or driver or five iron. Each of the questions can help you discern God's will for your life, but certain ones will be particularly helpful depending on your circumstances.

Is It Consistent With Scripture?

God will never lead us to make a decision that violates Scripture. His Spirit will never lead us to do something that His Spirit has already told us not to do in Scripture. God's Word reveals God's Will.

One evening, I sat down on the couch to enjoy my favorite pastime—channel surfing. While I was surfing, I came across a segment by Dr. Phil. Dr. Phil had a guest on his show who had a beautiful wife and 5 children. Interestingly, the guest refused to work. He said, "The Lord told me to keep trying to make a go at my gardening business." His gardening business had netted double zero for the last several years.

In the meantime, his family was living in a house with no heat; they were constantly borrowing money from their families, yet this guy maintained that that the Lord didn't want him to get a regular job so he could make a living for his family. Dr. Phil invited a guest pastor on the show as well. He provided a different perspective on the situation. In love, the pastor told the lazy husband and father, "God will never tell you to do something that contradicts His Word." Shortly thereafter, he quoted a Scripture verse...1Timothy 5:8 which says, "A man who doesn't provide for his own household is worse than an unbeliever." Regardless of what this man claimed to be hearing from God, his decision to stay at home and be a bum was violating God's Word. In trademark fashion, Dr. Phil told him to get off his butt and go find a job.

Psalm 119:105 says, "Your word is a lamp to my feet, and a light to my path." The psalmist says God's Word is like a light that gives us direction while traveling on a path. Caryn, my wife, has decorated our house with night lights. I don't guess they're technically considered decorations, but we have enough of them in our house that makes you feel like you're in New York City.

Caryn got really excited about night lights after traumatizing her toes a few times. Sometimes we have to get up in the middle of the night to check on our sons. After stumping her toes a few times in pitch darkness, Caryn quickly became a fan of night lights. I thought it was a good idea, too, after I ran head first into a closed door. It's hard to get around without any light. Interestingly, the metaphor used in Scripture to describe God's Word is light. God's Word is like a light—it gives us direction. It shows us which way to turn. It can protect us from a lot worse things than a stumped toe or a busted nose. The Scriptures can prevent us from experiencing a never ending list of regrets and will guide us to God's best path for our lives.

Is It Wise?

When you are at a point of decision, ask yourself this question, Is this decision wise? Remember that wise decisions are attached to long term thinking rather than short term thinking. God will never lead you to make a decision that would be unwise for the long term. We have to view today through the lens of tomorrow. If the decision you are about to make at this moment could be one you regret in 10 years, it probably isn't the wisest decision.

The decision may not revolve around whether something is "right or wrong." There are plenty of grey areas in life where the Scriptures are silent. That is, they don't speak explicitly about the particular situation that we find ourselves in. Though we may not find a specific verse dealing with our situation, Scripture does encourage us to use the wisdom test. Ephesians 5:17 says, "Therefore do not be unwise, but understand what the will of the Lord is." In Scripture, being wise is closely associated with thinking about the long term ripple effects of your decisions.

It isn't wrong for me to have a loaded gun in my house. It's perfectly legal to have a loaded gun in my house. But is it wise to have a loaded gun in my house with two younger children in our home? It might pass the legal test, but it will not pass the wisdom test.

Maybe you're thinking about buying a new car. You and your husband drive to a local car dealership and a charismatic salesman meets you on the lot. Before long, he shows you a car that you both fall in love with. It's only $15,000 above your budget. The salesman runs the numbers and he can qualify you to purchase the car. After you take a test drive, the salesman says, "You know, if you don't buy this car today, I have a feeling it will be gone by tomorrow." Sold!

You sign the dotted line and the car belongs to you. There's just one problem. The salesman never told you that virtually every single penny you make will have go toward paying for your new car.

Three weeks after you drive the car off the lot, your one year old child gets sick with what you think is a standard upset stomach. After several days of being sick, you take your young daughter to the doctor. The doctor says, "This is not an easy fix. Your daughter is going to have to have surgery." Thankfully, insurance is going to pay the bulk of it, but it still leaves you with the balance of $300.00. While you sink into your plush leather car seat, you think, "I don't have $300.00. All my money is tied up in this car."

Several months later, your husband has a very important business banquet that he would like for you to attend with him. Your formal dresses have seen their better day, so you go to a department store, but all you can do is stand in the aisle with tears rolling down your cheeks. You know you can't afford a new dress. Your expendable income is attached exclusively to your beautiful new car.

Your anniversary rolls around. You start thinking about having a nice romantic dinner out with your husband. You start day dreaming about how to make this evening memorable and exciting. The day before your anniversary, you sit down to balance your checkbook. After crunching the numbers, you know the anniversary dinner is now in the largest catalogue in your mind, "The Things We Can't Do."

You would love to go somewhere memorable for your anniversary, but you don't even have enough money to go to a nice restaurant. Think about it. You got exactly what you wanted, the new car, but you never thought about where that decision would take you. Now, you can't enjoy some simple pleasures because of one decision that was made in haste. If you would have asked yourself, "Is this wise for the long haul," you would have probably made a different decision.

When the salesman said, "If you don't buy this today, it probably won't be here tomorrow," perhaps you thought, "Maybe this is God telling us to act quickly." Before you come to that conclusion, remember an indispensable part of God's character is patience. Whenever we feel rushed to make a decision, more than likely we are not in step with God. There's not a single example in the Bible where God says, "Rush! Hurry up! Decide now!" God would much rather you make the right decision than to make a quick decision. If you feel pressured to make a decision quickly, more than likely, it's not a prompting coming from God.

Wise decisions are also the result of having the proper facts. It's impossible to make a good decision with bad information. Before we make a decision, we need to go on a fact finding mission. Jesus calls us to "count the cost" before we start to build. Some people consider the facts only after the decision has been made. If you are unclear about a decision, there's probably a lack of information that needs to be gathered. When the facts are in, it's much easier to gain clarity about your decision.

Is it an Opened Door?

God uses opened and closed doors to direct us into the middle of His Will. You have more than likely experienced a fair share of closed doors. You have your eye on the beauty queen that lives directly across from your dorm. You've met her a few times, and her personality is just as appealing as her physical beauty. You decide to make the big ask. You're convinced this is the woman you are destined to marry. When you ask her out, she brushes you off like a pesky mosquito. Bang! The door is slammed air tight.

But you have probably also experienced your fair share of opened doors. You interview for the job that seems tailor made just for you. During the interview, you are poised, relaxed, and exhilarated about this opportunity. Your skills are a perfect match with the job description. You walk out feeling so good about what just happened. The next day, you get a phone call, and the company president offers you the job. It's a wide opened door.

If you want to read a classic example of how God guides us with opened and closed doors, spend some time reading Acts 16. Paul and Timothy are traveling through Asia, which would be modern day Turkey. They're moving throughout the country going to different regions to proclaim the good news about Christ. As they move from region to region, closed doors are slamming all around them. In every direction, God seems to be redirecting their steps.

Door "A" wasn't opening as they had planned. Finally, Paul had a miraculous vision during the night. Through the vision, God showed them Door "B." God opened a door for Paul and Timothy to go to Macedonia. It's a perfect case of the opened and closed door strategy God often employs to direct our footsteps. Door "A" is not always going to open as we had hoped and planned. God surprises us with Door "B." Though it differs from our original plan, God still has good things planned for us as we walk through this new door.

We have an aversion to closed doors because it means we have to wait on God to open another door. We're Americans. We hate to wait. We don't like to wait in traffic, restaurants, airports, or in doctor's offices. For many of us, waiting is not our strong suit, and that includes waiting on God.

In studying Scripture, I've discovered an amazing truth about God. He is never in a hurry, but He's always on time. God came to Abraham when he was 75 and He said, "I'm going to make you a father." God promised him a son. How long was it before God came through on the promise? Only 24 years. When the Israelites were suffering at the expense of the Egyptians, God told the Israelites, "I've heard your cry; I've seen the affliction of my people; I'm going to free you from Egyptian bondage." How long did they have to wait? Only 400 years.

God promised the Israelites He would lead them to the Promise Land, the land flowing with milk and honey. How long would they wait before the promise was fulfilled? Only 40 years. They wandered forty long years in the desert before they tasted the milk and honey. God promised in the Old Testament that the Messiah would come. But Israel had to wait, generation after generation, century after century, but guess who finally arrived? The long awaited Messiah-Jesus Christ. God is never in a mad dash, but He's always on time.

There's one other item to note about the open door test. Just because you have an open door standing before you, doesn't necessarily mean God wants you to walk through the door. A case in point is Jonah's experience. God said, "Jonah, go to Ninevah." Jonah didn't like the idea, so instead, he set out for Tarshish. Tarshish was in the opposite direction of Nineveh. Jonah was going in the opposite direction of God's will. At first, everything seemed to be perfectly aligned for him. Jonah went down to Joppa, and found a ship that just happened to be going to Tarshish. It appeared to be an open door. One slight problem, though, is that the ship was going in the wrong direction. It should be a reminder to us that opened doors and favorable circumstances are not always a sign of God's approval. It certainly wasn't God's will for Jonah to be going to Tarshish. Open doors are not always opened by the Lord. If something appears to be an open door for you, but you have to violate God's commandments to walk through it, trust me, it's not a door God has opened. If you have to turn off your conscience, ignoring the lack of peace you have, mark it down—it's not a door God has opened for you.

Is It Affirmed By The Right People?

God never meant for you to make a big decision in life on your own. You can decide what kind of cereal to buy at the grocery store by yourself; that's why God gave you a brain. But what if you're deciding on where to go to college, who to marry, a career change, what house to buy, or what kind of medical treatment to pursue? God never intended for you to make these life defining decisions all by yourself. God wants you to get help and advice from mature believers.

Proverbs 11:14 says, "Where there is no counsel, the people fall; but in the multitude of counselors there is safety." This doesn't mean you go up to a total stranger and say, "Hello, I've been thinking about making this decision, what do you think about it?" Instead, go to several people who are mature followers of Christ, and ask for their feedback regarding the decision.

God doesn't want us to get our advice from ungodly people. Of course, this doesn't mean we don't love ungodly people. We love ungodly people; we just don't get our advice from them. God typically uses godly people to confirm His direction in our lives. It's important to talk with someone who has nothing to gain or nothing to lose in the decision.

This is why sometimes getting direct feedback from your family and best friends is not always the best place to begin. Family members and friends are often biased, hoping that the decision will not make them feel uncomfortable. It's important to talk with someone who is objective, someone who can keep his emotions in check as he reflects on the decision.

At times, it's common to have opposition to your decision because your decision forces others to leave their comfort zones. You can even face opposition from people who love you. Don't make the mistake of personalizing the opposition. Most likely, they're not against you, or even what you're about to do. Your decision creates ripples that shake people up. Perhaps you are struggling with a call into missions, a distinct impression from God to adopt a child, or to make a career change, to move several states away from your parents. These decisions force everyone around you to adjust and adapt.

As I think back over my leadership; virtually every big decision I've made which has impacted the Kingdom in a positive way has been met with some opposition. It's because when I chose to stretch myself, it meant the people around me were also going to be stretched.

In one leadership position, I was evaluating how our church could strategically do a better job at reaching the unchurched. After prayerfully considering ways we could reach out, I designed a different kind of worship service with a different style that we held in our gym. I knew it was the right decision. As I was casting the vision for the service, I had numerous people who said, "Clay, don't do it. You're just adding more and more to your plate." Others said, "We don't think this is going to work." In spite of the opposition, we started the new service and called it "The Vine." Over time, we were able to reach unchurched people for Christ that, otherwise, we probably would not have reached.

I think of Ross Price. Ross Price was a young man in his twenties. He came to Christ through The Vine. When Ross first started attending the service, he was strung out on drugs. Thankfully, he heard the gospel, and Ross gave his life to Christ. Ross happened to be a gifted guitar player and eventually became a part of the band who led us in worship. Sadly, it seems like yesterday that I was conducting his funeral.

After playing in the band for about a year, Ross was tragically killed in a car accident. I remember driving home after the funeral thinking about the incredible part The Vine service played in helping Ross come to Christ. After the funeral, I met with his girlfriend to try to comfort and console her. During our conversation, she assured me that she was turning to Christ for comfort and hope. I asked, "Tiffany, when did you give your life to Christ?" She said, "About 3 months ago at a Vine worship service."

What if I would have allowed the opposition to The Vine service to derail my decision to launch it? I wonder where Ross would be today. I wonder if Tiffany would have come to Christ. Someone may oppose your decision, but if you know you're in alignment with God's plan, don't allow a naysayer to disrupt you from pursuing God's will.

Is it Fixed in Faith?

Whenever God is leading us to make a decision about something, we're not going to have all the details in advance. If we had all the details, then we wouldn't have to trust God. God lovingly says, "I'm not going to give you all the details because I want you to learn to trust me. I want you to live by faith, not by sight." When God is leading us in a particular direction, it's always going to involve an element of faith on our part. The Bible says, "It is impossible to please God without faith."

On many occasions, the decision you're contemplating creates a crisis point in your faith. When the 10 spies returned from surveying the Promised Land, they gave a report, "We've been to the land of Canaan; it really is a land flowing with milk and honey. The fruit is unbelievably luscious. The whole land is incredibly fertile. There's just one problem. The people are way too big. We'll never be able to possess the land." However, Joshua and Caleb didn't believe the report. Instead of focusing on the obstacle, they chose to focus on the God who was bigger than the obstacle.

Do you know the only difference between the 10 who said, "No, we can't," and the 2 who said, "Yes, we can?" Faith. The 10 who brought back the pessimistic report only saw the obstacle. Joshua and Caleb saw the obstacle, but they saw it through the eyes of faith. The greatest enemy of your dream is not your fear, lack of resources, or opposition; the greatest enemy of your dream is unbelief. The 10 spies feared the obstacle more than they trusted God.

At some point, you are going to have to move forward in faith, trusting God with the details you don't have. Maybe God has given you the dream of becoming a nurse. You sense this is God's plan for you, but you have a lot of doubts surrounding the dream. You're unsure how you're going to arrange your time; you're scared to death you may not make the grades. Sure, there are looming details you're uncertain about. But would you see the obstacle through the eyes of faith? Don't forget one important factor—God. Are you assuming you're pursuing the dream all by yourself? No wonder your obstacle looks so big. What if you're not going to be by yourself? What if the all-powerful, omnipotent God of the universe is going to be your partner as you go after your dream? Then, your obstacle, sized up to God, is not that big at all.

When God is leading you in a particular area, He's not going to reveal everything to you. He will, however, give you enough light to take the next step. When I was a child, my older brother and I liked to walk through the woods at night time. There was a pond behind our house, and a well-worn path lead down to the pond. We would take our flashlights and walk down the trail, finally reaching the pond. Our flashlights didn't show us the whole trail. The flashlights simply showed us the next little part of the trail. They threw enough light to take the next step, and the next step, until we reached the pond. God's will works much the same way. God doesn't show you His whole plan all at once. He's not going to show you how everything is going to work out on the front side. But God will give you enough light to take the next step, and the next step, until you reach the final destination.

Is it Confirmed by God's Peace?

You're not going to be able to find a Bible verse that tells you exactly what to do every time you have to make a decision. What happens when you're offered several different scholarships at a college? What do you do when you're offered several different jobs? The question becomes which school do I go to? Which job do I take? You won't be able find a specific answer to that decision in a verse of Scripture. If you do, you're reading something into the Bible. Perhaps you're single, and you've been praying about someone to date. You won't find a verse which says, "Date Roger," or "Don't date Roger." You'll find general principles which might eliminate Roger. One that comes to mind is Scripture's admonition, "not to be unequally yoked with an unbeliever" (2 Cor. 6:14). The Bible teaches believers only to date other believers. However, what if Roger is a rock solid follower of Christ?

Several days after Roger asks you out, Malcolm comes along and invites you to go out to dinner. Malcolm is also a committed follower of Christ. You won't find a specific verse telling you whether to go out with Roger or Malcolm. Just because you can't cite a chapter and verse number doesn't mean God isn't interested in guiding you in the decision you make. God wants to guide us through the direction of His spirit. As we seek God through prayer, God will either provide a sense of peace or an absence of peace about a particular decision we're contemplating. Peace is one way God confirms we are in full alignment with His will. At the same time, if we have an absence of peace, it's usually God telling us to stop dead in our tracks.

Col. 3:15 says, "Let the peace of God rule in your hearts." The word for "rule" in this great verse was often used to describe what an umpire did at sporting events. What does an umpire do? An umpire makes the final call. In baseball, the umpire either calls you "safe" or "out!" The coach doesn't make the final call. That's not up for the players to decide. It's the umpire who makes the final call.

Like the umpire, there will be plenty of times in life when we have to let the peace of God make the final call in our lives. If God wants us to move forward, God will provide a peace in our hearts about the decision. If God wants us to go in a different direction, God will create a lack of peace about the decision. The lack of peace is an indicator God wants us to go in a different direction.

Life is at its best when you're in the sweet spot of God's Will. God has a general will, and He also has a specific will for our lives. His general will is the same for all of us. You can find His general will in the Bible. His general will is expressed in the form of His commands and standards. God wants every one of us to follow His commandments. In addition to His general will, God has a specific will for us. His specific will is different from person to person. This is God's unique, tailor made plan just for you. When you are in full alignment with God's general will and His specific will, you're in the zone—the bull's eye of God's best plan for your life.

Decision 4: Will I Choose To Be Grateful Today?

CHAPTER 10

Life Is Too Short to Be Ungrateful

LIFE IS SHORT. AN AVERAGE lifespan will spot you roughly 28,470 days on earth. Maybe you've never thought about it, but one of the greatest ways to improve those 28,470 days on earth is by practicing gratitude.

There are plenty of things you can do to improve your life. We've already talked about a few key areas that have the potential of changing your life dramatically. Your perspective on your problems, attitude about life, and your decisions position you to make the most of each day. However, very few things will enrich your life more like the power of personal gratitude. If you learn to practice gratitude, every one of your 28,470 days will get better.

Gratitude matters. At least we know it matters to Jesus. Look no further than His encounter with ten lepers. Remember this dreadful disease? Most likely, when the ten lepers came to Jesus, they didn't even look like human beings. Their faces were disfigured. Sores oozed from their bodies. Taking on the classic "lion look," these lepers probably resembled animals more than human beings.

On a particular day, the lepers hear that Jesus is coming to their village. They had already heard about this miracle worker who caused the blind to see, the deaf to hear, and the lame to walk. When they see Jesus coming through town, they raise their voices saying, "Jesus, have mercy on us." It was a soft, subtle request for healing. Jesus tells all ten lepers to go to the priest and show the priest they have been healed (this, of course, was before they had actually been healed.) In faith, they start walking down the road. This is one road trip I wish I could have been on. One by one, the lepers start to notice their skin, "Guys, look at my skin. It's like baby skin. No more sores." "Look at me; I have all my fingers and toes." "You think that's something, I've got my nose back. I can't believe what a big honker I have."

The good news is all ten lepers were healed; the bad news is only one man made a bee line back to Jesus to say thank you. When he returns to express his gratitude, Jesus asks him a question, "Where are the other nine? Weren't there ten lepers healed?"[31]

You know what we learn from this story? Gratitude matters to Jesus. Jesus noticed the one and only leper who returned to Him to say thank you. Gratitude is the heart's memory. It says, "God, I'm not going to forget what you've done for me." Apparently, Jesus also noticed the other nine who had a short memory and never returned to say thanks. He exclaimed, "Where are the other nine?" The implication is, "I did something good for you. Don't you even recognize it?" Developing a keen awareness of God's goodness is one of the essentials of a fulfilling life. If you will be determined to lift your level of gratitude, it will automatically elevate your level of joy. You'll be a happier person.

The goal is to graduate to a level of gratitude that enables us to be conscious of blessings all around us. It's great to make enough passing grades in college to earn a diploma, but it's quite different when you are able to walk across the stage with honors. Graduating with honors means you have excelled way beyond the basic standards for graduation. Let's consider three levels of gratitude, and how we can graduate to the point of operating at the highest level.

Cum Laude Gratitude

When a student graduates cum laude, they are graduating with basic honors. Cum laude means "with honor." Cum laude gratitude is the most basic kind of gratitude. This is when we learn to say thank you to fit in with appropriate social norms. We learn from childhood that saying thank you is common courtesy. Interestingly, it's surprising how few people actually practice this basic kind of gratitude.

31   Luke 17:11-19.

How well do you say thank you? When you go to a restaurant, do you express gratitude to the person serving your table? I read an article once about a business owner who used gratitude as an integral part of his interview process. Before he hires any new sales person, he takes them out to eat at a restaurant. He purposefully pays attention to how the prospective employee interacts with the waitress. When the waitress fills up his tea or when she brings the food to the table, the owner listens to see if he says, "Thank you." The owner says if the prospect doesn't say thank you in the restaurant, he's probably not going to be a great employee. Reflecting on his years of hiring, he said his greatest employees have always been people who practice gratitude.

We have an opportunity to express gratitude whether we are eating at a restaurant, shuffling paper at work, or sitting at home in our living room. We have an opportunity to convey gratitude every time we send an e-mail, write a letter, or have a phone conversation. Wherever there is a human being, there is an opportunity to express gratitude.

We will never graduate to the next level of gratitude until we practice this basic kind of gratitude. It starts with the simple things. Instead of taking things for granted, every day we can notice the simple things people do for us. When your administrative assistant helps you accomplish a project, acknowledge it by saying thank you. Not only will it mean the world to her, it will help build a nourishing culture in your work environment. Imagine what would happen if everyone where you worked decided to appreciate the people around them.

When your wife cooks a meal…when your husband does the laundry…when your kids pick up their toys…when your students work hard on an assignment…when your direct reports stay consistent on the job, a simple thank you recognizes your appreciation for the people God has placed around you.

Magna Cum Laude Gratitude

When students graduate Magna Cum Laude, it means they're graduating with high honors. Magna Cum Laude means "with great honor." Magna cum laude gratitude is when we express thanks for obvious blessings. It's important we don't overlook obvious blessings that take place routinely in our lives. The one leper who returned to say thank you to Jesus was practicing Magna Cum Laude gratitude. Earlier in the day, he had leprosy. After his encounter with the Messiah, his whole world changed instantaneously. He was once and for all healed from this dreadful disease. He didn't overlook this obvious blessing. He returned to say, "I recognize what you did for me." Some blessings are hard to miss.

One Wednesday morning, my wife and I received a phone call from the Sheriff's department. The message basically said an 88 year old woman with Alzheimer's had wandered away from her house. She lived in our general area, and the Sheriff's department asked everyone in the surrounding neighborhood to be on the lookout for her. It just so happened that this lady, named Mrs. Harrison, along with her family, were members of our church. Mrs. Harrison wandered away one Tuesday evening. She spent Tuesday night wandering around outside during the cold wintry night. The police asked everyone to be observant, and if anyone spotted Mrs. Harrison, we were told to call the police.

About 1 o'clock in the afternoon, I was on my way back to the office, and out of the corner of my eye, I saw Mrs. Harrison. She was walking through someone's backyard. I turned my car around as quickly as I could. I pulled into a driveway, and started walking toward Mrs. Harrison. Even though she had Alzheimer's, ironically, when she saw me, she recognized me. When I found her, she was three miles away from her home.

Fortunately, I was able to coax her into my car, and I took her home. Her family was so thankful she had arrived home safely. As you can imagine, they thanked me profusely. When I called the police, the officer on the phone was elated that Mrs. Harrison had been found. After I took her home, I was driving back to work, and the first thing that came to my mind was, "God, thank you! Thank you Mrs. Harrison is okay. Thank you for putting me in the right place at the right time." Some blessings are glaringly obvious.

Summa Cum Laude Gratitude

A student graduating summa cum laude is at the top of the class. Summa cum laude literally means, "With highest honor." Practicing summa cum laude gratitude is when we learn to be grateful for everything that is good. Achieving this highest level of gratitude takes place when we embrace a principle given to us by James, the half brother of Jesus. In James 1:17, he reminds us, "Every good and perfect gift is from above, coming down from the Father of Lights." People who live at this highest level of gratitude have developed a keen awareness of the goodness of God. Every day they go looking for God's goodness in the smallest and simplest details of life.

Sometimes life gets so crowded and we get so wrapped up in our own agendas, we miss the goodness of God which is all around us. If we go looking for God's goodness, it's not hard to find. Developing a conscious awareness of the goodness of God is the key to developing a grateful disposition in life.

Whether I'm looking into the eyes of my children or at the flashing cursor on my laptop, whether I'm walking in my neighborhood or driving on the interstate, whether I'm sitting in a worship service or sitting in a doctor's office, whether I'm paying the bills or having a quiet conversation with a friend, I can learn to see God's goodness. I want to spend the remaining part of the chapter describing ways you can cultivate gratitude.

Start with the Simple Things

God's goodness is often revealed in the simple things we take for granted. When we awaken in the morning, a good place to start is by acknowledging that the day is a gift. I don't manufacture each day. I don't create each day. I don't sustain the day—God does. Practicing gratitude before your feet ever hit the floor is a great way to start the day.

I have found expressing gratitude for the simple things sets my emotional temperature for the day. When you get in the shower, you can express your gratitude, "God, thank you for this warm shower today. So many people in the world won't get a shower today or even this month." When you put your clothes on, you can breathe a simple prayer, "God, thank you I have clothes to cover my body." When you get in the car to drive to work, you can express your gratitude, "God, thank you for this car, and that I have job to drive to today. Most people in the world will never have either one." By acknowledging that everything is a gift from God, it helps to create the right perspective for each new day.

Think Old School: Send a Letter

Getting a handwritten or typed letter in your mailbox is a rare experience these days. If you take the time to write someone to express your gratitude, more than likely the letter will never be forgotten. Instead of sending a message through Facebook or email, send your letter so the person you are writing gets the privilege of picking it up out of their mailbox. It's one more way to distinguish the message you're trying to convey.

Writing a note to express gratitude is a powerful tool to encourage others. I'm convinced one of the major reasons Paul wrote his letters in the New Testament was to encourage the people he was writing. Almost all the encouragement we know about in the early church took the form of written encouragement. Paul wrote encouraging letters to churches scattered throughout the Roman Empire.

Though most writers don't hand out assignments, I have one for you. Select 3 people who have made a difference in your life, and write them a letter. Express your gratitude, and explain why they are significant to you. I have a friend who tries to write 3 of these each week.

Several years ago, I wrote my father a letter which he received on his birthday. The letter was written at a time when my father was facing one of the greatest challenges of his life. I wrote a letter entitled, "How Can I Say Thanks," to express my gratitude for him. Here is my letter to my dad:

How Can I Say Thanks

Daddy, on your birthday, I want you to know how valuable you are in my eyes. The human vocabulary seems so inadequate to express my gratitude for you. Let me begin by saying thanks for being there! I never had an absentee dad who didn't make time for me. You were there in the good times and the bad times.

I can still picture you sitting in your lawn chair at my baseball games. On many occasions, I can recall an encouraging word from you just before I stepped up to the plate. I can remember making plays from second base thinking, "Daddy will be proud of that!" It never failed, when I walked in the house from a late game, you brought it up, "Son, what a great play tonight." Interestingly, every bad play I made never seemed to catch your eye. Though I know you saw them, you never drew attention to them, so as not to discourage me. I noticed that too!

Thanks for letting me work at Sports Corner. I have so many memories of chewing Gatorade gum, tagging merchandise, and hearing the alarm go off and having it scare me to death. The skills you taught me early on like greeting customers, shaking hands, and thanking people for their business are priceless skills I use every day in my ministry. I will forever be grateful to you for including me in your business.

Thanks for supporting me in every goal I have ever had! I can picture you at Crowe Park, behind the net, throwing me countless pitches because I wanted to play college baseball. I see you holding a fungo bat with buckets of balls around your feet. The countless hours you invested in me required you to sacrifice at work and with leisure activities, but you did it to help me achieve a dream. And then when I went to college and decided not to play, you never interrogated me about my decision. You invested a whole summer preparing me to play, and then when I chose not to play, you never said a word.

I have never had a goal you didn't support. When I wanted to go back to seminary to work on my doctorate, you bought me a computer so I could write from my home. Thanks for being in my corner no matter what the goal!

Thanks for teaching me about adding value to people. Your love for people and for the underdog has been passed down to me. I saw when a questionable person patronized the store; you didn't treat them with disdain or contempt. You treated them with value, respect, and showed worth to each person.

Thanks for modeling character in front of me. Like most virtues, character is caught more than it is taught. I also learned from you that discipline is crucial to excel at anything. You taught us: "The only time success comes before work is in the dictionary." You worked hard and taught us that anything worth doing is worth doing well. We learned that 90% is 10% short! God deserves our very best.

Most of all, thanks for your spiritual leadership in my life. My view of God, and my ability to love, trust, and obey Him, as well as my desire to grow in Christ-likeness, can be attributed to your influence. Without question, the relationship with my earthly father has helped me in my relationship with my heavenly Father. That's the way it's supposed to happen. The desire to know Christ and to make Him known will always stand as your greatest achievement.

This year of your life has been without question the most difficult one. The same could be said for me. Each of us now walk with a limp, but we will still walk. I have learned this from you. Winners never quit, and quitters never win. Even through this time of suffering, you have demonstrated an unfaltering commitment to Christ and His Word! We will hold tenaciously to the promise that "His grace is sufficient." His grace gets us up in the morning, and His grace offers us hope.

Recently, I added a plaque on my wall in my office. I have deemed it, "My Wall of Gratitude." On the plaque, I have the names of certain people who have made the biggest difference in my life. Guess who is at the top of my list? My Dad!

Christ has you in the palm of His hand! He is sovereignly working out His plan in your life. He has used you greatly in my life, and I wanted you to know I love you!

Love,

Clay

Written encouragement never dies. You can speak an encouraging word to someone, and occasionally they remember what you say. However, sometimes what you say is forgotten in a matter of moments. But when you write a note, it never goes away. Most people keep encouraging letters for a lifetime.

Reduce Your Complaining Quotient

Whenever we fall into the trap of grumbling and complaining, it's a telltale sign we are living outside the realm of gratitude. Each of us has the proclivity to notice what's wrong and complain about it. Yet, if we are honest with ourselves, we would have to agree that complaining changes nothing. All it does is release negative emotional energy. It doesn't change anything. Philippians 2:14 says, "Do all things without complaining." There's no shortage of things we can complain about. You can complain about your boss, teachers, spouse, children, school, church, and even your food.

Just recently, I watched a young lady in her twenties return to a fast food restaurant. She came back to complain that the restaurant failed to put cheese on her roast beef sandwich. I heard her say she drove 15 minutes back to the restaurant because she didn't get her sandwich the way she ordered it. She demanded a new sandwich with cheese on it. Wouldn't it have been much easier to simply eat the sandwich without cheese and be thankful for it? Wouldn't it be much smarter to overlook these petty items instead of taking our precious time to complain about them?

I once read about a particular principal who told all of his teachers to write down their New Year's resolutions. The principal told the teachers he was going to post their New Year's resolutions on their first day back to school after their break. He instructed everyone to meet at the bulletin board and they would talk about their resolutions for the New Year.

The first morning back at school, all the teachers gathered around the bulletin board. Suddenly, the principal noticed one teacher started to raise her voice. It quickly escalated into a full blown scene. The teacher behind the commotion made her way over to the principal. She started to complain profusely about why her resolutions were not posted on the bulletin board. She was throwing such a temper tantrum that the principal decided go back to his office to see if he misplaced her resolutions. Sure enough, he found her list of resolutions on his desk. He glanced down at her list, and was astounded to see what was number one on her list. Her #1 New Year's Resolution for the year: not to let little things upset me. Suffice it to say, she wasn't off to a good start on her resolutions.

When we complain about petty things in life, we're choosing to focus on all that's wrong instead of focusing on all that's right. When we develop a habit and lifestyle of complaining, we start to see all of life from a negative perspective.

By reducing our daily complaining quotient, we will be far more productive. Take work for example. It's easy to go to our jobs, congregate around the coffee pot, and hear a co-worker complain about something at work. If we're not careful, without giving it much thought, we can chime in with our own set of complaints. So much time is wasted on the job because of grumbling.

Even if we aren't doing the complaining ourselves, we can lose precious time by standing around listening to everyone else complain. If you refuse to listen to people complain, you will probably save 2 minutes in the morning, 3 minutes in the afternoon, and 4 minutes after lunch. At the end of the day, by refusing to participate in gripe sessions, you will probably save an hour of your time. Let's do the math. An hour a day, 5 hours a week, equals 250 hours a year. Believe it or not, that's over 6 weeks you have saved in a year simply by refusing to be sidetracked by complaining.

When Life Is Mysterious, God is Still Good

I don't have answers for all the mysteries, perplexities, and enigmas of life. I can't explain why a tornado strikes a community and kills one family, while their next door neighbors are completely unharmed. I don't understand why one person in the hospital prays for healing and he recovers and goes home, while the person in the next room prays a similar prayer but never returns home.

I was in Haiti six months after the horrific earthquake decimated the capital city. If you go with the conservative estimate, over 100,000 people were killed. I was in the capital city working with an orphanage. One afternoon, I spoke to a group of Christian leaders. After my talk, we did a question and answer session with the workers. After they got comfortable with me, one man from the corner of the room raised his hand. In broken English and tears streaking down his dark skin, he asked, "Why did God allow 100,000 Haitians to lose their lives in the earthquake?" Instead of offering a hollow answer, I simply said, "I don't know the answer to that question. I know we can trust God with all we don't know, but that's a question no human being can answer." Life is full of mysteries, perplexities, and enigmas. There are things we will never figure out.

In theology, we sometimes refer to the unknowability of God. There are aspects of God which remain unknown. We can know a lot about God. God has revealed Himself in creation, the Bible, and ultimately in His Son, but there are still things about God and His plan that remain unknowable to us.

Though I don't fully understand all the mysteries, perplexities, and enigmas in life, I do understand something far more important. I understand life is a gift. The good days are a gift. The bad days are a gift. The days filled with pleasure are a gift, and the days filled with pain are a gift. Every day contains a little bit of good and a little bit of bad. Our faith allows us to accept both as a gift. Here's something else our faith allows us to do. Faith allows us to stay more focused on the good than the bad. Even when your days are confusing and heartbreaking, if you go looking for the goodness of God, you will find it. Even in your hardship, you will discover God is still expressing His goodness to you.

Chapter 11

One Day with Alvin

CAN ONE DAY WITH A practical stranger change your life? Years ago, I would have answered with an emphatic "No!" But that was before I met Alvin. Alvin was a part of a search committee that had contacted me about a job offer. We had several phone conversations before we met, and on the phone, Alvin was always very kind and gracious with his words.

Alvin invited my wife and me to take a trip to Brevard, North Carolina so he could show us the community. Surrounded by beautiful mountains, Brevard is home to some of the most pristine waterfalls in the country. My wife loves the mountains. As we drove into Brevard, I could see her eyes sparkling with excitement. Though we had only been married a short time, I knew her well enough to know she was daydreaming about our potential new home. The thought of living in this beautiful scenic area was thrilling to her.

We arranged to meet Alvin at a restaurant in downtown Brevard. We drove into the parking lot of the restaurant, only to find a middle age man sitting in a wheelchair, with a contagious smile spanning the globe. As we walked up the sidewalk, this middle age man quickly wheeled his chair in our direction. Reaching out for my hand, he said, "Hey Clay, I'm Alvin." After entering the restaurant, we found a quiet place in the corner of the room where we could talk.

Over lunch, Alvin told us about his disease. He recounted the day he sat in the doctor's office. Alvin said, "An eerie silence filled the room before my neurologist started talking. I felt like it was the calm before the storm." He was right. Alvin's doctor began to explain that he had Amyotrophic Lateral Sclerosis (ALS), often referred to as Lou Gehrig's disease.

Since we didn't know very much about the disease, Alvin described some of the details about his brutal illness. ALS is a neurological disease that affects nerve cells in the brain and spinal cord. With time, the effects of the disease grow worse and worse. Alvin's doctors told him the disease would eventually destroy his brain's ability to control his muscles. After becoming totally paralyzed, his doctors told him the dreadful disease would take his life. Alvin said the worst part about the disease was the way it forced gradual losses on his body. He had already lost his ability to walk, and his doctors informed him he would eventually lose his ability to talk.

I'm so grateful we met Alvin before he lost his ability to talk. As I listened to him talk about his disease, I was struck by Alvin's enthusiasm for life. Though he spoke briefly about the disappointing effects of his disease, the conversation revolved largely around his love for life.

After we left the restaurant, he wanted to show us around town. I offered to drive, but I could tell Alvin really wanted to drive. Later on, it dawned on me why Alvin was so adamant about driving; he knew that before long, the ability to drive would be taken from him as well. He told us to climb into his Bronco while he went through his ritual of getting positioned in the car. It took him quite a few minutes, but when he emerged in the driver's seat, his smile could have covered the earth. He was like a sixteen year old who was overjoyed at the thrill of driving.

As Alvin drove us around, he pointed out his favorite scenic areas. He would drive a little, and then slowly pull over to the side of the road. "Look," he would say, pointing to the mountain stream, "Isn't that gorgeous?" A little further down the road, he pointed to a cascading waterfall, "Nothing beats this—this is one of my favorite places." With each mile, Alvin made sure we noticed the fall colors on the trees, butterflies, birds, and his favorite mountain cabins.

At one point, Alvin drove us into a wooded area deep into the mountains. As we drove up the unpaved road, Alvin pointed out his window, "See those woods? Through the years I've spent a lot of time in those woods hunting deer." With a deep sense of pride, he said, "I still enjoy hunting. This wheelchair is not going to stop me. It's harder now, but my friends help me get in and out of the woods." Everywhere Alvin looked, he found something to be grateful for.

After driving us around for several hours, we went to discuss the terms of the job. As we covered pertinent facts about the job, Alvin kept a contagious smile on his face the whole time. He seemed to be grateful for the chance to have the conversation. As we finished our meeting and were preparing to leave, Alvin reached out to shake my hand. I looked into his eyes only to discover several tears running down his cheeks. I was unsure how to respond to his tears, but after spending the day with Alvin, I knew exactly why he had tears in his eyes. For Alvin, each moment was sacred. Each moment was something to be relished and grateful for.

I didn't take the job in Brevard, but there was a big part of me that wanted to simply because Alvin was there. Though my encounter with Alvin took place many years ago, I have never forgotten him. Neither has my wife. We have referenced Alvin in our conversations on many occasions. Though we only spent one day with Alvin, it was one of the most important days of my life.

Through Alvin, I learned an invaluable lesson. Regardless of what has been taken from us, we can be thankful for what is still left. Alvin didn't focus on all that ALS had taken from him; instead, he focused on all he still had left. He still had his Bronco. He still had his license. He still had friends who made sure he could go hunting. He still had gorgeous waterfalls to take in. He still had sunsets, flowers, and butterflies to behold. And He still had two new friends he could spend the day with. In spite of all he had lost, Alvin was more focused on all he had left. From his perspective, he still had so much to be grateful for.

A Lesson From Morrie

In almost paradoxical form, sometimes losses enhance our sensitivity to God's goodness. A best-selling book that confirms that is entitled, *Tuesdays with Morrie: An Old Man, a Young Man, and Life's Greatest Lesson.* Morrie Schwartz (the old man) was a sociologist, professor, and author who faced the same thundering words Alvin heard, "You have ALS." Like Alvin, the disease began to attack Morrie's body unmercifully. Morrie, the consummate overachiever, had one final goal. He decided to meet with one of his former students, Mitch Albom (the young man), for ten weeks; they would discuss important subjects pertaining to the meaning of life. Mitch decided to ask Morrie about fear, regrets, greed, death, and a host of other topics. As a wise sage, Morrie provided timeless answers that ended up changing Mitch's life. One particular week, Mitch sat down to talk with Morrie about perspective:

> *"The truth is, Mitch," [Morrie] said, "once you learn how to die, you learn how to live ... Most of us all walk around as if we're sleepwalking." [Mitch asked,] "And facing death changes all that?" "Oh, yes. You strip away all that stuff and you focus on the essentials. When you realize you are going to die, you see everything much differently." ... He nodded toward the window with the sunshine streaming in. "You see that? You can go out there, outside, anytime. You can run up and down the block and go crazy. I can't do that. I can't go out. I can't run. I can't be out there without fear of getting sick. But you know what? I appreciate that window more than you do ... I look out that window every day. I notice the change in the trees, how strong the wind is blowing. It's as if I can see time actually passing through that window-pane. Because I know my time is almost done, I am drawn to nature like I'm seeing it for the first time."*[32]

It's Morrie's comment about sleepwalking through life that caught my attention. I don't want to sleepwalk through life. I want to be awakened, just as Morrie was, to all the wonderful blessings of each day. Even when losses occur, there is still so much to appreciate. We need a new set of eyes that will awaken us to God's goodness which is all around us. We have to train our minds to go looking for the goodness of God.

32　Mitch Albom, Tuesdays with Morrie: An Old Man, a Young Man, and Life's Greatest Lesson (New York: Broadway Books, 1997), 82–84.

People who experience the greatest levels of happiness learn to extract joy out of small things. I've learned this from my wife. She is an expert at finding joy in simple things. I've watched her squeeze joy out of a conversation with a friend, a song on the radio, a casual encounter with someone at the doctor's office, a sunset, and an evening stroll through the neighborhood. My wife doesn't need the bright lights of the big city to find enjoyment. She's satisfied with the joy she finds in simple things.

You may remember in the classic movie *Chariots of Fire*, one runner coveted winning above everything else. Winning is all he thought about, but the other runner, Eric Liddel, simply enjoyed the gift of the wind against his face and the feeling of his feet flying over the ground. For him, winning was not the point; the point was appreciating the experience.

When we overlook the simple things, it becomes more difficult for us to enjoy our own lives. This brings me to an important subject-contentment. To develop a new level of sensitivity to God's goodness, we will have to learn contentment. Scripture teaches contentment is something we don't get naturally. Contentment is something we have to learn.

> *"Not that I speak in regard to need, for I have learned in whatever state I am, to be content. I know how to be abased, and I know how to abound. Everywhere and in all things I have learned both to be full and to be hungry, both to abound and to suffer need."* **(Philippians 4:11-12) NKJV**

It's virtually impossible to recognize God's goodness in life without fostering a spirit of contentment. Benjamin Franklin once said, "Contentment makes a poor man rich and discontentment makes a rich man poor." It's so easy to complain about the kids bouncing off the walls, instead of being thankful they're healthy and full of life. It's easy to complain about our jobs, instead of being grateful we have one. It's easy to complain we don't have new furniture, when millions of people still sit on their dirt floors. We can complain that our houses aren't large enough, when there are plenty of people in the world who will never have a house.

Contentment: With The Rooms We Have

I've heard more than one person say, "I would be content if I just had a bigger house." You may not live in a 30 room house, but you can thankful for the one bedroom apartment you have. Do you really think having a bigger house is going to make you happier? You should ask yourself, "How many rooms do I need to be happy?" Do I really think that having one more room is going to make life better for me? The secret to being content is to be thankful for the rooms you already have.

The first step in learning contentment is appreciating whatever God provides. Hebrews 13:5 says, "Be content with such things as you have." In Paul's statement about contentment, he said he learned "how to be abased and how to abound." Undoubtedly, there were times in Paul's life when he had a lot at his fingertips, and other times when he had virtually nothing at his fingertips. Whether he was managing prosperity or adversity, he learned to be content.

You might be thinking, "You must be kidding me! How can I live like that? I'll never get anywhere. I have ambition, drive, and white-hot passion. I'm not going to sit back and let the world pass me by!" Contentment is not letting the world pass you by. That's not the picture of contentment painted by Scripture. To be content is not to be passive. You can be extremely motivated, have great personal drive, and still be content.

Don't confuse contentment with mediocrity. This is not a proof text for mediocrity. Being content doesn't mean you shouldn't have godly ambitions. Never be satisfied with mediocrity. Never be satisfied with being the secretary when you could be the president of the company. Never be satisfied with making D's when God has given you the brain power to make B's. Never be satisfied with playing 3rd string when God has given you the ability to be an All-American. Contentment is not the ultimate bob sled ride where you perpetually coast through life.

The word Paul uses here for contentment was actually a secular word; it was often used by the stoic philosophers. If you had a class in college in philosophy, chances are good you spent some time talking about stoicism. The stoics basically taught that nothing should move you emotionally. Even today we describe people who are "stoic," meaning they seem to be indifferent to pain or pleasure. They appear to be emotionless. The stoics essentially taught that we should be able to reach a point when we don't care about anything. According to the stoic philosophers, you reach this point of nirvana by subduing your emotions. If a vase broke in their house, the stoic would say, "I don't care." If they lost a pet, the stoic would say, "I don't care." If one of their own children died, they would say, "I don't care." But there is a major problem with stoicism—we do care.

Contentment is not getting to the point where you don't care about anything. Paul took this secular word and he gave it a Christian meaning. Contentment is not reaching a point of emotional numbness where you are ambivalent toward life. It's reaching a point where you recognize everything you need to be happy is contained in the goodness of God. The happiest people I know have learned to reduce their wish list. They have learned to be grateful and content with the things God has already provided. In his letter to his young associate, Paul reminds Timothy the way to be rich is to be content.

> *"But godliness with contentment is great gain. For we brought nothing into this world and we can take nothing out of it. But if we have food and clothing, we will be content with that" (1 Tim. 6:6-8).*

Happiness isn't getting whatever you want. Happiness is enjoying whatever you have. John Ortberg says using a bit of self talk can do wonders to foster contentment. He recommends using the phrase, "It could be worse," to re-frame your circumstances. Though playing the comparison game is typically counterproductive, this is one time it can be helpful.

When you leave work tomorrow, you will walk to your car. Upon arriving at your car, you might be tempted to think, "If I just had another car, a nicer car, a newer car, a bigger car, then I would be happy." We're bombarded with that message all the time, but the next time you're tempted to think that, say to yourself, "It could be worse."

When you get in your car to drive home from work, you will probably pull into your driveway. You'll glance up at your apartment or house. You might be tempted to think, "If I just had a different house, a newer house, a bigger house, then I would be happy and content." We're bombarded with that message as well. However, the next time you're tempted to have those thoughts, re-frame them. The moment you take the first step in your house, be determined to say, "It could be worse. It could be much worse."

Tomorrow morning, when you wake up, roll over and look at your spouse; you can say, "It could be worse." On second thought, you better keep that to yourself. Contentment is a state of mind where we are satisfied with what we have, knowing things could be much worse.[33]

Research shows that cancer patients, regardless of their condition, have a better outlook when they are able to call to mind another patient who is much worse off than themselves. Finding someone else who is suffering at a far greater level allows them to gain a better perspective.[34]

Personally, using "It could be worse" has been a lifesaver for me. There have been plenty of occasions where I have felt overwhelmed by the health condition of my sons, and in particular, Graham's condition. Like Alvin and Morrie, Graham has had his own fair share of losses. I've had to watch things slowly be taken from Graham. When Graham was seven, he played on a recreational baseball team. I coached his team, and he loved it and so did I. Graham made contact with the ball almost every time he was at bat. Now, I still play baseball with Graham in the backyard, but he rarely is able to make contact with the ball.

At one time, Graham could sit across from me at the dinner table and carry on a meaningful conversation. He was always the one I called on to say the blessing before our meals. Today, he may

---

33   Leadership Message at Summit by John Ortberg

34   Daniel Coleman, Emotional Intelligence (New York: Bantam Dell, 1995), 74.

only say 7-10 words in a day. It would mean so much to me to have Graham say the blessing again, but now someone else prays.

Though Graham was delayed in being potty trained, he finally reached this important milestone. Then, the seizures progressed and became uncontrollable, and Graham regressed. He has been in pull ups now for several years. As his father, it's been tough to have a front row seat to all these losses. I still have memories of all Graham could do when he was younger.

When I have felt overwhelmed about these losses, I have occasionally taken a trip to a nearby children's hospital, located just blocks from my office. I walk the hallways, and I see children who are paralyzed. I see children undergoing intense forms of chemotherapy for cancer. I see children with trachs and feeding tubes. I see children who have never spoken a word. In addition to praying for these children while walking the hallways, I usually drive back to work with one thought echoing in my mind, "It could be worse...It could be worse." I've learned to celebrate the things Graham can still do rather than focusing on all he can't do.

Though being overly comparative can be dangerous, sometimes it can put things into perspective. It all depends on our reference point. In our own minds, we all define who we are. And we usually define who we are by comparing ourselves to other people. We can either compare up, or we can compare down. We can compare our lives to people we think are doing better than us, or we can compare our lives to people we think are doing worse than us. When we're trying to define who we are, we either compare up or down.

A Lesson From Bronze Medalists

There's an MIT professor who did a very interesting study with Olympic athletes. After an Olympic competition, we know who performed the best. Obviously, the gold medalist performed the best, the silver medalist is the second best, and the bronze medalist is the third best. The MIT professor did this study to determine the level of happiness of each medalist.

Who do you think was the happiest medalist? Naturally, the gold medalist scored the highest on the happiness scale. Who do you think was second happiest medalist? It only makes sense that it would be the silver medalist; after all, he came in second place. Actually, in the study of all these athletes, the bronze medalist was the second happiest athlete.

Here's what the MIT professor discovered. The bronze medalist compared down. He thought, "Wow, I almost didn't get a medal at all. I'm so grateful for what I have. I have this bronze medal." But guess who the silver medalist compared himself to? He compared up. He compared himself to the guy who won the gold medal. He started to think, "Man, look what I could have had. If I only had that gold medal, then I would be happy." The bronze medalists were happier than the silver medalist because of their gratitude. How we compare ourselves, either comparing up or down, can make a big difference in our outlook. When you're facing hardships, "comparing down" to others who are facing greater hardships can help to reframe your circumstances.[35]

Interestingly, when it comes to our finances, do you think we compare ourselves with people who are doing better than us financially, or to people who are doing worse than us financially? Typically, we always compare up. We tend to compare ourselves to people who are doing much better than us. We start to think, "If I had what he had, then I would be happy, too." We're no different from the silver medalist, looking up at the gold medalist saying, "If I had what you have, I would be happy, too."

Let me give you an indisputable fact. If we ever hope to achieve a high level of contentment, we have to break this cycle. Instead of comparing up, we need to compare down. We need to see just how blessed we are compared to the rest of the world. The hard core facts should cause gratitude to bubble up quickly.

If you have food in your refrigerator, clothes on your back, and a roof over your head, you are wealthier than 75% of the people in

---

35   *When Less Is More* (Journal of Personality and Social Psychology, 1995, Vol. 69, Nov. 4. 603-610.)

the world. If you have any money in your wallet, or even some spare change in a dish somewhere, you are in the top 8% of the world's wealthiest people. Every one of us is incredibly blessed, but until we acknowledge that, we will never take a step in the direction of gratitude.

If you happen to fall into the trap of thinking you have it worse than everyone else, here's a few questions to pose to yourself...Do you live inside? Do you have a roof over your head? Do you sleep in a bed? Do you have covers on the bed? Do you have a TV? How many TV's do you have? Do you have cable? Do you own a set of golf clubs? Do you eat out at restaurants? Do you have plenty to drink? Do you drink coffee? Do you go to Starbucks? Gratitude reminds us to appreciate what we have compared to the rest of the world.

And we can practice gratitude regardless of where we are. Maybe you've heard of Brother Lawrence. He wrote one of the great Christian classics called, *Practicing The Presence of God*. Brother Lawrence was a French monk, and he lived in a monastery. His primary responsibility in the monastery was to work in the kitchen. Amazingly, Brother Lawrence believed he could do every one of his kitchen tasks with gratitude. He believed God was with him when he was in the kitchen as much as God was with him when he was in the sanctuary. Brother Lawrence developed a deep sensitivity to God's presence. He saw his kitchen as a holy altar. Whether he was preparing food, taking an order, or cleaning a pot, he practiced gratitude in the presence of God.

Jesus once told a story about a businessman who was never satisfied with what he had. This corporate executive was incredibly successful; he was a master at forecasting the market; other co-workers came to him because of his business brilliance. Because he had accumulated so many resources, he believed his only option was to keep building bigger and better barns to store all his resources in. But when everything was said and done, the successful businessman didn't exactly reach "hero status" in Jesus' story.

Jesus made a frank assessment about his life. Jesus called him a fool. It's one thing if someone else calls you a fool, but when Jesus calls you a fool, you know you're in real trouble. Why would Jesus use such a harsh word? He was foolish because he could never be satisfied with what he already had. He kept building bigger and better barns for himself. It never dawned on him that he had enough, and he could build someone else a barn. We can focus so much on what we want that we forget about what we already have.[36]

---

36   Luke 12:13-21

CHAPTER 12

Praise Without Filet Mignon

HABAKKUK. WHEN I FIRST HEARD the name, I thought it was probably a character in Star Wars. I was thinking maybe it was an obscure figure overshadowed by Luke Skywalker, Chewbacca, Yoda, Darth Vader, and R2-D2. As a new follower of Christ, I soon discovered that Habakkuk was actually a book in the Bible.

If we all blew the thick layer of dust off the book of Habakkuk at one time, the worst dust storm in the history of the universe would occur. Habakkuk is not a book we turn to very frequently. Habakkuk, the prophet, never made it into the "Who's Who" of Bible characters. He never had his name flashing in neon lights. He doesn't exactly get a lot of press coverage. But in the book of Habakkuk, we learn some invaluable lessons about gratitude.

Habakkuk was no stranger to bad news. God told this Hebrew prophet that a foreign nation was going to attack and destroy Judah. His home place would be turned into a mound of rubble. For Habakkuk, it was a time of testing and a proverbial dead end.

Ever found yourself there? That is, standing at a dead end? You're at a dead end when the physician says, "I've done all I can do." You're at a dead end when your spouse says, "I'm leaving, and I'm never coming back." You're at the very end of the road when your boss comes in and says, "We're downsizing and your job is being eliminated." A dead end is when a tragedy occurs, and it throws every one of your dreams out the window.

In America, we've had our fair share of national tragedies. One of the worst tragedies occurred when Timothy McVeigh bombed the government building in Oklahoma City. Timothy McVeigh placed a 5,000-pound bomb, hidden inside a Ryder truck, just outside the

Alfred P. Murrah Federal Building in Oklahoma City. The explosion caused enormous damage to the building and killed 168 people, 19 of whom were children.

After the tragedy, officials knew the building was so badly damaged it would have to be demolished. I happened to be in Oklahoma City the day after the government building was torn down. I was on my way across the country to help plant a church in Las Vegas, Nevada, and we stopped in Oklahoma City for the day. One afternoon, my friend and I decided to go see where the building once stood. We pulled into a parking lot adjacent to where the bombing occurred. Shortly after we pulled in a parking space, another car pulled in the lot and parked beside us. Very soon after the car parked, we glanced over only to notice a woman in the car with her face buried in the steering column. She was alone and weeping uncontrollably. On the back windshield of her car, she had written in bold letters, "We miss you."

As I drove away from that scene, I had a string of thoughts rambling through my mind. I thought about what it must have been like for this woman when she first learned about the tragedy. I can only imagine the shocking horror of hearing the news that her son, daughter, or husband had been killed in the bombing. No one can prepare for tragic news; it comes without any warning.

I imagine Habakkuk felt similar to this woman when he first heard the devastating news that destruction was on its way to his home town. Habakkuk heard the news that God was going to send the Babylonians to invade his homeland. Scripture records his natural response.

> *"I trembled inside when I heard all this; my lips quivered with fear. My legs gave way beneath me, and I shook in terror. I will wait quietly for the coming day when disaster will strike the people who invade us"* (**Habakkuk 3:16, NLT**).

When Habakkuk heard the bad news, he gave a clear indication of how he responded: "I trembled inside...my legs gave way...I shook in terror." As a pastor, on numerous occasions, I've been the first one to arrive after someone has received tragic news. It's one of the unpleasant parts of my job. It's difficult to watch as people tremble under the weight of distress. I've watched parents tremble over the loss of a baby; I've watched a mother tremble as her grown son took his last breath; I've watched a spouse collapse after finding out her marriage partner had betrayed her.

Habakkuk might have been a prophet, but he was also a man. When he received the bad news, he found himself trembling under the pressure. One of the first things we experience when we get bad news is fear. Every one of us has fears. We can try to camouflage our fears or cover them up; some people even try to medicate them. But if we're honest, we can't deny that we all have fears.

Franklin D. Roosevelt said, "We have nothing to fear but fear itself." That's a good piece of golden mouth oratory, but I'm not convinced it's anywhere close to the truth. Most of us will spend our entire lives managing various hidden fears. One of the best ways to deal with fear is to replace the fear in our lives with the truth. The more we fill our minds with God's truth, the less room we'll have for fear.

In the middle of his fear, Habakkuk's words are laced with hope. Habakkuk says, "I will wait quietly." Even though Habakkuk felt the full effect of the bad news, he could say, "I am going to wait calmly and quietly for God to show up in these circumstances." Why would Habakkuk demand quietness from the deepest part of his soul? Habakkuk knew the truth about God. He knew the God of Abraham, Isaac, and Jacob was in complete control of his circumstances.

The Practical Side Of God's Sovereignty

We want to believe we're in control, but we're not. Give it some serious thought, and you'll reach the conclusion that all the major things in your life are things you don't control. You couldn't control who your parents were; you couldn't control where and when you were born; you couldn't control your DNA makeup; you couldn't control the abilities and gifts you were given. You can't control when you're going to die. You can't control the ebb and flow of the economy; you can't control the weather, and you can't control the future. You can't even control what's going to happen to you in the next 30 minutes.

Though you can't control the circumstances of your life, here's the good news—You can control whether or not you trust God with your circumstances. You can control whether or not you approach life in faith. You can choose to believe that in spite of the bad news, God can bring good out of the bad. Anyone can bring good out of good, but only God can bring good out of bad. You can choose to believe that God is still on His throne. You can choose to believe God is still calling the shots in your life. The secret to crisis control is to believe that God is in control.

The truth you learn in the light should never be denied in the dark. Reaching the firm conviction that God is in control, helps you when life spins out of control. Settling that God is in control of the details of your life is better to do now. Later on, when bad news comes, this singular truth alone will serve as a safety net for you.

One afternoon, the disciples were in a boat with Jesus. With very little warning, a terrible storm hovered over the lake. The boat started to take on water, but the entire time these things were happening Jesus was snoozing. He must have been in "REM" sleep, the deepest level of a sleep pattern. Thunder, lightning, and crashing waves didn't seem to faze him, reminding me of when my wife is sleeping. Finally, the disciples ran to Jesus and said, "Jesus, you've got to get up and save us from this storm." You know what Jesus did? He calmly walked out to the deck of the boat and rebuked the winds and the sea. Suddenly, you could hear every bird chirping. Everything was calm.

What was Jesus trying to show the disciples? He was trying to teach them He was in absolute control over everything around them. Most of the miracles Jesus performed were not done to razzle and dazzle his audiences. He didn't do his miracles to draw big crowds. Most of the miracles Jesus did pointed to the indisputable fact that He was in control. He makes the rain fall; He makes the sun shine;

He makes the stars twinkle in the sky. And not a single detail of your life is beyond His control.[37]

Habakkuk didn't live in denial; he fully embraced that "facts are our friends." He stated the facts, and they were not pleasant. Amazingly, after his appraisal of the impending judgement, he moves quickly to gratitude and praise.

> *"Even though the fig trees have no blossoms, and there are no grapes on the vine; even though the olive crop fails, and the fields lie empty and barren; even though the flocks die in the fields, and the cattle barns are empty, yet I will rejoice in the Lord. I will be joyful in the God of my salvation"* **(Habakkuk 3:17-18, NLT).**

Habakkuk describes the desolate condition that would affect the land of Judah. Not only would the Babylonians take control over the people, but they would also desecrate the orchards and vineyards. The Babylonians would destroy all the cattle. God showed Habakkuk that when the Babylonians came to town, they were coming to take over. After they were done with Judah, the land would resemble the remnants of an earthquake. No figs on the trees, no grapes on the vine, and no cattle in the stall. Here's my translation, "No ribeye steaks. No filet mignon. Get ready to eat Ramen noddles until they're coming out of your ears."

From Habakkuk's viewpoint, everything had been taken away. There were no figs on the trees, no grapes on the vine, no cattle in the stall, but like Alvin and Morrie, Habakkuk didn't focus on what was lost; he focused on what was still left. One of the best ways to deal with adversity and depression is to live in gratitude. Gratitude has a way of helping us break through the fog of depression. It's very difficult to be grateful and depressed at the same time. When you start to feel depressed, sit down and make an appreciation list. Thank God for all the things you appreciate. Count your blessings. List them one by one. After this exercise, you'll find the dark clouds of despair and depression will start to break up.

---

37   Mark 4: 35-40.

When everything around him was crumbling, Habakkuk said, "The Lord God is my strength. " Come what may, Habakkuk believed God would give him the strength to endure his hardship. He compared the strength he would receive to the strength of a deer. If you know anything about deer, you know they have strong legs; their strong legs enable them to run with blazing speed.

I was driving home one day when I spotted a little fawn on the side of the road. I could tell this baby deer had been just been hit by a car. She was still alive, but she couldn't stand up on her feet. Given the situation, I knew if I didn't try to help her, the deer would die. I figured I would try to get her to my car, and then find the nearest vet. I tried to grab her front legs and pull her toward my car, but she started kicking her legs so fast I couldn't keep my hands on her legs. I tried the back legs, but she did the same thing. Her strength caught me by surprise. I finally got her inside my car, and then drove her to a vet. Of course, by then she had kicked me so many times I looked like I had been in a boxing match with the heavy weight champion of the world. I had black and blue bruises on me for weeks. That's when I first learned about the strength of a deer. Comparatively speaking, when we are weak, God says He offers us that same kind of strength. It's a supernatural strength that often catches us by surprise.

When The Odds Are Against Us

I've picked up on a pattern I see throughout the Bible. Sometimes God waits to display His strength until something is humanly impossible. God loves to show up when the odds are impossible. Think Gideon. Gideon had an army of 32,000 men. His army was up against the Midianites, and God tells Gideon he has far too many men to win the battle. I'm sure Gideon thought, "Say what…did you mean far too few, because I thought I heard you say far too many?" God said, "You heard me correctly; you have far too many men for me to deliver you." Most generals would rather have too many soldiers than not enough. God instructed Gideon to thin the ranks. He tells Gideon to give an honorable discharge to all his soldiers who are afraid. Talk about thinning the ranks! Within 30 minutes, he lost about half of his army. Then, the Lord said, "Gideon, you still have too many men.

Let all the soldiers go get a drink of water and the soldiers who bend down and drink their water like a dog, I want you to release all those soldiers." When the dog lapping exercise was over, Gideon was only left with 300 soldiers.

At this point, the odds had to be a billion to one, yet Gideon's army won the battle. Why did God size the army down? It was for one profound reason. If Gideon fought with 32,000 soldiers and won, guess who would get the credit? You guessed it! Gideon and the soldiers. However, when an army of just 300 men defeats a massive army, guess who gets the credit? God gets the credit. God alone gets the glory. Sometimes God allows the odds to be stacked against us so that He can get all the glory. When the odds are stacked against you, you're more likely to depend on God than at any other time.[38]

In Genesis, we have the mysterious account of Jacob wrestling with God. And Jacob says, "I will not let go until you bless me." He gets the blessing, but He also gets a burden. God touches His hip, and for the rest of his life, Jacob walks with a limp. You may walk with a limp too. Maybe it's not a literal physical disability, but there could be a hard side to your life. I'm convinced everyone has a hard side to life. For one person, it's a health challenge. For someone else, it's a career which has never taken off, or a marriage that seems to always be on the brink of disaster. The hard side of life keeps reminding you how much you need God.

One of the most misquoted ideas in the Bible is that God will not give you more than you can handle. That's not the promise at all. The promise is that God will not give you more than He can handle. I'm convinced God allows plenty of circumstances in life far greater than what we can handle. This is by design. The hard side of life is what drives us to God. These circumstances which are way bigger than us keep us dependent on God.

Just ask Jehoshaphat. He is one of the consummate underdogs of the Old Testament. Jehoshaphat is surrounded by 3 armies. He knows he is completely overpowered. The odds are stacked against

---

38   2 Judges 7.

him. He knows he doesn't have the man power to win the battle. That's when God offers this consummate underdog a word of encouragement, "The battle is not yours; the battle is mine." Ever felt like Jehoshaphat? Ever felt like you were surrounded by 3 armies? The odds are stacked against you. When you feel overwhelmed, you can easily try to fight your battles in your own strength. Out of sheer will-power, it's not uncommon for us to bow our backs and say, "I'll save this marriage... turn my kids around... conquer this addiction... solve my financial difficulties." God says, "Time out! This is not your battle. It's Mine."[39]

Remember when the odds were against Abraham? He was 99 years old and God comes to him and says, "Abraham, you're going to have a son." You know what he did? Abraham did what you would have done if God told you that you were going to have a child when you were 99. He started to laugh. He knew that it would be humanly impossible for him to have a child when he was 99. When Sarah, Abraham's wife, heard the news, she responded the same way. She started to giggle and laugh. But then God spoke another word to Abraham; He said, "Is there anything too hard for the Lord?"

That is a great verse for us to memorize. This is one Scripture that we desperately need in our memory banks. "Is anything too hard for the Lord?" When the odds are against us and we're tempted to doubt what God can do, we should challenge our thinking. Ask, Is anything too hard for the Lord? You know the answer. No! Nothing is too hard for the Lord. Abraham and Sarah had the promised child because the odds are never against God. Jeremiah expressed his unwavering faith when he said, "Ah, Lord God! Behold, you have made the heavens and the earth by your great power. There is nothing too hard for you" (Jeremiah 32:17). God is a miracle working God. A miracle is only a miracle to us; it's not a miracle to God. God, by definition, is supernatural. God specializes in miracles.

Last winter, we couldn't have our worship services at church one Sunday because of a winter storm. Since we were snowed in on Sunday, I decided we could have our own little worship service at

39   2 Chronicles 20

home. We all gathered in the living room and sat on the sofa. Caryn played the keyboard, and we sang songs as she played. We prayed together. We had a puppet show, and to top it off, Lawson did a jig for us. He danced to one of his favorite songs. We had a lot of variety in our service.

At the end of our service, I read a story out of a children's Bible. I read the amazing story about Jesus feeding the multitudes with only 5 loaves of bread and two fish. Jesus fed over 5000 people, and that's just counting the men. If you counted everybody, the ladies and the kids, it was probably up around 20,000 people. What do you think are the mathematical odds of feeding 20,000 people with 5 loaves of bread and 2 fish? It's not too good. Yet Jesus, the Son of God, wasn't ever limited by mathematical odds and He still isn't. Jesus would take this little boy's lunch box, and He would miraculously feed all these people. Jesus said, "According to your faith, be it unto you." Sometimes God doesn't do the impossible until we believe He can do the impossible.[40]

When Your Dreams Are Shattered

Ever had a dream that didn't turn out the way you had hoped? When I was a young boy, my dream was to be a professional baseball player. I played a lot of baseball growing up, and as I grew older, it looked like my dream could possibly come true. When I reached my junior year in high school, I started getting letters from Division I Colleges about possibly playing baseball for them. I was so excited going into my senior year. This is where the story goes south. During my senior year, to put it in no uncertain terms, I choked! I choked big time. It seemed like I couldn't buy a hit. About half-way through the season, the college coaches and scouts turned ice cold. They stopped coming to my games. That was the year my dream when up in smoke.

We can look back on many of our childhood dreams and smile, but other unrealized dreams become a source of great pain. More than one person has been catapulted into a mid life crisis because of a shattered dream. Most of us wake up at some

40   Matthew 14:13-21

point in life to discover that many of our dreams are not going to occur. We get a phone call, a letter, or a diagnosis and we watch our dreams turn to a pile of rubble. What do you do when your dream dies?

David, the King of Israel, knows something about dying dreams. He was probably sitting in front of his fireplace when he started to develop his dream. David's dream was born out of what seemed to him as an obvious injustice. David was living in a beautiful house, when the ark of God was residing in a tent. The ark of God in Old Testament represented the presence of God. David said to himself, "It's not right that I should live in this extravagant house, yet the ark of God is housed in a little tent." So David develops this noble dream of building a house for God. His dream was to build a temple to honor God. Very soon David shared his dream with his personal confidant, Nathan. Nathan encouraged him to pursue the dream with total abandonment.

God, however, didn't buy into the idea. At least, not the way David envisioned the dream happening. God said, "David, there's nothing wrong with your dream, but it's not going to happen in your lifetime." God told David He was going to raise up his son, Solomon, to build the temple. At this very moment, David's dream went up in a ball of flames. Amazingly, after learning his dream had just gone up in smoke, David responds with unpredictable gratitude.

"Then King David went in and sat before the Lord and prayed, Who am I, O Sovereign Lord, and what is my family, that you have brought me this far? And now, Sovereign Lord, in addition to everything else, you speak of giving me a lasting dynasty. Do you deal with everyone this way, O Sovereign Lord? What more can I say? You know what I am really like, Sovereign Lord. For the sake of your promise and according to your will, you have done all these great things and have shown them to me" (2 Sam 7:18-21).

After David hears his dream is not going to happen, David goes and sits before God. In gratitude he says, "God, You have brought me so far. You have done great things in my life. You've taken me from leading a flock of sheep to being the King of the nation." Dream or no dream, David knows he is a blessed man. In the middle of his disappointment, David chooses the way of gratitude.

When his dream went belly up, David didn't put his fist in the face of God. He didn't turn his back on God. Nor did He become bitter. David didn't run away from God; He ran to God. When your dream dies, take the same path as David. Let your disappointment drive you to God.

How do you respond when you realize one of your dreams is not going to come true? Some people resort to the bottle; others start popping pills. Some people get angry. And over time, their unresolved anger turns into bitterness.

I remember talking with a lady who was going through a divorce. In her own words, she described how her dream of a lifelong marriage had been shattered. Though she meant it when she said, "I do," she couldn't live out the same commitment for her husband. Her husband wrecked her dream. Essentially, she told me since he had wrecked her dreams, she was going to spend the rest of her life wrecking his dreams. Then, I decided to pose a classic AA question to her, "How's that working for you?" My question hung in the air like a giant disco ball. She couldn't get around it. Seconds later, she broke into tears.

Bitterness never works for me, or for you, or for anyone. It always works against you. Bitterness is like poison in your soul. It will contaminate your whole life. David's disappointment didn't drive him to become bitter; His disappointment drove him to God. David didn't stop believing in God simply because his dream died. In gratitude, he looks back and expresses thanks for all God has done for him.

When life is tough, it's good to go back and remember how God has blessed us. It's like looking in the rearview mirror. Most of the time, we drive looking forward, but every once and a while it's good to glance in the rearview mirror so we can see what's behind us. In the fog of his shattered dream, David looks in the rearview mirror of his past. He says, "God, I know my dream is not going to come true, but when I look back and see all you've already done for me, I'm so grateful."

Dream or no dream, David chooses to reflect on the great things God has done for him. His response is one to remember, "Who am I?" If there is ever a time to express gratitude, it's when there are no figs on the tree, no fruit in the orchards, and no cattle in the stall. When our dreams lie in ruins, it's the perfect time to say, "God, who am I?" "Who am I that I have a roof over my head?" "Who am I that I'm warm in the wintertime?" "God, who am I that that I should have this job?" "Who am I that I have eyes to see?" "Who am I to have legs to walk?" "God, who am I that I should have plenty of food in my cabinets." Who am I? When we look back, God's goodness is glaringly obvious. In fact, if God chose never do another kind thing for me, He has already done enough. Fig or no fig, fruit or no fruit, cattle or no cattle, God has been good to me.

Decision 5: Where Will I Get My Worth From Today?

CHAPTER 13

Warped Mirror, Warped Self

I ALWAYS LOOK FORWARD TO the state fair. I enjoy pigging out on all the high fat, high cholesterol foods that are sure to clog every artery in the body. It's a good thing I only go once a year. While I was walking around at the fair this year and looking at some unique things, I came across a warped mirror. If you've never seen one, a warped mirror basically distorts what you look like. It makes you look bigger, skinner, and taller all at one time; it does crazy things with your forehead, nose, lips, and cheeks. When you look into a distorted mirror, you get a distorted image of yourself. When you first glance into a distorted mirror, it's hilarious. But let me mention something not so hilarious. It's not funny when someone looks into a distorted mirror of themselves everyday. Yet, untold numbers of people live each day with a distorted view of themselves. It usually ends up holding them hostage.

Breaking free from this stronghold seems virtually impossible. When you were growing up, you developed your view of yourself in large part from the adults around you. They were your mirrors. What they said to you about you is one of the first ways you started to develop your self image. Maybe you were told you were dumb and stupid. You could have been told you would never accomplish anything with your life. All of that data was stored in your mind. Your distorted image of yourself developed because of what others said to you about you.

You can also develop a distorted image by what you tell yourself about yourself. This is what psychologists call limiting beliefs. This is when you limit yourself by what you believe about yourself. This is when you say or think things like, "I'll never accomplish anything with my life"; "I'm unwanted and unloved"; "No one in my family could ever achieve something great." These are limiting beliefs. You are limiting yourself by your own beliefs. If you see yourself as a failure, it usually gets reinforced by your decisions. Surprisingly, it's very easy to maintain a distorted view of yourself. Something may not be true, but you can become so used to it that it starts to feel like it fits.

To a large degree, the way you see yourself is determined by what you think the most important person in your life thinks about you. This is why it's so critical to make God the most important person in your life. The truest thing about you is what God says about you. Building your identity and self image around God is one of the most important decisions of each day. If you can begin to see yourself the way God sees you, your self image will no longer be warped.

Some people make statements, and their statements are immortalized. In 399 A.D., Augustine made such a statement. Augustine said, "People travel to wonder at the height of mountains, at the huge waves of the sea, at the long courses of rivers, they wonder at the vast compass of the ocean, at the circular motion of the stars, and yet they pass by themselves without ever wondering" (Saint Augustine, in 399 A.D).[41]

What Augustine said is true. People go to great lengths to see the ocean, and they travel far and wide to see snow-capped mountains; they also spend massive amounts of money to travel so they can see the Grand Canyon and Niagara Falls. They stand in complete awe of God's creation, but they never stop to appreciate God's crowning achievement in creation. God's crowning achievement in creation is you. Have you ever been told you are a piece of work? You really are—you are God's work. You are a special creation of God.

I want to introduce several life changing truths about the way God sees you. If you can grasp and internalize these truths, this could be one of the most important days in your life. This new data should replace the old data. The best way to reverse a curse is by replacing wrong thoughts with correct thoughts. Regardless of the curses spoken over your life, the truth can set you free. Because of God's grace, you no longer have to have a distorted image of yourself. What God says about you is what is true. In Romans 5, one of the Magna Carta passages of the Bible, God tells us the truth about ourselves.

> *"Therefore, having been justified by faith, we have peace with God through our Lord Jesus Christ, through whom also we have access by faith into this grace in which we stand, and rejoice in hope of the glory of God…Now hope does not disappoint, because the love of God has been poured out in our hearts by the Holy Spirit who was given to us… Much more then, having now been justified by His blood, we shall be saved from wrath through Him"* (**NKJV, Romans 5:1-2; 5, 9**).

God Says You Are Accepted

One of the most important concepts in the New Testament is justification by faith. We derive the concept from the idea of being "justified." The term is actually a legal term. In the general sense, it means to be declared right, and in the particular sense, it means to be declared right before God. The moment you place your faith in Christ, God declares you're right in His sight. He issues a once and for all verdict of "not guilty." The Judge of the Universe declares you fully righteous and fully acceptable. This acceptable position is now your standing before God. It's important to notice how we are declared right before God— by faith. Scripture doesn't say it's by good deeds, lofty accomplishments, advanced degrees, or social status. We are declared right before God the moment we place our faith in Jesus Christ.

When I was sixteen, some of my friends invited me to go dove hunting. There was just one problem. I didn't have a gun. I went home and gave my best sales pitch to my mom, and several hours later, we were in a pawn shop looking at guns. After a few minutes, I spotted a 20 gauge shotgun that seemed to fit me perfectly. My friends told me I also needed to buy a hunting license. After we left the pawn shop with my new gun, we went to Wal-Mart so I could buy my hunting license.

I got up early on Saturday morning, and went to meet my friends in the field. We were having a great time until late in the afternoon when I spotted a man dressed in a uniform. Later on, I found out he was called a game warden. It was all new to me. He was going from hunter to hunter to make sure everyone had a license. As he was walking around, I noticed the game warden was also looking at each gun.

When he came up to me, I gladly showed him my hunting license. Then, he asked to see my gun. He started shoving shotgun shells in my gun. After about six or seven shells in my gun, the game warden turned to me and said, "Son, you don't have a plug in this gun." A plug? The only type of plug I knew about was the kind that went into the wall. My friends told me about the hunting license, but no one told me about a plug. The warden explained that a plug only allows you to have three shells in your gun. It's illegal to have more than 3 shells in your gun at the same time. He said, "Son, I'm going to have to write you a ticket." I said, "How much is this going to cost me?" He said, "I don't know. You'll have to wait and see what the judge says." I gulped, "The Judge?" He said, "Yes, this is a serious violation, and you're going to have to go to court." I went home and told my parents what happened. They knew this was the first time I had ever been hunting. My father assured me he would talk to his attorney first thing on Monday, and my dad's attorney agreed to be at the courthouse on the day of my court date.

On the day of my court date, I drove nervously to the courthouse. I found my way through the narrow hallways and entered the courtroom. After several hours of waiting, the clerk called my name. I walked up and stood before the judge, and he read my offense. Then, my father's attorney came forward. He said, "Your honor, this was Clay's first time hunting. He had no idea what a plug was. He has no criminal record; he's a good boy; he's the president of his class at school. We're asking you to forgive this first-time offense."

Suddenly, I glanced over in the courtroom and saw a familiar face. It was the game warden who issued my ticket. He stepped up to the microphone and said, "Your honor, this young man has broken the law. This is a serious violation. A dove is a migratory bird, and I believe this young man needs to be punished for breaking the law." The judge listened to both sides and then issued his verdict. Guilty! He slapped me with a $90.00 fine and made me do 24 hours of community service. On this day, in the courtroom, I experienced just the opposite of justification. I wasn't declared innocent. I was declared guilty, and I had to pay for my violation.

A Different Kind of Courtroom

Thankfully, in the courtroom of God, justification plays out very differently. Even though we are guilty before God, God issues us a once and for all "Not Guilty" verdict. We are declared righteous before God because of our faith in Jesus Christ. This is the radical nature of grace. Grace is when God gives you what you don't deserve.

Forgiveness and salvation are free. The metaphor Scripture uses to describe salvation is a gift. You can't earn or work for a gift. Neither can you buy a gift. It's something freely given to you by someone who loves you.

If you randomly ask one hundred people, "In your opinion, what does it take for a person to go to heaven?" you will get a lot of different answers. The vast majority of answers though could be summarized this way…"How do we get to heaven? Well, you have to be a good person, a moral person, and an upstanding citizen. You have to live by the Ten Commandments and the laws of the land." Essentially, they're suggesting you have to do more good things in life than you do bad things. If your good pile is higher than your bad pile, God's going to say, "Good job, come on in to heaven."

However, the Bible has a different message. It doesn't teach that we are justified by our deeds, or good works. Scripture teaches we are justified and declared right before God by faith in Christ. We will not be able to work our way to heaven. If we could work our way to heaven, when we arrived, we would all brag about what we did to get there. It would be one big braggafest. We would each try to out do the next person with our stories about what great people we were while we were on earth. If salvation is truly a gift given to us by God, then bragging and boasting about it is illogical. We didn't do anything to earn it. It is given to us as a free gift. What do we do with a gift? We can accept it. We can be grateful for it. We can celebrate it, but the one thing we'll never be able to do is brag that we earned it.

There are only 2 spiritual paths you can take in life. One is to spend the rest of your life trying to earn God's acceptance by your own human effort. The other is to enjoy God's acceptance by embracing His grace. How do you embrace grace? By faith. You turn to God in faith and say, "God, I believe there's nothing I can do to earn your acceptance. I believe there's only one way to be forgiven of my sin and that's through your son, Jesus Christ. Right now, I receive your grace." The moment you turn to Christ in faith is the very moment you are justified. God declares you righteous and you are fully accepted by God.

This is good news since most of us spend our entire lives trying to be accepted. We want to be accepted by our parents, peers, co-workers, and even by total strangers. Though we're often unaware of it, behind many of the decisions we make is the desire to be accepted. The all-consuming desire to be accepted can influence the way we dress, the kind of car we buy, where we live, and what kind of career we pursue.

People do crazy things to be accepted by other people. Remember when you were a kid and one of your friends dared you to do something crazy? I can't count the number of stupid, dangerous, idiotic things I did when I was younger. I said yes to a lot of "dares" because I wanted to be accepted by my friends. This childhood phenomena can spill over into adulthood. Our self-worth can be attached at the hip to how much approval we get from our friends. If we have their acceptance and approval, we feel good about ourselves. However, the moment the opinion polls drop, we start to feel deflated and depressed.

This often leads to perfectionism. When we find our worth in human approval, we think, "If I can just be perfect, then everyone will accept me." Here are the brutal facts. Even if you could be perfect (which is not an option), everyone wouldn't accept you. The reason I know this is because Jesus Christ was perfect, and everyone didn't accept Him. Jesus was the most loving, compassionate, graceful, truthful person ever to walk planet earth, yet plenty of people rejected Him.

Perhaps you grew up in a home and you could never please your parents. No matter what you did, it was never good enough. In their eyes, you never made the cut. You never measured up. You never hit a homerun. It was an endless cycle of continual strikeouts. In the back of your mind, you can hear a voice, "You're never going to amount to anything." "You're a loser." "You're an accident." As you entered into adulthood, your singular focus has been to prove your parents wrong. Since you didn't get their acceptance as a child, you're determined to earn it as an adult. Your parents could live in another state. They could be dead, but your insatiable desire in life is to silence their condemning voice.

No one deserves to have these lingering messages embedded in their minds. Yet, in all likelihood, if you didn't get your parents' acceptance as a child, you will probably never get it. Their acceptance is not something you can control. It's probably a deep source of pain for you, but their lack of approval doesn't have to control the rest of your life. The good news is that you have a Father in heaven who accepts you. Because of His grace, God accepts you just as you are. Psalm 27:10 says, *"Even if my mother and father forsake me, the Lord will receive me."*

God says You are Valued

Paul reminds us that "…we have access by faith into this grace in which we stand" (Rom. 5:2). The moment we place our faith in Christ, we have access to God. In the Old Testament, access to God was tied directly to one's status in society. For example, when a Gentile (that's anyone who is not a Jew) entered the temple, they were restricted from going beyond a certain point in the temple. There was actually a sign in the temple warning the Gentiles, "If you go beyond this point, the penalty will be death." Gentiles were considered less valuable than Jews.

Jewish women could go a little further than the Gentiles could go, but they couldn't go all the way into the temple. Jewish women were restricted because they were considered less valuable than the

Jewish men. Even Jewish men couldn't go all the way into the Holy of Holies, as this was something strictly reserved for the High Priest. There was a religious hierarchy which reminded everyone who was considered valuable and who was less valuable. However, when Christ came to take away our sin, this system changed. When Jesus died on the cross, the veil in the temple was torn in two, symbolizing that everyone who comes to Christ has full access to God. Because of His grace, we each have equal worth before God.

A healthy self image should begin with God, not man. We were made by God and for God. Until we understand this truth, we will never have a healthy self image.

William Ernest Henly was a 19th century British scholar. He was a well-known humanist. Henly wrote a famous poem called, "In Victus." It's often read at high school and college graduations. With just a cursory reading of a few lines, you can spot that the poem is laced with humanism.

> *Out of the night that covers me, Black as the Pit from pole to pole, I thank whatever gods may be For my unconquerable soul. In the fell clutch of circumstance I have not winced nor cried aloud. Under the bludgeonings of chance My head is bloody, but unbowed. Beyond this place of wrath and tears Looms but the Horror of the shade, And yet the menace of the years Finds and shall find me unafraid. It matters not how strait the gate, How charged with punishments the scroll I am the master of my fate: I am the captain of my soul.*[42]

The poem may sound good at a high school and college graduations, but it's a poor philosophy to live by. Its humanism personified, and it suggests that, "I am the captain of my soul." Taken to its logical conclusion, humanism says I'm the center of the universe. It typically leads to narcissism, demanding that everyone bow down at the altar of my personal preferences. Everyone is looking for significance and

---

value, but often they begin at the wrong starting point—themselves. To truly find purpose and significance in life, we have to begin with God.

Scripture teaches that each one of us is made in the image of God.[43] There's so much truth contained in this one statement. It would take volumes to treat the expansive nature of this one theological truth. In the deepest sense, the statement means you have intrinsic worth. Because God made you in His image, you are valuable to Him.

God didn't have to bring you into this world, but He did. Regardless of the circumstances surrounding your conception, you are not a mistake. Above the human circumstances which led to your conception was a sovereign God who chose to bring you into this world. There might be accidental parents, but there are no accidental children. God could have prevented you from being conceived, but He didn't. If God chose to create you, it means you are valuable and significant. Psalm 139 says, "You have been wonderfully and fearfully made." God put you together detail by detail. This includes every detail of your intellect, personality, and body. You have been custom built.

Tailor Made by God

When I was leading a church outside of Charlotte, North Carolina, one of the members scheduled an appointment to see me. I was unsure exactly what he wanted to talk about. Shortly after he walked into my office, he asked me somewhat of a bizarre question. "Clay, have you ever had a tailor made shirt?" Caught off guard, I said, "No, I've never had a tailor made shirt." He said, "Would you like to have one? I would like to buy one for you." Since he was buying, I said, "I would love to have one… I've always wanted one."

About a week later, a sales representative came to my office and worked me over with a tape measure. He measured my neck, arms, and my torso. He even measured my left wrist where I would normally be wearing a watch. He wanted to make sure the sleeve

43   Genesis 1:26-27; Gen 2:7

would fit perfectly over my watch. Everything about the shirt was going to be tailor made. Several weeks later, the shirt arrived. It's my only tailor made shirt, and I've been wearing it for over ten years. The reason it's so comfortable is because it was built just for me.

Detail by detail, this is exactly the way God built you. You're not a product of random choice. God put you together piece by piece. And as one of my friends says, "God doesn't make junk."

How much are you worth? I'm not referring to your net worth. I'm referring to your self-worth. Your net worth has nothing to do with your self-worth. In life, we normally judge value and worth by what someone is willing to pay for it. For example, how much is your house worth? It's only worth what someone is willing to pay for it. You may have paid $250,000 for your house, but what if someone is only willing to pay $200,000 for your house? Then, that's the worth of the house. The value is determined by what someone is willing to pay for it.

That leads me to an important question. What was God willing to pay for you? God paid the ultimate price for you. Your salvation cost Him His very own son. Romans 5:8 says, "God demonstrated His love for us in that while we were sinners, Christ died for us." If you want to know how valuable you are, take a long hard look at the cross. Jesus stretched His arms out on the cross and said, "This is how valuable you are to me." Jesus died for you because you matter to Him. If you were the only person on earth who needed to be forgiven, Christ would have still come to pay the price for your salvation.

God says You are Loved

The moment you receive God's grace, here's the truth about you, the love of God has been poured out in our hearts(Romans 5:5). Through the Holy Spirit, God has poured His love into your heart. God's love is very different from human love. God's love is consistent, whereas human love tends to be inconsistent. God's love is predictable, whereas human love can be very unpredictable. God has never been caught saying, "I like you today, but I want you to get lost tomorrow." God has never gotten up on the wrong side of the bed. He's never had a mood swing. God's love is consistent because His love is unconditional. God's love isn't based on your performance.

As human beings, we try to give unconditional love, but we fail miserably. We end up giving conditional love. Conditional love says I love you "if." I love you if you treat me well...I love you if you don't hurt my feelings... I love you if you are a Republican...if you are a Democrat...if you are conservative...if you are liberal... if you are from my social class. We use qualifiers and filters when we're determining to give or withhold our love.

God doesn't use qualifiers. He doesn't use filters. God doesn't use the "if" word. "If" never enters His mind. God says, "I love you period!" No conditions. No strings attached. No caveats. You never have to wonder if God will love you today. You never have to wonder if God will love you tomorrow. You never have to ask, "Will God love me even if it's been a while since I read my Bible?...even if I haven't prayed for weeks?...even if I have been disobedient to God?" God loves you period! His love isn't based on your performance. Grace means there's nothing you can do to make God love you more, and there is nothing you can do to make Him love you less.

God says You are Forgiven

When Jesus died on the cross, which of your sins did He die for? Christ died for all of your sins. This includes the sins you have already committed and also the ones you don't even know you're going to commit next week, next month, or next year.

Some Christians assume every time something goes wrong in their lives that God is paying them back for their sin. They presume God is trying to get even for the foolish, stupid things they did the previous week. But God doesn't direct His punishment toward you because all your punishment was paid for on the cross. Because Jesus paid your punishment, you don't have to pay for it yourself. According to Paul, grace covers your sin. Romans 5:9 says, " we shall be saved from wrath through Him." Because of God's grace, you have been saved from His wrath. His judgment is not directed at you because it was directed at Christ when He was on the cross. God is not mad at you. God has forgiven you.

In his book called, *Rising Above the Crowd*, Brian Harbour tells the amazing story about little Ben Hooper. Ben Hooper was born in the hills of east Tennessee. He was born into a very dysfunctional family. Little Ben didn't even know who his father was, and years ago, not knowing your father created a major social stigmatism. Ben was repeatedly ostracized by his classmates. During recess, the other kids went outside and played on the playground, but not little Ben. He usually sat at his desk and studied because the other kids didn't want to play with him. At lunchtime, Ben would take his lunch and eat it in the corner of the room, all by himself. He felt like no one wanted to sit with him.

When Ben was 12 years old, a new pastor came to town. He pastored a church just down the road from where little Ben lived. Ben started to hear about this new preacher. He heard that the new pastor was a kind and gentle man. He had heard that whenever someone was around this pastor, he made them feel like they were the most important person in the world.

Even though Ben had never been to church a day in his life, one Sunday, he decided to go. Little Ben arrived at church late, and he left early before anybody could speak to him. But while he was at church, he experienced something for the first time in his whole life—hope. The next Sunday, Ben went to church again. Like before, he got to church late, and then he left early. This went on for 5 or 6 weeks, but on the 7th week, the pastor's message was powerful, and it was so intriguing to Ben that he lost all track of time. Before Ben knew it, the service was over and he stood up and expected to run out like he had done the other Sundays. Before he could get out, Ben felt a hand on his shoulder. He turned around, and it was this new pastor.

The pastor asked Ben a question that was on the minds of everyone who had seen him at church. He said, "Hey son, whose boy are you?" Ben grew deathly quiet. The pastor picked up on the fact that little Ben didn't answer the question. He smiled and said, "Oh, I should have known. The family resemblance is incredible. I know who you are. Why you are a child of God." Many years later, Ben Hooper said that was the day He was elected the governor of the state of Tennessee.[44] Little Ben Hooper went from being a child of an unknown father to being a child of the King. When Ben started to see himself the way God saw him, everything in his life started to change. Though you may never be elected the governor of your home state, I promise you, if you will see yourself as God sees you, you will no longer have a distorted view of yourself. Every day will change for the better. When you interpret your entire life within the framework of God's grace, everyday takes on a whole new meaning.

44   Brian Harbour, *Rising Above the Crowd* (Baptist Sunday School Board, 1988).

CHAPTER 14

Who Is In Your Jury Box?

CHILD ABUSE IS HEART WRENCHING, especially when you have to view pictures of it. I still remember the horrifying pictures I saw of a little girl who had been abused by her father. I was one of the jurors, sitting in the deliberation room, scanning the pictures with tears in my eyes. During the attack which took place in their home, the father took an extension cord and beat his daughter unmercifully with it. After the attack, the father was arrested and later brought to trial. During the investigation, the police had taken pictures of this young girl's abused body. As a juror, I remember cringing when I saw the whelps, lacerations, and bruises all over her body. At one point, during the attack, the father took the extension cord and wrapped it around his daughter's neck and started choking her with it. As I viewed the pictures of her neck, I could see the burns and bruises around her neck.

The trial lasted for two days. After we heard the evidence, the judge then gave us a series of instructions, and we went to deliberate. We had a choice of 3 verdicts. We could find the father guilty of felony child abuse, misdemeanor child abuse, or we could find him not guilty. When we went into the jury room, it was obvious that every juror believed the father was guilty. At first, most everyone was ready to settle on a felony child abuse conviction. As we continued our discussions, some of the jurors expressed doubts about the felony charge.

As the judge described it, felony child abuse had to inflict serious injury, suffering, and pain on the child. The misdemeanor charge, according to the law, was defined as causing harm but not serious harm. As the jury, we were responsible for deciding what should be deemed as "serious injury." Since the law didn't specify what "serious injury" involved, we had to settle on how we were going to define this subjective definition.

A few of the jurors commented that they didn't believe the young girl suffered serious pain and injury. One lady said, "She didn't spend the night in the hospital; she didn't have any broken bones. Therefore, she didn't suffer serious injuries." My definition of serious, however, was very different from her definition. As I stared at the pictures, it certainly looked serious to me, not to mention that serious suffering wasn't just relegated to the physical pain she endured. I reminded the other jurors about the emotional pain inflicted on this young girl. It was emotional trauma. She was attacked around her throat by her own father. In the trial, she testified that she could barely breathe while her father was choking her with the extension cord.

Some of the jurors, though, were not buying my "wider version" of serious injury. At one point in our deliberations, I held up the pictures of the girl's battered body and asked, "If this happened to your son or your daughter, would you classify it as being serious?" Most of the jury members said, "Yes, if that happened to my son or daughter, I would consider it serious." Unfortunately, when it happened to be someone else's daughter, it was no longer serious. Though I tried to persuade the others, I could tell some of the jurors were not going to go for the felony child abuse charge.

I knew I didn't want to be the cause of a hung jury. Even though I knew a misdemeanor would bring a lighter sentence than a felony, my hands were somewhat tied. I decided to concede with the other members of the jury and issue a misdemeanor conviction.

We reassembled in the courtroom, the judge read our verdict, and then we waited for the judge to issue the sentencing. Before the judge issued the sentence, he asked to see the prior criminal record of the father who had abused his daughter. He had eight prior convictions, three of which were assault charges against women. Once the whole courtroom saga was over, several members of the jury came up to me and expressed their regrets about our misdemeanor charge. One juror said, "Clay, knowing what we know now, with his long term track record of abuse, I wish I would have agreed to go along with the felony charge."

I walked out of the courtroom tremendously disheartened. Not only was I frustrated over the misdemeanor charge, I couldn't get this little girl off my mind. I stayed awake the entire night after the verdict. I thought about what life must be like for this little girl. In a way, I felt I had failed her myself. If only I would have been more successful at persuading the other jurors, perhaps I could have bought her a few extra years of peace, without the threat of another attack. Then again, I was just one juror. There were 11 other opinions that were considered just as valid as my own.

Now I understand why selecting a jury can take weeks in high profile cases. In fact, consultants make great financial gains by helping attorneys select their juries appropriately. Jury consultants are often retained to help choose the jurors who they believe will tip the scales in their favor. When you're on trial, who you have in the jury box makes a big difference. What the people think about you in the jury box is of utmost importance.

When it comes to finding your worth and building your own identity, it's like having your own jury box. Your jury box is not in the corner of a courtroom; it's in the corner of your mind. Think of it like a mental jury box. We place certain people in the jury box, and if we gain get their approval, we feel good about ourselves. If we don't achieve a favorable opinion in their eyes, we feel unaccepted and less valuable.

The people we place in the jury box are typically the people whose approval we desperately want. Who's in the jury box? Probably your parents. I've never met a child who didn't want the acceptance and approval of mom and dad. Somewhere along the way, you probably placed some of your school teachers in your jury box. This is probably why you've never forgotten the 2nd grade teacher who told you that you were the brightest math student in her class. You could tell she believed in you, and you started to believe in yourself, too. Most of us place our bosses in the jury box. The trajectory of our income usually depends on our boss's view of us. Perhaps you have other moms in your neighborhood in your jury box. It's important to you that they think you're an excellent mom.

Over time, the jury box can get overcrowded. We put way too many people in the jury box. Over time, we start to allow our mental jury box to control the verdict we give ourselves. If we can get everyone to give us their approval, we feel good about ourselves. At the same, if people in the jury box start to reject us or develop an unfavorable opinion about us, we feel devastated. Our worth and value is often attached to what kind of verdict we're getting from the people in our jury box.

We don't need a host of people in our mental jury box. We only need one person in the jury box— God and God alone. In the end, God's opinion of us is the only one that truly matters. In 1 Corinthians 4, it's clear that the apostle Paul had resolved who was going to be in his mental jury box.

> *"But with me it is a very small thing that I should be judged by you or by any human court. In fact, I do not even judge myself. For I am not aware of anything against myself, but I am not thereby acquitted. It is the Lord who judges me. Therefore do not pronounce judgment before the time, before the Lord comes, who will bring to light the things now hidden in darkness and will disclose the purposes of the heart. Then each one will receive his commendation from God." (ESV, 1 Corin. 4:3-5)*

This is a mental courtroom scene. For Paul, God and God alone was the judge of his earthly life. What the Corinthians thought about him was secondary. He wasn't trying to impress them; His goal was to please God. Paul wasn't trying to win their approval; He was more concerned about living for God's approval.

Unfortunately, plenty of people base all their decisions on one underlining question: what will other people think? I see this especially in young people. When they're making a key decision about something, the first thing that often comes to mind is, "What will everyone around me think about my decision?" You could be at a party, and suddenly everyone begins to take a few puffs from a joint. You're invited to take a few puffs yourself. Ultimately, the decision you make will depend on whose approval you're seeking. If you're seeking the approval of everyone around you, more than likely, you'll take a few hits yourself. Yet, if your goal is to have God's approval, then the decision you need to make will be very clear. Most of the big decisions, especially the ones that have moral implications, are determined by whether we want someone else's approval, or whether we want God's approval.

Several years ago, I decided to further my education and apply to enter the doctoral program at seminary. To be admitted to the program, I had to do a number of things. I had to write a few book reviews. I had to go through a personal interview with a few professors. I also had to do well on a few standardized graduate entrance exams.

I took one of the graduate tests at the seminary. An administrative assistant was administering the exam. She would walk in and tell me how long I had to complete particular sections, and then she would leave the room. When the time was up, she would return to the room and tell me to stop.

On one particular reading comprehension section, I had to answer 70 questions. The administrative assistant told me the time I had to complete it, and then she left the room. Unfortunately, I misread my watch. When she returned to tell me to stop, I had only answered 38 out of the 70 questions. I couldn't believe it; it was my mistake. At that moment, I knew my chance at getting into the program was probably a long shot.

I still had several other sections to complete on the exam. When the secretary walked out of the room, I could have gone back to the other section, and circled in all those blank answers. To be honest and totally transparent, I vividly remember considering this as a viable option. I remember sitting at my desk, distinctly thinking about filling in those blanks. Sitting in a seminary classroom doesn't make you immune to temptation.

Thankfully, that wasn't the decision I made. I went on to the next section, still wondering about all those blanks that would be counted against me. By God's grace, I decided whether I got into the program or not, I wanted God's approval above the title "Dr." that might one day sit in front of my name. I can remember walking off campus thinking, "God, I probably won't get into this program, but at least I honored you by doing what was right." In a surprising string of events, I was admitted into the program. (They needed some extra students.) Actually, some of my other scores outweighed the bad section of the exam. I mention this, not because I always get this right. I don't. On more occasions than I would like to admit, I still fall prey to seeking after man's approval rather than God's. I mention this because on this particular day I made the right decision for one simple reason. I had the right person in my jury box.

The vast majority of us attach our worth to human approval, but that can be a dangerous mistake. There's a phrase used in Scripture to describe being pre-occupied with the opinions of other people. It's called "the fear of man." Proverbs 29:25 says, "The fear of man is a snare." The Hebrew word for snare pictures a bird that is caught in a net. The bird is helpless because he's trapped. What a sad image. Someone who is living to please human beings rather than is God is trapped by the opinions of other people.

It's possible to be in bondage by constantly thinking about what other people think about you. You can develop an addiction to human approval. By now, you might be wondering, "Am I an approval addict?" Here are a few symptoms that may reveal that you have a human approval addiction If you're always trying to impress other people, you probably have a problem. If you're constantly asking yourself, "I wonder what they (the people in my jury box) think about me," then you probably have a problem. If you habitually compare yourself to other people, you're placing too much emphasis on human approval. If you live to receive the next complement or live to receive public praise, you most likely are caught in the trap.

If you want to read the mission statement of every approval addict, read Matthew 23:5. Jesus summed up his view of the Pharisees in this one verse, "They do all their deeds to be seen by others." He whittles down his assessment of the Pharisees to one simple statement, "Everything they do, they do to be seen by other people." No wonder Jesus repeatedly said, "Don't be like the Pharisees. "

Jesus said, "When you give, don't be like the Pharisees." The Pharisees brought their monetary gifts to put them in the treasury at the temple. The treasury was made up of 13 funnel shaped metal cones. The worshippers would come up to the treasury and drop them into the funnel, and their coins would spiral downward into the base of the treasury. Some of the Pharisees would take whatever money they were going to give and have it changed into the greatest number of coins. It would be like taking two quarters and having it changed into 50 pennies.

The Pharisees were notorious for coming to the treasury, standing back, and then tossing all the coins into the metal funnels. The noise from all the coins hitting the metal cones sure did generate a lot of attention. Everyone standing close by thought, "Man, he must really love God. Look how much money he's putting into the treasury." No wonder Jesus said, "When you give, don't be like the Pharisees. They give to be seen by men" (Mt. 6:1-4). It was all a show. Jesus didn't have a problem with what the Pharisees did; He had a problem with why they did what they did. He had a problem with their motives. Their motives were skewed because they were trying to impress other people. They loved the applause of man more than the applause of God. They had the wrong people in their jury box.

Some people have a poor view of themselves because they have believed a myth. The myth says, "If I want to be happy, I have to be liked by everyone." Yet, no matter how hard you try, everyone is not going to flash the thumbs up sign in your direction. Sometimes they may flash another finger at you. Jesus was a realist. He knew it was impossible for us to please everyone. Jesus even said, "Woe to you when all men speak well of you." If everyone is giving us the thumbs up sign, Jesus seems to think it's not a good sign.

Even God can't please everyone. When it rains, fifty percent of the people complain because they can't go out and play golf. When it's sunny outside, fifty percent of the people say, "Boy, we sure do need some rain around here." God can't even please everyone. Why do you think you can do something God can't even do? Instead of finding your value and worth from human approval, base it on something that is far more stable.

It's never wise to get your self-worth from something that can be taken from you. Does your self-worth come from your friends? Because you have a bunch of friends, does that make you valuable? Does your self-worth come from your career? Do you think you are who you are because of your successful job? Does your self-worth come from your house? Is your value attached to the value of your house? Does your worth come from the labels inside of your clothes? I hope not. Everything I just mentioned can be taken from you. You can lose your friends, your job, your house, and your clothes. If your worth is attached to those things and you lose them, you also lose your self-worth. Attach your worth to God. His love, grace, and acceptance can never be taken from you.

No one wants to be rejected by other people, and every one of us wants to be liked. Those two facts are a common denominator for all of humanity. Some people, though, exclusively find their worth from the people around them. Teenagers tend to find their worth from their peers. This is why when someone says to a teenager, "Did you know your upper lip is bigger than your lower lip?" it sticks with them. They start to think, "I might be able to do something with my life if my upper lip wasn't bigger than my lower lip." The desire to have everyone's acceptance is really coming from a deeper desire. Our deepest desire is to be accepted by God. In Christ, you have been fully accepted. His acceptance is irrevocable. It can never be taken from you.

Paul could say, "It's a small thing that I should judged by you" because he knew one day he would be judged by the Lord, not by other people. He feared God, not man. We enjoy a healthier identity when we develop a fear of God, rather than the fear of man. The fear of God is a biblical concept repeated frequently throughout the Bible. Psalm 34:9 says, "Oh, Fear the Lord, you His saints... " Proverbs 1:7 says, "The fear of the Lord is the beginning of knowledge." The fear we should have of God is not the kind of fear that causes us to sweat or shake in our shoes. God is not a boogeyman hiding in the closet, waiting to pounce on us.

When we fear God, we start by acknowledging who God is. He is the all-powerful God of the universe. We stand in awe of Him. A quick cursory glance through the Bible helps us get a grasp of what the fear of God looks like. When God appeared to Moses in the burning bush, the Bible says that Moses was afraid. When God sent the plagues on Pharaoh, the Scriptures affirm that he was afraid as well. When Jesus came to the disciples, walking on the water, the gospels record that the disciples were afraid. When Jesus was on the mountain and His appearance was transformed like the sun, Peter, James, and John fell to ground because they were afraid. Why were Moses, Pharaoh, and the 12 disciples afraid? Because when they got a glance of God and His power, they were in complete awe of who God was. They were overwhelmed with His power, purity, and greatness.

Fearing God also means I recognize I'm accountable to God. Paul wasn't overly concerned with human judgments; He was more concerned about divine judgment. He lived in light of the final judgment of God. In America, we understand accountability. April 15th in America is a day of accountability. On this day, we have to cough up everything we owe to the government. We have to give an account of how much we've made and how much of it belongs to the government. No matter what we do to delay this day of reckoning (filing extensions or looking for loop holes) April 15th still rolls around every year.

God has an April 15th on His calendar. God has a day when we are held accountable for our lives. Hebrews 4:13 says, "Nothing is hidden from God's eyes. Everything is uncovered and laid bare before the eyes of Him to whom we must give account." It's sobering to think that one day I will stand before God to give an account of every word I've spoken and every deed that I've done. Interestingly, I think about this day on a regular basis. Not in a morbid way, but in a healthy way. I find that this day also has a big influence on the decisions I make each day. I find it influences how I choose to spend my time and money. Remember this day of accountability doesn't prevent me from stumbling. I still strike out. I still mess up. I still fumble the ball. At the same time, remembering my day of accountability helps to put some extra guard rails around my decisions.

I remember reading a story about the legendary Babe Ruth. Babe was at bat one day, and the pitcher threw the first pitch. He swung and missed. The pitcher threw the second pitch and he swung and missed. He dug in a little deeper, and the pitcher threw the third pitch and Babe Ruth didn't move. The umpire said, "Strike Three! You're Out!" Bath Ruth turned around to the umpire and said, "There are 40,000 people here, and all 40,000 of them know that last pitch was a ball." The umpire said, "Maybe so Babe, but my opinion is the only one that counts. You're out!" When we have a healthy fear of God, we realize the opinion that really matters is God's opinion. In the flyleaf of one of my Bibles, I wrote, "I have nothing to prove, no one to impress, nothing to lose, just one person to please."

One day, God will ask me about my life. I don't want to get to the end of my life and have to say, "God, I was planning on doing your will. I just never quite got around to it. I was planning to use the gifts, skills, and talents you entrusted to me, but I was too busy." God will say, "Wrong answer! That's not what I was looking for." I don't want to get to the end of life only to find I'm standing on a mountain of regret. One of the ways we can minimize our regrets is by living with the end in mind. A lot of people live their whole lives and never think about what's going to happen at the end of life. They make decisions and choices, and they never think about the day when they'll be held responsible for those decisions. When we fear God, we live with the end in mind.

Solomon was one of the most powerful men to rule over ancient Israel. Unfortunately, he learned an important principle of life a little too late. In his personal diary called Ecclesiastes, Solomon described what he lived for: power, pleasure, and possessions. He set a record for taking the most thrill rides of any man of his time. He seemed to have so many pleasures at his fingertips, but near the end of his life, he had so many regrets. He had spent so much of his life trying to please himself rather than please God. After burning up decades of his life, Solomon looks back and he whittles life down to one basic principle: "Now all has been heard; here is the conclusion of the matter: Fear God and keep His commandments, for this is the whole duty of man" (Eccles. 12:13).

God preserved the words of Solomon for us so we wouldn't make the same mistakes. God doesn't want us to get to the end of life, only to glance back over the landscape of our lives and see it's littered with regrets. Solomon said the best way to minimize your regrets is by "fearing God and keeping His commandments." Fearing God in Scripture is closely associated with His judgment.

It's important to have a healthy balance between the great truths of the Bible. Two tall truths presented in Scripture are the love of God and the judgment of God. Both His love and His judgment can be traced throughout the Old and New Testament. We have to balance these two great truths. Some Christians have an out of balance view of God. If you fall too far on the side of the judgment of God, and you don't factor in the love of God, more than likely, you will become a legalist. You will probably reduce Christianity down to a list of do's and don'ts. You will have the tendency to view God as a monster who enjoys zapping Christians when they get out of line. God is viewed as someone who enjoys blowing people away with one blast of His nostrils.

At the same, some Christians can fall too far on the love side. In their minds, they reason that God loves them unconditionally. Therefore, because of His unconditional love, they can throw all restraint to the wind and live any way they like. To them, God is like a giant teddy bear in the sky. Because of His softness, He doesn't care how you live your life. Neither view is correct. This is why it's so important for us to balance these two great truths about God. Yes, God loves you unconditionally. The Bible says, "God is love." Love is the quintessential character trait of God. God loves you, yet the Bible says the same God who loves you is the same God who will judge you. Both truths have to be balanced.

In the end, God really is both judge and jury. His opinion of your life isn't measured by 11 other equal opinions. In eternity, there are no jury consultants. No defense attorneys. No court of appeals. God's opinion is final, irrevocable, with no chance of it being overturned. The next time you catch yourself thinking about what someone thinks of you, remember, in the courtroom of heaven, only one person is in the jury box. Live to please the One who is both judge and jury.

CHAPTER 15

Big Shots Get Shot

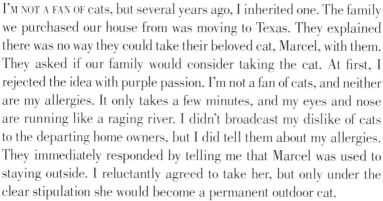

I'M NOT A FAN OF cats, but several years ago, I inherited one. The family we purchased our house from was moving to Texas. They explained there was no way they could take their beloved cat, Marcel, with them. They asked if our family would consider taking the cat. At first, I rejected the idea with purple passion. I'm not a fan of cats, and neither are my allergies. It only takes a few minutes, and my eyes and nose are running like a raging river. I didn't broadcast my dislike of cats to the departing home owners, but I did tell them about my allergies. They immediately responded by telling me that Marcel was used to staying outside. I reluctantly agreed to take her, but only under the clear stipulation she would become a permanent outdoor cat.

After we moved into the house, one of our neighbors warned us about a wild cat roaming around in the neighborhood. She informed us that this wild feline enjoyed traveling the neighborhood, beating up the other cats. One night, we were in bed and I suddenly heard the loudest screeching noise imaginable. I went outside, took one look at Marcel, and knew Rocky Balboa had gotten the best of her. She was beaten up so badly that a large chunk had been taken out of her right ear.

Several weeks later, Rocky returned for a few more rounds. This time when I went out to check on Marcel, the neighborhood bully was still lingering around. I scanned the backyard with my flashlight, and there he was hissing. Rocky was the biggest cat I've ever seen; he was intimidating just to look at. When I first laid eyes on him, I considered running back inside myself. He had been in so many fights that one of his ears was barely attached. Rocky thought he was a big shot, whipping up on all the other cats. In fact, he also enjoyed fighting the dogs. I saw more than one dog run in the opposite direction when they spotted Rocky. Without any debate, he was the undisputed heavy weight champion of the neighborhood.

Well, I may not be a cat lover, but I am the man of the house. I'm supposed to protect my family-Marcel included. I became a vigilante and decided to buy a cheap BB gun at Wal-Mart. I made three different targets, and went to the backyard to practice my shooting. I was determined to take BB marksmanship to a whole new level. The next time Rocky Balboa came around, I was going to show him that Marcel was not his personal punching bag. Just as I expected, in several days, the heavyweight champion came back for some more action. But this time he would lose his title. When duty called, I had to respond. Wearing my Ninja uniform, I blended in perfectly with the darkness. I told my wife if I didn't return in one hour to please call 911. I took my BB gun, aimed it at his big belly, and pulled the trigger. This time, Rocky didn't walk away as a big shot. Instead, He hobbled off, finally getting a taste of his own medicine. Rocky learned that big shots aren't as big as they think they are. Big shots usually end up getting shot.

What's true of cats is equally true of human beings. We all have the tendency to drift toward "big shotitis." In its rawest form, big shotitis means we want to stand above the crowd and be recognized by others. The world's perspective on greatness hasn't changed a lot in 21 centuries. To reach big shot status, it comes down to having power, prestige, and position. This faulty view of success and greatness often leads to a life of emptiness.

Jesus had two disciples who had a bad case of big shotitis. Matthew records the day James and John got stars in their eyes:

"Then the mother of James and John, the sons of Zebedee, came to Jesus with her sons. She knelt respectfully to ask a favor. "What is your request?" he asked. She replied, "In your Kingdom, will you let my two sons sit in places of honor next to you, one at your right and the other at your left?" But Jesus told them, "You don't know what you are asking! Are you able to drink from the bitter cup of sorrow I am about to drink?" "Oh yes," they replied, "we are able!" "You will indeed drink from it," he told them. "But I have no right to

say who will sit on the thrones next to mine. My Father has prepared those places for the ones he has chosen." When the ten other disciples heard what James and John had asked, they were indignant. But Jesus called them together and said, "You know that in this world kings are tyrants, and officials lord it over the people beneath them. But among you it should be quite different. Whoever wants to be a leader among you. must be your servant, and whoever wants to be first must become your slave. For even I, the Son of Man, came here not to be served but to serve others, and to give my life as a ransom for many" (**Matthew 20:20-28 NLT**).

The mother of James and John came to Jesus with an audacious request. She asked if Jesus would allow her sons to sit in a place of honor in the future kingdom. The same story is recorded by Mark, but in Mark's account, the mother of James and John wasn't the one asking Jesus for this special privilege. In Mark's gospel, James and John are the ones asking Jesus if they can sit on His right hand and left hand. So which is right? Both of them are right. Most likely Momma spoke up first, then James and John chimed in. Their request was obvious, "Give us the highest position in your kingdom."

James and John were looking for status; they wanted to be deemed the President and Vice-President of the kingdom. In their minds, greatness was measured by a position, but Jesus didn't equate greatness with name recognition or social status. Jesus equated greatness with service.

In one of his most famous statements, Jesus said, "Whoever wants to be a leader among you must be your servant." A servant in the first century was someone who did menial labor, like house cleaning and waiting on tables. The servant was described as the lowest level of hired help. Yet, Jesus elevated the servant to a place of significance. Jesus could have selected any word to describe greatness, and He purposefully chose this one. When the disciples heard Jesus equate success with being a servant, they were stunned. Servant? "Jesus, you mean greatness is like that guy over there? He's wearing an apron around his waist. No one even knows his name; no one has ever done an interview with him." Jesus said, "Yeah, that's right; he is a wonderful picture of greatness."

To amplify His teaching on servanthood, Jesus went one step further by saying, "And whoever wants to be first among you, let him be your slave." The reference to being a slave referred to a *doulos* slave.[45] A *doulos* slave had no rights; he was considered the lowest rung on the social ladder. A slave was in a much lower position than a servant. A servant was paid, but a slave was owned. A servant was free to go where he wanted, but a slave could only go where his master wanted him to go. A slave's life was spent focusing on others. It wasn't exactly what James and John had in mind when they requested CEO status for the kingdom.

Most people look at success like a pyramid and the person at the top of the pyramid is the one who is successful, and everyone below him on the organizational chart is considered less successful. Everyone below him is responsible to serve him. Jesus comes along and He turns the pyramid upside down. Jesus teaches that the person who is truly successful is the one who is serving others. Being a servant means wherever you fall on the organizational chart, you're determined to serve the people above you and below you.

Jesus compared greatness to a humble servant. Through His example and teaching, Jesus radically altered the way society looked at the virtue of humility. John Dickens, a professor of ancient history, researched extensively how humility emerged as a social virtue. In ancient society, and also in ancient Israel, humility before God was appropriate; humility before judges, kings, and priests was also considered appropriate. However, it was culturally unacceptable to humble yourself before an equal, or someone socially inferior. Jesus changed the way the Roman world, and eventually the Western world saw humility. Deliberately lowering yourself to an equal or someone

---

45   John Grassmick, "Mark," *The Bible Knowledge Commentary* (Wheaton: Victor Books, 1983), 158.

socially inferior started to be considered a beautiful virtue. Jesus created this ripple effect.[46]

Not Getting What We Ask For

I find it interesting Jesus flatly denied their request for these places of honor. It's a sure indicator that some of our prayer requests are not answered because they're inappropriate. James and John seemed to have a knack for asking for things that were inappropriate. One day when the disciples and Jesus were traveling through a Samaritan village, the people in the village refused to let them pass through their town. James and John were livid. They turned to Jesus, and asked, "Jesus, why don't you call down fire and destroy this village?" Now I know why they were called "the sons of thunder." Having a throne beside Jesus and dropping a pyrotechnic show on top of a village were two requests Jesus flatly rejected.

I'm glad God hasn't answered every one of my frivolous prayers. God knows what is best for me, and when I ask for something not in my best interest and His best interest, God declines my request. Can you imagine what the world would be like if God answered yes to everything? God loves us far too much to say yes to everything. Have your children ever come to you and asked for something you knew wouldn't be good for them to have? Did you still give it to them? No. To reflexively say yes to every request would destroy your children. I've been around parents who thought it was their responsibility to give their children everything they asked for. In the end, it misrepresents the natural rhythm of life. We don't always get what we want.

Since my father owned a sports goods store when I was growing up, I often made requests for certain items in the store. His store contained all kinds of sporting equipment for sale. One day, I got the bright idea to ask my dad if my older brother and I could each have a pair of the boxing gloves. When I made the request, my dad said, "Son, I don't think that would be a good idea." He explained, "I don't believe you and Brandon can box without it turning into a real fight." I quickly turned to the art of persuasion, "Come on Dad, we're

---

46   John Dickson, *Humilitas* (Grand Rapids: Zondervan, 2011), 99-110.

just two teenagers trying to have some fun. Just think of all the other things we could be doing to get into trouble. We just want to box." My persistence paid off, and my dad finally gave in. He let us both have a brand new pair of boxing gloves. Before we started our boxing match, we made a few rules. The most important rule was that no one could punch in the face.

Our first couple of rounds went great. Then, when we reached the fourth round, the downward spiral began. Everything was going by the book until one of my punches missed my brother's shoulder and hit him right square in the nose. Without giving you the blow by blow details, let's just say that didn't go over so well with my brother. In a matter of moments, I thought I was in the ring with Mike Tyson. It's one those memorable times I wish my dad wouldn't have given me what I asked for.

Looking back many years later, I'm sure James and John were grateful Jesus said no to their selfish request. They believed their value in the kingdom was directly related to their position in the kingdom. Jesus exposed their erroneous thinking. Jesus spooked them by suggesting that merely obtaining a prominent position doesn't necessarily make someone great. Our self-worth isn't determined by how many toys we have in the closet or how many cars we have in the garage. Neither is it determined by how many initials are to the right of our names. When God measures success, He doesn't put the tape measure around the size of your house, bank accounts, or the square footage of your executive office. God puts the tape measure around your heart. Do you have a heart of a servant?

Servants Don't Need Status Symbols

Servants don't have to cover their walls with plaques and awards. They don't insist on being called by titles. Servants don't need status symbols to prop up their image because their worth isn't attached to power, prestige, or a notable position. Their worth is attached to a person. They find their worth in being a servant of Jesus Christ.

When Paul wrote his letters in the New Testament, he often opened his letters by introducing himself. His simple, "Paul, a servant of Jesus Christ," was his default introduction. Paul could have taken

2 or 3 chapters to talk about his credentials, but Paul didn't resort to self-promotion tactics. It was as if Paul was saying, "I only want you to know two things about me. First, my name is Paul, and second, I am a servant of Jesus." His identity was built around being a servant of Christ. Knowing who you are usually determines what you do. When you start to see yourself as a servant, you're more likely to start behaving like one.

When Jesus equated greatness to servanthood, He was talking about serving other people. Ironically, some people want to serve God, but they don't want to serve other people. In actuality, the only way to serve God is by serving other people. Do a cursory reading of the words of Jesus. You'll find a mother lode of fog-cutting statements about the impossibility of serving God without serving other people. Matthew records some of His landmark statements:

> *"Then the King will say to those on his right, 'Enter, you who are blessed by my Father! Take what's coming to you in this kingdom. It's been ready for you since the world's foundation. And here's why: I was hungry and you fed me, I was thirsty and you gave me a drink, I was homeless and you gave me a room, I was shivering and you gave me clothes, I was sick and you stopped to visit, I was in prison and you came to me.' "Then those 'sheep' are going to say, 'Master, what are you talking about? When did we ever see you hungry and feed you, thirsty and give you a drink? And when did we ever see you sick or in prison and come to you? Then the King will say, 'I'm telling the solemn truth: Whenever you did one of these things to someone overlooked or ignored, that was me—you did it to me'* (**Matthew 25: 43-40, The Message**).

Jesus is painting a picture of an event that will take place in the future. He is describing the Day of Judgment, when all the peoples of the world will be gathered before Him. Like my favorite professors, Jesus tells us exactly what to expect on the final exam. There will be no surprises. He is going to separate everyone like a shepherd separates sheep from goats. He says the sheep are going to heaven, but the goats are not. What makes a sheep a sheep and a goat a goat?

As a pastor, this is a subject I get a lot of questions about. Little kids in the church ask me, "Will my grandpa be in heaven?" "Yes, of course, Billy. Your grandpa will be in heaven. He was a follower of Jesus Christ." Then I get more complicated questions, "Will my dog be in heaven?" "Well, I'm not exactly sure about that one, Billy." "How about my cat?" "No, Billy, I'm sure about that one! Cats don't go to heaven."

Everyone wants to know the answer to that question: who is going to heaven? At the final judgment, Jesus says the sheep are going to heaven. These are the people who have fed the hungry, clothed the naked, and visited and cared for the sick. These are people who did more than have good intentions. Their intentions were translated into action. Jesus isn't teaching we can earn salvation by what we do, but He is teaching that our salvation is revealed by what we do. Someone who has real, saving faith will demonstrate it by their service to other people. Genuine salvation isn't measured by what we say, what we feel, or by what kind of bumper sticker we have on our cars. Jesus said it's measured by what we do. My love for God is measured by my love for other people.

Don't get twisted up here. You are not saved by your good works, you are saved by grace. God in His grace makes His forgiveness available to you as a free gift. We simply reach out and receive it by faith. The moment you place your faith in the finished work of Christ, you are accepted and declared right before God. Too many people are confused about this today.

We should never confuse the fruits of the gospel with the gospel itself. Why do we feed the hungry? Why do we care for the poor? Why are we compassionate to the least of these? Because these actions are the natural outgrowth of what happens when the gospel has impacted our lives. Feeding the hungry, caring for the poor, and showing compassion to the least of these is not the gospel; these actions are the outgrowth and fruit of the gospel.

The Gospel

The Bible teaches we are saved by the gospel. So we beg the question, what is the gospel? The word "gospel" didn't start out as a religious term. The word gospel (*euangelion* in Gk) referred to an announcement. The word was used originally to make an announcement about military victories. During a war, Greek Generals would often send news that their armies had been victorious in battle. The General would send a designated soldier out to make the announcement. The carrier of the good news would say something like this, "I bring you the gospel of General Ptolemy-we have been victorious in battle." It was a declaration of what had been accomplished by the army. Later on, this term, *euangelion*, was applied to the good news of Jesus Christ. The gospel is a declaration of what God has accomplished in Christ. Through His death and resurrection, God liberated us from the penalty of sin and death. By faith, we're invited to personally embrace the good news of Christ. Paul said, "I declare to you the gospel that Christ died for our sins…that He was buried, and that He arose again the third day " (1 Corin. 15:1-4).

The gospel is not about what we should be doing for God; it's about what God has already done for us. When we emphasize what we're supposed to be doing for God more than what God has done for us, the gospel can become confusing. It can be confused for a nice, prepackaged set of good works. Churches can unknowingly confuse worshippers by overemphasizing what we are supposed to be doing for God.

Some churches focus primarily on social justice; other churches focus on marriage enrichment; some churches are known for their focus on verse by verse Bible teaching. What is truly important in the church? Without question, every healthy church will teach the Scriptures, engage the community with compassion, and seek to build winning families. However, every one of those things are the result of what happens when the church stays focused on what's primary—the gospel.

Jesus is saying when the gospel (the announcement of the grace of God) has truly impacted your life, it's going to express itself. It's going to come out by feeding the hungry, clothing the naked, and helping the hurting. Philippians 2: 3 says, "Work out your salvation in fear and trembling." The Christian life is not a passive life. We don't just sit back and say, "Well, God saved me from hell, so I'm just going to coast the rest of the way into heaven." No, the Bible says to work out your salvation. Don't overlook the little preposition in this verse. The Bible doesn't say work "for" your salvation; it says work "out" your salvation. Your salvation was accomplished by the work of Christ not your work. Yet, the moment you embrace God's grace, God calls you to live out your salvation with a life of service.

In the picture Jesus paints of the final judgment, it's important to note what Jesus didn't say. He didn't say, "I was sick and you built me a ten story hospital"; "I was hungry and you reformed the welfare system"; "I was lonely and you established a cutting edge big brother program." Jesus isn't emphasizing grandiose ideas here. He mentions simple acts of service like feeding someone who is hungry, visiting with someone who is lonely, and loving someone who feels ostracized. Sometimes when we think of serving someone, we think of doing something big for them. But most of the time, service takes the form of little acts. Though the ripples are felt, the actions are often never noticed.

Non-Flashy Service

Service rarely involves jumping in front of someone to take a speeding bullet in their place. It's a lot less dramatic and subtle. It's going to see a friend in the nursing center. It's writing a note or email to someone who needs encouragement. It's having prayer with someone who was just diagnosed with cancer. It's taking food to a homeless shelter. It's sponsoring an underprivileged child in an under resourced part of the world. It's serving in the children's ministry at church. It's making time in your schedule for someone. It's inviting someone to church; it's communicating the good news about Christ to a coworker. When we serve, we are trying to improve somebody else's life.

The ultimate standard for greatness is Jesus Christ. Jesus didn't come to be served, but to serve others. Make Jesus your hero in life. Don't let anyone tell you that you don't need some heroes in your life. You do. I do. We all do. We need people who model great lives before us, but if you're a Christian, your ultimate hero is Jesus. How did he live? Did He demand that everybody meet His needs? No, He was busy meeting everyone else's needs.

If you're going to be successful, you need a hero. You need someone to pattern your life after, someone who has demonstrated true greatness. You can veer way off course by making someone other than Christ your standard for greatness. Christians can get way off base by making a top executive, sports figure, or a beautiful model their ultimate standard for greatness. It's possible to get to the end of life only to think, "Man, how did I miss the bull's eye by so far?" No one sets out to intentionally miss the mark. How does that happen? It happens when we choose the wrong heroes. It happens when our standard for greatness is the wrong one. If you will make Jesus your ultimate example for greatness, you may not hit the bull's eye, but at least you'll be shooting at the right target. That's coming from a BB marksman—who will never forget the day Rocky Balboa gave up his throne.

Decision 6: Will I Place Value On Everyone I Meet Today?

Chapter 16

Everyone is a 10

One evening I sat in my father-in-law's house getting ready to make the biggest request of my life. I wanted to take the traditional route and ask for his daughter's hand in marriage. I can recall sitting in his living room. It was just me and Charlie. Everyone was gone, and I figured this would be the perfect time to spring the question on him. I had already rehearsed in my mind what I was going to say. All I needed was the perfect opportunity to make a smooth transition.

When we stopped talking about fishing, I thought, "Here's what I've been waiting for, my golden opportunity to broach the subject." Just about the time I was determined to start speaking, I could feel my heart pounding in my chest. My breath was short, and I began sweating profusely. I could feel the sweat under my arms running down the side of my rib cage. Remember my encounter with the snake? When I'm afraid, I sweat and I mean a lot!

When all these physiological responses kicked in, I thought I better give myself a chance to calm down. Just about that time I calmed down and was ready to launch into my speech, Charlie would bring up another subject he wanted to talk about. We would talk some more until we exhausted the next topic of conversation. There would be a brief moment of silence. Then, just as I would start to speak, my heart would start pounding again. The sweat started to drip from underneath my arms. I huffed and I puffed, but I couldn't get anything to come out. Finally, after about two hours, I got the courage to ask his permission to propose to his daughter. Shortly thereafter, I had to go change my t-shirt because it was soaking wet.

Sometimes when you're trying to communicate your love for someone, it can be thorny and complex. Communicating your love for someone is actually easier than tangibly expressing it. True love goes far beyond our words. True love is expressed through our actions. In 1 Corinthians 13, we have the most comprehensive description of love in the entire Bible.

"Love is patient and kind; love does not envy or boast; it is not arrogant or rude. It does not insist on its own way; it is not irritable, or resentful, it does not rejoice at wrongdoing, but rejoices with the truth. Love bears all things, believes all things, hopes all things, endures all things" (1 Corith 13:4-7 ESV).

Every description Paul uses to describe love is a verb. Remember what your English teacher taught you about verbs? Ironically, my mother was the one who taught me English in middle school. I'll never forget the day she dropped me off at the school so I could see who my teachers were going to be for the upcoming school year.

I looked up at the list, scanned down to my name, and found out who my teachers were. I had Mrs. Yelton for social studies, Mrs. Hardin for math, and Mr. Cook for P.E. All was going well on the list until I saw the name of my next teacher. For English, I would have Mrs. Waters. When I saw her name, I thought, "Well, I know one class where I won't be missing any homework." Needless to say, I was a little intimidated about having my mother as my English teacher. Yet, as I sat in her classroom, I discovered she was a great English teacher.

My mother taught me the mechanics of the English language. She taught me how to diagram sentences. She taught me how to find a subject and predicate. She showed me how to distinguish between different parts of a sentence. She taught me about nouns and adjectives. Her favorite speech, though, like most middle school English teachers, was the one she gave about verbs. If I heard her say it once, I heard her say it one hundred thousand times, "A verb always shows action."

That's the whole point of 1 Corinthians 13. Love is not a feeling; it's not something you say; love is something you do. In America, the word love has all kinds of connotations. When you were in elementary school, you probably sent letters to your sweetheart, saying, "I love you. If you love me, please check the box that says you love me too." You called those "love letters" because you had warm, fuzzy feelings toward your sweetheart. In our culture, you might hear some people say, "I love pizza." But I don't think they have those same warm, fuzzy feelings toward pizza as they did for their childhood sweetheart. They simply like to eat pepperoni pizza. Sometime ago, I saw a man driving a truck, and he had a bumper sticker on it that said, "I love country music." I don't think he had warm, fuzzy feelings for country music. He was merely saying, "My favorite music is country music." In the Bible, love is more than a feeling, or a strong desire, love is an action. To use English terminology, love is always a verb. Love is always expressed through our actions.

Love has to become the prevailing life principle that fuels our lives. Everyone has a prevailing principle they build life around. Some people build their lives around money. Others build life around fame. Others build life around success or sex. Everyone has prevailing principles that stand at the center of life. God wants the prevailing principle of our lives to be the principle of love.

Love Is Expressed Through Value

What is the greatest expression of love? Is it diamonds? Is it chocolates? Is it flowers? How about a trip to Hawaii or a new car? Each of these items can be an expression of love, but the greatest expression of love is value. When you value someone, you believe they matter to God and to you. Here's an undeniable fact—you can never express love to someone until you value them.

One of the most important decisions we make each day takes place before we ever get out of bed. Before we ever put on our slippers, we've probably already made the decision—will I express value and worth to everyone I encounter today? If we're going to express love to the people around us, we have to make the right assumptions about people. One assumption we have to make is that every single person on planet earth is valuable and important.

A good place to start is in the very beginning. Genesis reminds us about the worth of each human being. Every human being is made in the image of God. That means everyone bears the stamp and imprint of the Creator of the Universe. Every human being has intrinsic worth. This is why we should be a voice for life. Every human being is valuable, regardless if they are in the womb or out of the womb. You have never laid eyes on another human being that didn't matter to God. Everyone is valuable to Him.

I've made a startling discovery. People who leave a lasting legacy of love place a high value on everyone they encounter. They assign high worth to everyone they meet. John Maxwell calls this, "putting a 10 on everyone." In your eyes, is everyone a 10? Does everyone matter to you, or only certain people who are from your same socio-economic group? It's possible for us to put labels on people the way designers put labels on clothes. We can put the Tommy Hilfiger tag on some people, while we label others with an Izod tag. If you're a 10, 9, or 8 in my eyes, you will know it. At the same time, if you are a 5, 4, 3 in my eyes, it will be obvious by the way I treat you. If you are not a 10 in my eyes, I won't be able to fake it. The value I place on you will determine how I treat you. Relationship expert, Les Giblin said, "You can't make the other fellow feel important in your presence if you secretly feel that he is a Nobody."[47]

The Pharisees got this wrong. Everyone was definitely not a 10 in their eyes. The Jewish men were a 10 but not the Jewish women. The Jewish women scored a 7. The Gentiles came in at 5. Below them were the female Gentiles, who hit the scales at 3. People with disabilities (especially lepers) scored a 2, and then there were notorious tax collectors, who were at the bottom of the pack with at a 1. In contrast to the Pharisees, there was Jesus. Follow His soft sandaled feet in the gospels; it's obvious that everyone was a 10 in

---

47   John Maxwell, *25 Ways To Win With People* (Nashville: Thomas Nelson Publishers, 2005) 122.

His eyes. Nothing increases our capacity to love like the value we place on each person we meet.

Our beliefs drive our behaviors. If you don't believe everyone is a 10, it will be impossible for you to express love to them. The reason some people have a tough time loving certain people is because they don't believe those people really matter. Their behavior is nothing more than a reflection of their beliefs about people. In order to change their behavior, they will first have to change the way they see people. This takes us back to the undeniable fact about love: you can't love someone you don't value.

Do the Custodians Know They Matter?

I had a great example of this principle when I was in college. One of my professors, Van Murrell, stood head and shoulders above the other professors because he expressed value to everyone he met. Dr. Murrell didn't know it, but I watched him walk through the hallways. When he passed a janitor in the hallway, Dr. Murrell always stopped to talk with them. Not only did he talk with them, but he also knew their names. He knew the names of their wives and the names of their children. The vast majority of the other professors, religion professors I might add, would walk by the janitors on campus and would barely notice them. But Dr. Murrell noticed them. They didn't need Dr. in front of their names to be important. From Dr. Murrell's perspective, everyone was important. He added value to them by letting them know they were just as important as everyone else. How we treat the custodian in the office, the waitress in the restaurant, or the bag boy in the grocery store speaks volumes about how we value people.

I've often said you can tell a lot about someone by the way they treat the fast food chef and the neurosurgeon. If we go to McDonald's and we're disrespectful and snobby to the fast food chef, but then we go see the neurosurgeon and give him our utmost respect, then we have a major problem in the way we view people. Everybody should be a 10. If we treat the fast food chef any different from the neurosurgeon, we're placing greater value on one person than on another person. The Bible has a name for that. It's called "favoritism" and God doesn't like favoritism.

James 2:1 says, "My brothers, show no partiality as you hold the faith in our Lord Jesus Christ." The New English Bible calls partiality "snobbery." A snob is someone who thinks he's better than everyone else. In the same chapter, James paints a picture of what favoritism might look like with a hypothetical church experience.

In the scenario, James introduces us to "the snobbish usher." He says if two strangers come into your church, and the first guest is dripping with wealth, but the other guest is poverty stricken, then make sure you treat them equally. How the usher treats them speaks volumes about how he values these two guests. In the hypothetical situation, the usher takes a look at the sparkling gold that's all over the rich man. He sees his Rolex watch. He notices his Armani suit. He says, "Hello sir, let me help you find a seat. Here's one; it's the best seat in the house." After a few minutes, another guest arrives for worship. This same usher takes one look at this man. It's obvious he's from the other side of the tracks. He is unshaven, unclean, and uncultured. He has holes in his slacks. He looks rough. He smells bad. I mean really bad. The usher has to make a decision. Where am I going to seat this man? The usher approaches the poor man and says, "Here's a place for you. I hope you don't mind sitting on the floor." In the story, James says the usher made a fatal mistake when he decided to give preferential treatment to the rich man. He was snobbish because he was playing favorites. One person was more valuable in his eyes.

Several years, I had an opportunity to lead a spiritual growth campaign in a medium security prison. Before our team could get clearance to go in and out of the prison, we had to go through an orientation from an official representative at the prison. The lady leading the orientation told us all the "do's and don'ts" of prison protocol. She also offered a series of suggestions about how we were expected to interact with the inmates. Toward the end of her speech, she made a striking statement. She said, "By the way, we would also like to recommend that you don't touch the inmates. Don't shake their hands and don't hug them."

After she was done, I asked the prison representative if I could have a few minutes alone with our team. When she left the room, I turned to all the guys on our team and I gave my own speech. "Guys,"

I said, "I know I invited you to be a part of this ministry team. If there are any of you who are unwilling to touch these inmates, to shake their hands and to hug them, then I would like to graciously uninvite you to participate." Then I explained myself, "Guys, there is no way to look at these inmates and say Jesus loves you, but I'm not willing to touch you. It's the ultimate message of rejection."

After my speech, every team member said in their own way, "Clay, you don't have to worry about us. You can count on us to reach out and touch them." We went through the 8 week campaign, and each week, it was such a joy to watch our team express value and love to every inmate.

Jesus loves with no strings attached. Jesus loves the man who lives behind bars as much as he loves the man who lives in a mansion. He loves the gangster in the street as much as He loves the graduate of the university. Jesus loves the homosexual on Bourbon Street as much as he loves the CEO on Wall Street.

Seeing People With New Eyes

I was reading recently in John's gospel about the way Jesus encountered the woman at the well. She had been through 5 marriages and 5 divorces, and the man she was living with was not her spouse. By now, she felt like she was a piece of worthless meat that was being passed around. She felt like she had no value. She probably had no self-respect. She was carrying a load of guilt and shame. When Jesus comes up to the well, He sees this woman on the other side of the well. When He sees her, He begins to walk over to the other side of the well where she was standing.

She's completely caught off guard. No Jew was supposed to rub shoulders with a Samaritan, not to mention a Samaritan woman. That was a double whammy. It would have been a definite "no, no" for any orthodox Jew. Yet, there went Jesus, as he went sailing across gender barriers, racial barriers, and cultural barriers. He reached out and started a simple conversation about water with someone who was supposed to be off limits. Eventually, He used the conversation about water to talk to her about the one thing that would quench her thirsty soul. For the first time in a long time, a man offered her something and expected nothing in return. Jesus offered her value. He offered her love. He extended grace to her. She was so overwhelmed and excited about this newfound love, she left her water pot at the well. She was never the same.[48]

Back in the day when I was working at my father's sporting goods store, I learned a ditty that has stayed with me. It helped me when I was selling Nikes, Reeboks, and Adidas tennis shoes. It also helped me later on when I worked a short time at Belk selling men's clothing. The sales ditty went like this, "If I could see Joe Jones through Joe Jones eyes, I could sell Joe Jones what Joe Jones buys." Read that again in slow motion.

If you follow the words, you can trace the meaning. Basically, the sales principle was about staying focused on the customer. If I could just get inside my customer and see his needs from their perspective, I would have a greater likelihood of making a sale. A good salesman isn't thinking about himself when he's making a sale; he's thinking about the needs of his customer. He's trying to see the world through the eyes of his customer. You don't have to be a salesman to live by this principle. As followers of Christ, our goal is to see people through the eyes of God. If we could see people the way God sees them, it would begin to radically change the way we value people.

Studies have been done to examine what causes us to like someone. Out of all the different factors, like physical attractiveness, IQ, and personality type, the dominant factor that determines someone's likeability is whether or not we think they like us. If we perceive that they like us, then we will decide to like them back. One of the best ways to increase your own likeability is by deciding to like others. Likewise, when we value others, we tend to get value in return.

Love Is Expressed Through Forgiveness

In the beautiful description of love in 1 Corinthians 13, Paul says, "Love is not resentful." Literally, "Love keeps no record of wrongs." In the original language, it's an accounting term. It describes a bookkeeper who is meticulously keeping records on his ledger. If it's tax time, it's good to have a bookkeeper who keeps meticulous records. However, Paul is saying when it comes to our personal lives, it's better to throw away the books. Don't keep score. Don't make a list of everyone who has wronged you. Throw away the ledger.

One of the most profound expressions of love is forgiveness. In life, we don't have an endless supply of emotional energy. Each day we have to decide the best way to expend our emotional energy. When someone hurts us, one of the most important questions to ask is, "Do I want to use my energy to get well or to get even?" If you choose to use your energy to get even, eventually your emotional tank will be on E. Getting even will take every ounce of your life away.

How often should we forgive? Peter asked the same question, "Lord, how many times should I forgive?" Peter offered his own answer, "Seven times?" Peter thought he was being very generous. Jesus said, "Try 7 X 70." That's a few more than seven times. That's 490 times to be exact. Does that mean when you get to 491 that Jesus thinks it's okay to deliver your best uppercut? Not exactly. Jesus wants us to keep forgiving.

It's natural to think, "But they don't deserve to be forgiven." You're right. They don't deserve to be forgiven; however, you and I don't deserve to be forgiven either. Yet, God in His grace forgives us. I'm not suggesting forgiving them because they deserve it. It's a bit altruistic, but I would suggest forgiving them for your own sake. If we fail to forgive others, we end up being imprisoned by our own resentment.

Galatians 6:1 says, "If you see a brother caught in sin, you who are spiritual restore such a one in a spirit of gentleness." When someone is trapped, God wants us to go on a rescue mission to restore them. We should go representing His grace. The word for "restore" is actually a medical term. It means, "To set a broken bone." It's putting things back together after it has been broken.

Have you ever broken a bone? Fortunately, I have never broken a bone, but since I played a lot of sports growing up, I did witness plenty of bones being broken. The worst one I saw took place when Matt Brown, a friend of mine, was playing 3rd base. The coach wanted Matt to play in on the batter because he thought the batter was going to bunt. The coach was surprised when the batter didn't bunt. He hit a scorching line drive that nailed Matt right in the nose. On impact, it shattered his nose. You could hear it break when the ball hit his face.

While he was lying there on the infield, with blood oozing out of his nose, there were a few things he didn't need. Matt didn't need a lecture. He didn't need me to say, "What were you doing? You should have never been playing that close to the batter." You know something else Matt didn't need? He didn't need to be ignored. He was hurting. He was losing an incredible amount of blood. He didn't need to be ignored. He needed someone to pay attention to his injury. Neither did Matt need a good kick in the rear. I mean he was already down. He didn't need a player to come along and kick him while he was on the ground.

As Christians, when someone fails, we can be guilty of mistreating them. For all practical purposes, they're on the ground with blood oozing out of them. They don't need a lecture, nor do they need to be ignored. Besides, a good kick in the pants is usually always counterproductive. Why shoot those who are already wounded? God wants us to go to them in gentleness and mend their broken lives. What they need from us is forgiveness and grace.

An Example of Grace

In his book, *I Was Wrong*, Jim Bakker recounts how Billy and Ruth Graham treated him after his fall from grace. Jim Bakker was the disgraced televangelist who was sent to prison for a series of crimes. It was such a public scandal that not only exposed Jim Bakker's crimes, but also his immoral behavior. Amazingly, during that time, Billy and Ruth Graham never stopped loving him. They knew that most everyone would turn their backs on Jim Bakker, but they wanted to offer him love.

When Jim Bakker got out of prison, Billy and Ruth Graham bought him a car. They paid for a house for him to live in. Jim Bakker, recalls his very first Sunday out of prison. He writes, "Ruth Graham called the halfway house I was living at the time, and she asked permission for me to go to church with her that Sunday morning. When I got there, the pastor welcomed me and sat me with the Graham family. The organ began playing and the place was full, except for a seat next to me. Then the doors opened and in walked Ruth Graham. She walked down that aisle and sat next to inmate 07407. I had only been out of prison 48 hours, but she told the world that morning that Jim Bakker was her friend."[49] That's love. That's forgiveness. That's grace. That's what our world needs more of.

One of the best ways to become more loving is to not be easily offended. If you are easily offended, you're probably not going to be a loving person, or a happy person. In Matthew 18, Jesus said for us to expect offenses. He remarked, "Woe to the world because of offenses. For offenses must come, but woe to that man by whom the offense comes" (Matt. 18:7). Jesus is telling us straight up that offenses must come. People offend us by what they do (those are sins of commission). People offend us by what they don't do (those are sins of omission). Jesus said either way, life is going to set up plenty of occasions where you are going to feel offended. We can take that to the bank. The happiest and most loving people I have ever met are good at overlooking offenses. They're simply not easily offended. They take the high road and develop tough skin. They give their offenders the benefit of the doubt, and they move on with life.

It also means we're willing to admit we are flawed sinners, too. Nothing will ever replace the art of saying, "I'm sorry." Those are two of the most important words in the English language. I was reminded of the power of these words while I was watching a web cast interview of a well-known Christian author. The author described how his father was in the CIA while he was growing up. His dad had a high ranking position in the CIA and traveled extensively around the world.

Behind the scenes, though, his father was an alcoholic. He described how hard it was to have a father everyone looked up to, but at home, no one respected him. At one point in the interview, the author was asked an intriguing question, "What's the biggest

49   Jim Bakker, *I Was Wrong:The Untold Story of The Shocking Journey from PTL to Prison and Beyond* (Nashville: Thomas Nelson Publishers, 1997).

difference between the way your dad interacted with you and how you're interacting with your children?" He paused for a moment; I could tell it was an unscripted moment. He said, "The biggest difference is I tell my children I'm sorry on a regular basis." He said, "I can't remember my dad ever saying he was sorry." He went on to elaborate, "I want there to be enough humility in my life that when I'm wrong, I have enough love for them to say I'm sorry."[50] Admitting when we are wrong is a powerful expression of love.

Forgiving Yourself

One of the toughest people in the whole world to forgive is yourself. Chances are good if you don't learn to forgive yourself, it will impede your ability to give and receive love from others. I've known people who were incredibly forgiving toward others but never quite got around to giving the same level of grace to themselves. Admiral Mike Boorda was one such man. Mike Boorda was the first enlisted man in the history of the Navy to become the chief of naval operations, the highest ranking officer in the Navy. He was appreciated and respected by everyone who served under him. Why then did he take a .38 caliber handgun, point it at his chest, and pull the trigger? Why did he take his own life? For one reason—he couldn't forgive himself.

According to newspaper and magazine reports, Mike Boorda supposedly made the decision to wear commendation ribbons on his uniform that he didn't earn. It was an error in judgment that, in the Navy, could be punishable by court-martial. Why would such a promising leader inflict a fatal gunshot to his chest? I imagine he was embarrassed. I'm sure he feared the great sense of dishonor that would have ensued if he had been fully exposed. In the end though, one thing killed Mike Boorda—unforgiveness. It was his own inability to forgive himself that lead to his tragic death.[51]

---

50   Michaelhyatt.com (interview with Ian Cron).

51   Chris Thurman, *Lies We Believe* (Nashville: Thomas Nelson Publishers, 1999) vii.

Do you think your sin is too great to forgive? If it's not too great for God, why should it be too great for you? Maybe you're embarrassed by something you've done, or maybe you're embarrassed by something you didn't do. From your perspective, your sin seems overwhelming. Your sin might be great, but it's not greater than the grace of God. When you come to Christ and confess your sin, He promises to wipe the slate clean. He promises to give you a clear conscience. God doesn't want you to live under condemnation. He wants to forgive you and release you from your guilt. Receive His grace and forgiveness by faith. You don't have to sweat it out and try to repay God for your mistakes. In Jeremiah 31:34, God says, "I will forgive their iniquity, and I will remember their sin no more." Why should you remember something God has already forgotten? When you continue to bring up a failure in your past and habitually ask God to forgive the sin, do you know what God is thinking? He's thinking, "What sin? What sin are you talking about?" He doesn't remember your sin. He gives out grace. Try giving some to yourself.

Roger Gosnell pastored a church in my hometown. Though we didn't attend Roger's church, he was a close family friend. Roger had a son my age named Tad. Tad grew up like myself and moved away from our hometown. He was working in a convenient store at the beach. One night, early in the morning hours, a man entered the store. Tad was the only person working the night shift. The man came in with a gun and demanded that Tad give him all the money. Tad did what he was trained to do. He gave the robber the money in the register, but for some strange reason, the money wasn't enough.

The gunman pointed his pistol at Tad and pulled the trigger. It was a fatal shot. Tad died just shortly after the bullet entered his body. The authorities caught the criminal and brought him to trial. Roger, Tad's father, drove several hours to be at the trial. The man who killed Tad was convicted of robbery and murder.

Before the sentencing, the judge asked Roger if he would like to say something to the man who was guilty of murdering his son. Roger got up from his seat in the courtroom, and he made his way over to the microphone. He looked intently and directly into the eyes of the man who killed his son. In a quiet tone, Roger said, "My son was a

Christian. Many years ago, he placed his faith in Jesus Christ, and God forgave him from all his sins. Because of his faith in Christ, I know Tad is in heaven." Then, with tears in his eyes, he stated to the judge, jury, and friends in the courtroom, "I don't want this man to die." He glanced over at the man who had taken his son's life. With brokenness and grace, he uttered 3 amazing words to his son's murderer, "I forgive you." And with those 3 words, Roger walked out of the courtroom a free man.

CHAPTER 17

Everybody Needs Somebody
In The Bleachers

I PLAYED BASEBALL WITH A teammate in high school named Steve. Steve was 6'4, and weighed about 225lbs. He was an amazing baseball player. Steve played the outfield and had an unbelievable throwing arm. His offensive game at the plate was as good as his defensive game in the outfield. Steve was a slugger, and he could hit his way out of any pitch. Every year, he led our team in homeruns.

During our senior year, it was common to have 4 or 5 scouts at each game watching Steve play. I remember the Atlanta Braves scouted him heavily, and they considered drafting him out of high school. Even though Steve was a standout baseball player, his parents didn't come to any of his games. In four years of baseball, his mom and dad never came to watch him play, not a single game. I knew both of his parents; they were physically able to come to his games, but they just never did.

Almost every game Steve would ask me, "Clay, are your parents coming to the game today?" He knew the answer to the question, but he asked the same question each game. "Yes, Steve," I would say, "my parents will be here." My parents came to all the games—home and away. I don't recall my parents missing a single game.

Steve knew his parents wouldn't be there, and he wanted to know that someone else would be there to support him. Steve knew my parents would be in the bleachers, cheering for him. After each game, my dad always found Steve so He could tell him he played a good game. He would brag about a good play Steve made in the outfield or complement him on a great at bat. Often, right before Steve stepped into the batter's box, he would look up in the bleachers to make sure my parents were still there. Steve knew the moment he dug his heels in the batter's box, my parents would start to cheer for him, "Let's go Steve Let's go Steve."

Steve went on to play baseball at college. His great baseball skills earned him a scholarship. While we were both in college, we lost touch with each other. We were in separate colleges, and our paths didn't cross except when we were on break from school. One evening, I got a surprise telephone call from Steve. After a few minutes of catching up, He said, "Clay, I'm playing my last collegiate baseball game on Friday night. Do you think you could come to my last game?" I told Steve I wouldn't miss the game for anything. I drove several hours to be there, thinking the whole time that surely his mom and dad would be at his final collegiate ballgame. I arrived at the stadium, took a moment to gaze through the stands, but the sad reality was his mom and dad were no where to be found.

All Steve ever wanted was to know somebody was cheering for him. He wanted to know that somebody was in the bleachers just for him. You know what I've become convinced of? Every one of us is just like Steve. We want to know somebody is in the stands cheering for us. When we look up in the bleachers, we want to know somebody will be there waving a flag just for us.

Every day we lock eyes with people who are facing something a lot bigger than a ball game—they're facing life. Let's be honest, life can be tough. At times, life has a way of beating us down and grinding us up. It's the very reason each one of us needs someone in the bleachers just for us. I don't know anyone who doesn't need a cheering section for life.

One Way To Be Remembered

It's been said, "If you criticize me, I may not like you. If you flatter me, I may not trust you. But if you encourage me, I will never forget you." If you want me to remember you, all you have to do is encourage me. If you're in the bleachers for me, I promise, I will never forget you.

Let me introduce you to someone who spent a lot of his time sitting in bleachers. He may not have the same celebrity status as other more glamorous Bible characters, yet he is one of the most significant people in the Bible. His name is Barnabas. Actually, his real name is Joseph, but the apostles got together and changed his name to Barnabas. If ever there was an encourager par excellence, it was Barnabas. The reason his friends changed his name is because he had an extraordinary ability to encourage people. Barnabas means, "Son of Encouragement." Barnabas may be the most remembered person in the Bible. Do you know why? We don't forget encouragers.

Just about anyone who has ever accomplished anything significant tells about a moment in their lives when someone encouraged them. Scores of athletes have been on the verge of quitting, but someone came along at just the right time to encourage them. Michael Jordan was cut from his high school basketball team, but fortunately, someone came along and encouraged him to keep playing basketball. Well-known writers have submitted manuscripts to publisher after publisher, only to receive one rejection letter after another. Plenty of them were ready to stop writing until someone came along and say, "No, you can't quit. Your writing will make a difference in the world. Stay at it."

We forget a lot in life, but one thing we don't forget are the people who encouraged us at just the proper time. Several years ago when my oldest son, Graham, had brain surgery, he spent the first night in the pediatric intensive care unit. Caryn and I were able to spend most of the time right by his bedside, but there were other times when we had to wait in the ICU waiting room. The intensive care waiting room, especially for pediatrics, is unlike any other place in the world. Everyone is polite. No one is rude. Everyone is pulling for each other's family members. No one notices things like race, social classes, or educational accomplishments. Everyone is in the bleachers, pulling for each other.

One evening in the ICU waiting room, I met another dad who had a son there as well. He looked very different from me. He had tattoos all over his arms and neck. He had ring piercings everywhere, including in his nose, ears, and lips. We struck up a conversation about why we were both in the ICU waiting room. I told him that

Graham had just undergone brain surgery. Then I asked him why he was there. He told me that his son had been born several weeks ago, and many of his organs were not fully developed. The doctors were trying to save his life by methodically rebuilding his organs.

As we were talking, the differences between us didn't matter. His tattoos didn't matter to me. His ring piercings didn't matter either. None of those external things were on my radar screen. The only thing that mattered to me was that he was pulling for me. The only thing that mattered to him was that I was pulling for him. We were there to do nothing but encourage each other. When you're in the ICU waiting room, very few things matter. Image doesn't matter. Education doesn't matter. Career status doesn't matter. Fashion doesn't matter. The ICU changes everything. Suddenly, you have a laser like focus on what really matters in life. What matters is people. Though I can't recall his name, I will never forget the dad with all the tattoos. While we were logging in hours in the ICU waiting room, I needed him. Maybe he needed me, too.

Learning to be an encourager is something every one of us can learn. You don't have to be rich to be an encourager. You don't have to be a genius or have a graduate degree to be an encourager. It all comes down to your desire to add value to the people around you.

Let's take a few lessons from Mr. Encouragement himself. As the gospel was spreading, the new believers in Antioch needed someone to teach and encourage them. What better person to send than Barnabas. We learn a lot about encouragement by watching Barnabas in action.

> *"The report of this came to the ears of the church in Jerusalem, and they sent Barnabas to Antioch. When he came and saw the grace of God, he was glad, and he exhorted them all to remain faithful to the Lord with steadfast purpose, for he was a good man, full of the Holy Spirit and of faith. And a great many people were added to the Lord. So Barnabas went to Tarsus to look for Saul, and when he had found him, he brought him to Antioch. For a whole year they met with the church and taught a great many people"* (Acts 11:22-26-ESV).

Encouragers See Potential In Other People

Encouragers believe in what others can become. When Barnabas was sent to Antioch, he was going to serve these brand new followers of Christ. He went to encourage the new believers because Barnabas saw potential in them. He knew God wanted to use them to spread the good news about Christ.

This is a traceable pattern in Barnabas. You don't have to look far to find him finding potential in other people. Once after Paul was converted on the Damascus road, Paul went to Jerusalem to join the disciples there. But when he arrived in Jerusalem, the disciples didn't exactly give Paul a warm reception. They were afraid of him. They had heard about this man who had persecuted followers of The Way. The disciples were so reluctant that they basically told Paul to hit the road. Fortunately, Paul had become friends with Barnabas. In true to form fashion, Barnabas took Paul and marched him before the disciples. He put his arm around him and said, "Fellows, I can vouch for this guy. Embrace him. He's one of us."[52] Encouragers have an uncanny ability to believe in others when no one else believes in them.

At every turn, Barnabas is finding potential in unlikely candidates. On one occasion, Barnabas and Paul were planning a mission trip. Barnabas thought they needed some help, so he thought he would invite John Mark to go on the trip. Paul didn't exactly agree with Barnabas. Since John Mark defected on a previous trip, Paul saw him as a mommy's boy. He didn't think John Mark could handle the rigors of a missionary journey. Barnabas was adamant that John Mark be allowed to go on the trip. Like two bull headed men, neither man would budge.

This disagreement led them to go their separate ways. Barnabas took John Mark with him, and Paul asked Silas to be his missionary companion. Barnabas wasn't doing anything different than his customary practice. He was trying to be an encourager. He wanted to give John Mark a second chance. When no one else believed in John Mark, Barnabas believed in him.

---

52   Acts 9:27-28.

Encouragers Speak Words That Bring Life

If you've ever done a cursory reading of the book of Proverbs, you know it has so much to say about the power of words. Proverbs speaks about the destructive things our words can do, but it also speaks about the constructive things our words can do. Just to give you a flavor, here's a few of my favorite Proverbs about the tongue.

> *"Death and life are in the power of the tongue." Proverbs 18:21*

> *"The mouth of the righteous is a fountain of life." Proverbs 10:11*

> *"The lips of the righteous nourish many." Proverbs 10:21*

> *"The tongue that brings healing is a tree of life." Proverbs 15:4*

> *"Pleasant words are like a honeycomb, they are sweet to the soul and health to the bones." Proverbs 16: 24*

The writer of Proverbs says there is "life in the power of the tongue." You can give life to someone by the words you speak. Can you imagine what would happen in our marriages if we would be more conscious of speaking words that bring life to our spouses? Solomon wrote the vast majority of the proverbs, but there's another book he wrote; it's sort of like a romance novel. Solomon wrote the Song of Solomon.

All you have to do is take 15 minutes and read some in the Song of Solomon. You'll discover all this talk about the power of words was not just hot air for Solomon. He practiced what he preached. In the Song of Solomon, he spends a significant amount of time praising his wife, Shulamite. In poetic language, Solomon praises her for her beauty, her clothes, and her character. He mentions a whole host of other things that will cause you to become more excited about the Bible.

One of the simplest ways to encourage someone, especially your marriage partner, is by giving your spouse heartfelt compliments. Compliments are like magnets. You are drawn to people who praise you. Criticism repels, but praise attracts. With the power of your words, you can push your mate away, or you can become more attractive to them.

We can easily spend more time criticizing our spouse than encouraging them. In a book called, *After Every Wedding Comes a Marriage,* I like the exercise suggested for you ladies. The author included one whole chapter called, The Other Woman.[53] Only a female author could get away with that title. In the chapter, she challenges each lady to imagine what the woman who is plotting to steal their husband might say to him. That other woman might say, "You look nice in that blue shirt today." She might say, "You are such a great listener." On second thought, I need to keep this realistic. She definitely wouldn't say that. But she might say, "You're the hardest worker in the office." Imagine what that other woman would say to your husband, and compare it to what you're telling your husband. Think there's any room for improvement? Probably so! Guys, imagine what the "other man" would say to your wife. It's a two way street.

Encouragers Invest Their Lives In Other People

Barnabas chose to invest his life in the new believers at Antioch. For one whole year, Barnabas stayed in Antioch pouring his life into this new church. Encouragers make disproportionate investments in people.

We have to decide if our goal is to impress people or invest in them. It's not difficult to impress people. You can do that from a distance. If your goal is to impress people, you don't have to get close to anybody. You can impress people from a distance, but you can only invest in people up close. You have to get close enough to them to be able to serve them.

---

53   Florence and Fred Littauer, *After Every Wedding Comes A Marriage* (Harvest House Publishers, 1997).

How do you invest in people? Much the same way you invest in your retirement. You do it a little bit at a time. You have your employer take out a certain amount each week or every other week, and you invest it. Slowly, as the years unfold, your retirement grows. You don't invest a year's salary in retirement; you do it a little at a time. That's exactly how we invest in people, a little at a time. Most of us can't spend 24 hours a day with someone, but we can take small steps to encourage them.

For example, you can encourage others by serving them with a smile. When you smile at other people, you're making a conscious decision to try to offer life to other people. Have you ever noticed that when you smile at other people, they usually smile back? We enjoy doing this with babies. Try smiling at a baby. More times than not, the baby will always smile back at you. What's true for babies is also true for adults.

Your smile can be an act of service. We don't always have to have to have fuzzy feelings before we generate a smile. When you smile at others, you're making the conscious decision to encourage them. I'm not talking about painting on a plastic, Hollywood smile to make people think you never have problems. I'm not referring to a fake, but a serving smile. You consciously smile to build others up.

Something so small can go so far. This was brought home to me several years ago when we befriended a man named Henry. Henry lived in an apartment complex close to where we used to live. He often rode his bike through our neighborhood, and we started to strike up regular conversations with him. We found out Henry lived alone. He had no family in the area. He moved to our city so he could get proper treatment for his health problems.

One evening, Henry was riding through the neighborhood, and Caryn and I were sitting on the front porch. When we saw him, we invited Henry over to the porch. We visited with him for no more than about 15 minutes. After the brief visit, Henry got back on his bike and road back to his apartment. The next morning I came into my office, and surprisingly, I had a voicemail from Henry. He said, "Clay, I wanted to call and thank you for taking the time to get to know me. You'll never know how much it meant to me to be able to sit on your front porch and talk with you and your wife. I just called to say thank you."

You know why 15 minutes on the front porch meant so much to Henry? Henry was lonely. Sometimes we think we have to do something spectacular or great to encourage someone. In reality, it's usually the small things that make a big difference. It could be something as simple as 15 minutes on your porch. Mother Teresa used to say, "If you can't do great things, do little things with great love."

Encouragement helps to alleviate loneliness. Some experts say loneliness affects 75-90% of our American population. It's often thought to be a problem that only older people struggle with. The truth is loneliness is cited as one of the primary reasons teenagers commit suicide. According to one study, loneliness reaches its highest peak in people between the ages of 18 and 25. Loneliness affects married people, attractive people, rich people, and even famous people. It has reached epidemic proportions. Too many people feel like they're flying solo through life.

In Genesis 2:18, God said, "It is not good for man to be alone." That's the first thing God said after He created Adam. Everything was perfect; sin hadn't entered the world yet. God pronounced that it is not good for man to be alone. God hates loneliness. Most people hate loneliness, too. Nobody wants to be lonely. Why do you think we have solitary confinement in our prison system? It's a form of punishment. Inside of every person, we don't want to be alone. Chronic separation from others tends to lead to discouragement.

The writer of Ecclesiastes describes how encouragement often comes to us. It often comes to us through a friend, someone who refuses to allow us to stay down when we're discouraged.

"Two are better than one, because they have a good reward for their toil. For if they fall, one will lift up his fellow. But woe to him who is alone when he falls and has not another to lift him up. Again, if two lie together, they keep warm, but how can one keep warm alone? And though a man might prevail against one who is alone, two will withstand

him—-a three-fold cord is not quickly broken" (Ecc. 4:9-12, ESV).

When we have fallen, often what we need is an encouraging friend. Solomon is right on target when he says, "Everybody needs somebody to pick them up when they fall down." That's what encouraging friends do.

Elijah, the prophet of the Old Testament, knew what it was like to fall down. Thankfully, he also knew what it was like to have someone there to pick him up. Elijah had just come down the mountain from defeating the 450 prophets of Baal. He prayed and God answered. The Lord gave him a great victory on Mt. Carmel. Then, shortly after his victory party, Jezebel issued a death threat. She told Elijah that in 24 hours she was going to turn him into dog food.

Elijah ran for his life. Finally, he slumped down under a tree and while he was there, He asked God to take his life. He was falling fast. What did God do? Interestingly, God provided a meal for him, and then in the very next scene, God gave Elijah a friend named Elisha. After his new friend arrived, there's a noticeable difference in Elijah's life. He has a renewed vision for what God could do through his life.

I wonder how many Elijahs are in our neighborhoods? In our offices? In our churches? I wonder how many people are desperate for a friend like Elisha? They're waiting for an encouraging friend to say, "I know you've fallen, but I won't leave your side until you're back on your feet."

People are like batteries. They give out a negative charge and positive charge. If we're totally honest, after we are around some people, it feels like have been hit by a Mack truck. You walk away emotionally drained. Your physical energy is completely depleted. What happened? You got a negative charge.

At the same time, have you ever been around someone and when you walk away, you are energized. What happened? You received a positive charge. I'm not suggesting to get rid of all the people in your life who have a negative charge on you. Jesus will never allow that because He wants you to learn to love the unlovable. Yet, it is important to make sure you're spending time with people who are putting something into your life, rather than always taking something out of it.

Surround yourself with people who speak life into you. Samuel was one of those life speaking friends for David. When Samuel came to Jesse's house to anoint a new king, each son walked down the runway, one by one, to see which son possessed King material. After God said no to all of Jesse's sons, Samuel asked, "Jesse, do you have any more sons?" Jesse said, "Well, actually there is one more... little Dave. Dave is just a teenager, and he's out tending the sheep."

Samuel said, "Go get little Dave." David came in from the fields, and Samuel looked him right in the eye, "David, God has a great plan for your life. God has a high and holy purpose for your life. God has seen something in your heart that He likes. You have destiny a to fulfill."

I don't know if you've ever had a Samuel speak words like that to you. I don't know if you've ever had a mother or a father, grandmother or grandfather, coach or mentor, pastor or teacher who has spoken similar words to you. Just in case they haven't, let me be your Samuel. You need to hear these words, "God has a plan for your life. It's a good plan. He has a destiny for you to fulfill. Your life really matters. It matters too much to give your life to something that's insignificant."

Samuel saw what David could become. He didn't discard David because he was young. Neither did he eliminate David because he didn't have the striking appearance that some of his brothers had. The Bible says he didn't select David on the basis of his outward appearance. Samuel saw beneath the outer shell and saw what David could be. Encouragers have this enormous capacity to look beyond the surface to what God can do with a human being.

Some people never take time to build encouraging friendships. They are too busy climbing the corporate ladder. They are ever networking but never connecting. If you want to have meaningful friendships, you have to start by making it a priority. No one ever stumbles into great friendships. It is a choice. We choose to develop friendships by making time for them.

I remember one person who was bemoaning the fact that she didn't have any good friends. I started to probe, "When was the last time you picked up the phone to call someone just to say something kind to them?" She said, "It's been a long time." I asked another question, "When was the last time you invited someone out to lunch?" Her response was the same, "It's been a long time." I stopped with a third question, "When was the last time you invited a friend to go shopping with you at Wal-Mart?" I thought for sure she would score a few points here, considering that most ladies could be inducted into the Wal-Mart Hall of Fame. She answered with her same melancholy tone, "It's been a long time." The longer we talked, the more I realized she was waiting for friendships to come to her.

Friendships don't happen unintentionally. They don't forge haphazardly. We have to pursue them. If you go looking for friends, you probably won't have too many friends. However, if you go looking to be a friend, you'll probably have plenty of friends. If you go looking for someone to encourage you, you'll rarely find encouragement. However, if you go looking for someone you can encourage, like a boomerang, encouragement will come back in your direction. And not only that, but you'll be remembered by a lot of people. We don't forget the people who sit in the bleachers and call our names.

CHAPTER 18

How to Love The Jerk In Your Life

SOME TIME AGO, I WAS invited by two of my friends to shoot clay pigeons at a gun club. There were certain days the gun club allowed non-members to shoot. The only stipulation for the non-members is that you were required to shoot with a member of the gun club. Since the three of us were non-members, we found a club member and asked if we could shoot with him. He agreed, and off we went to the range.

The club member we were shooting with was shooting with a gun that cost over ten thousand dollars. As you might imagine, he was quite the marksman. He hit practically ever clay pigeon that was thrown. As for me, it was my very first time to ever shoot clay pigeons. Unlike the club member, I was shooting a gun that came from a pawn shop. I hit a few of the clay pigeons, but I missed a whole lot more than I hit.

As we continued to shoot, the club member decided to give me some pointers to improve my shooting. At first, I welcomed his shooting advice, and even his correction. After a few more minutes, though, his correction turned into cutting, sarcastic remarks. He actually started to make fun of my shooting. He said, "I hope you never get drafted into the army. We'll be in trouble if you do." "My grandmother can shoot better than that." One digging comment really got under my skin. He quipped, "Are you shooting a BB gun?"

That's when I turned around and shot him. I'm just kidding, but I have to admit the thought of mistaking him for a clay pigeon did enter my mind. The only reason I didn't pull the trigger is because I thought it might interfere with my role of being a pastor.

Ever had a jerk come bee bopping into your life? If you have lived very long at all, you've encountered some jerks yourself. As a child, perhaps you were mistreated by a school bully. Every day when you arrived at school, the school bully took your lunch money, and embarrassed you in front of your friends. Or maybe you were mistreated while you were playing a recreational sport. Even though you were the better player, you didn't play first string. The baseball coach had a son that played the same position as you. That landed you a place on the pine. Recently, a new boss has come to your department. Instead of expressing his gratitude for all you do, your new boss is constantly breathing down your neck for what you didn't do. The bully, the baseball coach, and the boss all have something in common. They make life difficult for each of us. Jerks aren't going anywhere. They're here to say.

Jesus is 100% committed to keeping some jerks in your life. About the time I get rid of one jerk in my life, God is faithful to send me a new one. You know why? God wants me to learn to love difficult people. Jesus said,

> *"You're familiar with the old written law, "Love your friend," and its unwritten companion, "Hate your enemy." I'm challenging that. I'm telling you to love your enemies. Let them bring out the best in you. If all you do is love the lovable, do you expect a bonus? Anybody can do that. If you simply say hello to those who greet you, do you expect a medal? Any run of the mill sinner does that" (Matt 5:43-47 The Message).*

When you study Jesus, you find He was such a practical teacher. He would present a truth, and then He would show how it works in real life. He was an advocate of applied theology. This is when we actually apply what we know. Some people make the mistake of knowing a lot about theology, but it's not applied theology. It's never applied to their lives; it's just intellectual information. It's like going to a shoe store and buying some shoes, but you decide only to buy one shoe for your left foot. If you have one shoe on your left foot, but you don't have one on your right foot, you're going to end up walking a little funny. You're going to end up off balance. The same thing can happen in our spiritual lives. We can know a lot about theology, but if we never apply it to life, we end up off balance. It takes the left shoe and the right shoe to be properly balanced.

To make sure you get plenty of practice at loving difficult people, God arranges plenty of situations in your life where you have to apply these verses. He wants you to wear the left shoe and the right shoe. He wants you to know the truth and apply it. It's one thing to say we love difficult people, but it's quite different to actually love them.

Here Comes A Jerk, Stay Under Control

One of the hardest commandments Jesus gave is this one, "Love your enemies— do good to them" (Luke 6:35). If you don't think this is hard, you obviously haven't tried it lately. Loving someone who is unlovable is counterintuitive and unnatural. I believe Jesus gave this commandment to drive us to God. He knew this is far beyond our pay grade. It's not something we can accomplish on our own strength. We need God's intervention to pull this off.

Jerks push our buttons. When a jerk shows up in your life, it's important to stay under control. The virtue needed most when dealing with a jerk is meekness. You read that right. I know it's a word that has a negative ring to it. If you call your boyfriend or husband meek, he will probably be insulted. We normally don't put this quality down on our resumes either. When most people think of meekness, they think of weakness. They think about someone who is passive and mild. But that's a skewed understanding of meekness.

Jesus said, "Blessed are the meek, for they shall inherit the earth." Tied up in the word meek is the idea of "power under control." The word was often used to describe a wild horse which had been broken. The horse, though it had immense power, was now under control.

When I was in my middle twenties, I helped to plant a church in Las Vegas, Nevada. Just several weeks before I left to go to Las Vegas, I met this knock out from Knoxville, Tennessee. I thought she was so gorgeous that I decided to marry her.

Since I had just met Caryn before leaving to go to Las Vegas, I wanted to fan the flames of this new relationship. So, after I arrived in Las Vegas, I wrote Caryn a letter every several days. Then, she would write me in return. This was before the day of email, texting, or cell phones. We wrote hand-written letters.

After a few weeks, I really started to miss Caryn. I put my creative energy to work and arranged for her to fly out to Las Vegas for a visit. While she was in Vegas, she stayed with an older couple who were supporting the church plant. I decided I would show Caryn the main attractions of Las Vegas and the surrounding area. We went to Caesars Palace, MGM, Hoover Dam, and many other attractions.

After she got the flavor of the bright lights of the big city, I arranged for something I thought was a bit more romantic. I arranged for us to take a horseback ride way up in the mountains, out in the desert. We had a special guide that took us up the winding trails of the rugged mountains. Interestingly, the guide put Caryn on a huge white horse. It was the biggest horse in whole fleet. He was beautiful, but the horse had a mind of his own. I think he was having a bad hair day. He was so unruly. The guide was repeatedly calling him down to try to bring him under control.

At one point during the trail ride, the horse started backing up into a bunch of thorny cactus plants. Caryn's horse was in front of my horse as the chaos started to develop. She screamed out for help, and as her new boyfriend, I wasn't exactly sure what to do. I had a quick vision of me dismounting off my horse, with my cape flying in the wind, only to run over, grabbing the reigns and saving the day. I knew this was bound to impress my new girlfriend. Just about the time I was getting ready to dismount off of my horse, suddenly the guide runs back, grabs the reigns, and proceeds to get the horse under control. I was so mad. He ruined my opportunity to impress my new girlfriend. I just sat there on my horse, stewing over the fact he had just stolen my thunder. There's only one thing worse than being on a horse that's out of control, and that's losing a golden opportunity to impress your girlfriend.

The best way to manage a horse that's out of control is for the rider to stay under control. If the horse senses you are flustered and out of control, things normally go from bad to worse. This is also the best way to manage the difficult people in your life. Even if they are out of control, you can stay under control. It's important to respond to situations instead of reacting to them. The moment we lose our control is the moment we are no longer in control.

If someone raises his voice at us, but we remain calm and collected, we are still in control of the situation. At the same time, the moment we strike back at the same decibel level as the person across from us, we are no longer in control of the situation. No wonder Scripture says, "A soft answer turns away anger." When we respond in a soft, calm manner, we're in control of the hostile atmosphere.

Victor Frankl, the famous Jewish psychiatrist, went through Auschwitz. He experienced the horrors of the Holocaust. He had everything taken from him. Reflecting back on his days in Auschwitz, Frankl said, "They took my clothes, they took my wife, they took my kids, they took my wedding ring. But the one thing they could not take was my freedom in the way I responded to them."[54]

That's one thing no one can ever take from you. You can't control how other people respond to you, but you can control how you respond to them.

I think of a lion that has been tamed. The lion weighs about 500 lbs, has claws 3 inches long, his roar can be heard for 5 miles, yet a 120 lb trainer can step into the ring with this furious animal. She usually has a little whip with her—that's all. This massive wild animal still has all of its strength, power, and teeth, but he has yielded his will to the will of his trainer. Meekness is when you yield your will to God. It's when we go to God and say, "God, tame this lion inside of me, the lion inside of me that can get so out of control so quickly. God, I yield my will to your will. Holy Spirit, I bring myself under your control."

---

54   http://www.purposedriven.com/blogs/dailyhope/index.
html?contentid=3726

Here's Comes A Jerk, Take the High Road

When someone offends us, we can respond in one of three ways. We can take the low road. This is when we treat them worse than they treated us. We can take the same road. This is when we treat them the same way they treated us. Or we can take the high road. The high road is when we respond to them with grace. We treat them a lot better than they deserve. Jesus recommended the high road.

Jesus taught us a lot about taking the high road. Jesus said, "Whoever compels you to go one mile, go with him two miles" (Matt. 5:41). In the first century, Palestine was under the control of the Romans. The Roman soldiers had the authority to command Jews to carry their back packs and other items on a whim. If you happened to be walking by, a Roman soldier could stop you and tell you to carry his possessions. You could be on the way to your own wedding, but if you were told to carry something, you were obligated to carry it for at least one mile.

When Jesus was walking down the Via Delarosa to be crucified, the Roman soldiers saw Simon, who was from Cyrene. They commanded Simon to carry the cross. He had no choice. He was obligated to carry it at least one mile.

The Jews despised being reduced down to puppets on a string. They hated this "one mile" compulsion so much they measured the exact amount of steps to equal a mile. It was one thousand steps exactly. Believe me, they counted every step. When they came to the very last step, they dropped the bag and left it for the Romans to pick up. Jesus came along and said, "If someone insists you go one mile, be willing to go two." It's where we get the expression, "Go the extra mile." Jesus is saying take the high road. Instead of reacting, try responding. Try responding in a way that reflects the love and grace of God.

Here Comes A Jerk, Get the Story Behind the Story

How can we be patient with peculiar people? One way is to get the story behind the story. When you take the time to find out about someone's background, it often increases your capacity to be patient with difficult people. As we start to look behind their behavior, suddenly some of their idiosyncrasies start to make sense. We stop saying, "Look how far they have to go," and we start saying, "Look how far they have come." Once we start to appreciate the story behind the story, we start spotting people more grace. It doesn't mean we excuse wrong behavior, but it does mean we try to understand why they do what they do.

Karen Covell is a Hollywood film producer. She's a follower of Christ, and has tried to be a positive influence for Christ in Hollywood. The executives of MSNBC wanted to do a documentary of a famous person. Karen attended a staff meeting where key executives were discussing who they might cover in the documentary. Since she was Christian, she suggested Billy Graham. The other executives shot down her suggestion in no time. The majority of the team wanted to pick someone who would raise eyebrows, so they went with Hugh Hefner. If you're looking to raise eyebrows, Hugh Hefner is a good choice. As the founder of Playboy magazine, he's been raising eyebrows for many years.

Karen was extremely bothered by the choice, but decided to make the best of it by slanting the documentary in a surprising direction. She set up the documentary to focus on why Hugh Hefner became the man that he is. During the interview, she delved into intriguing facts about his background, his upbringing, and his parents.

When the cameras started to roll, Karen couldn't believe his story. Hugh Hefner stood with Playboy bunnies all around him, answering questions about his upbringing. To her own surprise, Karen discovered Hugh was raised in a religious family. He said his parents believed in a rigid God, but he never heard much about a God of grace and love. Hugh also mentioned that his parents never told him they loved him. They never hugged him. His mother never kissed him because she had such a phobia of germs.

In the interview, Hefner told Karen about a childhood blanket. He said, "I did have a blanket though that was my security blanket. I remember holding the blanket because it was the only thing I had to hold. It had bunny rabbits all around the border I started calling it my bunny blanket."

Hugh Hefner told Karen that when he was a little boy, he wanted a puppy, but his mother refused because she said dogs spread germs. When his parents discovered Hugh had a tumor in his ear, they finally decided to let him have a puppy. Little did he know that just five days after he got the dog, his newfound friend would become deathly ill and die. He took his bunny blanket, his most precious childhood possession, and wrapped his little sick dog in his blanket. When the puppy died, his mother took his bunny blanket, the only thing that brought him security, and she burned it. His mother told him his bunny blanket had too many germs on it to keep it.

After Hugh finished recounting memories about his childhood, he closed with a heartbreaking statement. He said, "I guess I'm still just a little boy trying to find love." Karen walked away from the interview with an incredible burden for Hugh Hefner. She decided to write him a letter and also send him a Bible. She had his name, Hugh Hefner, engraved on the front cover. In the letter, Karen told Hefner that in spite of all he had accomplished, there was one person he needed to get to know, one person who would love him unconditionally—Jesus Christ. The documentary about Hugh Hefner is a telling reminder: often there really is a story behind the story. That story has a way of increasing our capacity to love and show compassion. It's certainly no excuse for Hugh Hefner's wrong choices, but it helps to explain why his story is such a sad story.[55]

Here Comes A Jerk, Try Sympathizing Instead of Criticizing

When we have a good understanding of ourselves, we tend to be less critical of others. When we pay attention to our own failures, we pay less attention to everyone else's failures. If I want to make an honest appraisal of myself, I have to take a look at "the real me."

Did you know you have two "Yous?" You have the ideal you— that's who you want to be. It's also usually the part of you that you project when you're around other people. The ideal you is the image you uphold in front of others. Then, there's the real you—that's the part of you that nobody else knows about but you. The ideal you is

---

55   Bob Reccord and Randy Singer, *Made To Count* (Nashville: Word Publishing Group, 2004), 128-131.

the one who has an argument all the way to church, but when you get to church and somebody says, "How are you doing today?" You say, "Praise God, I am so blessed. This is the day the Lord has made, I will rejoice and be glad in it." That's the ideal you— the one you project toward others.

Here's the danger between "the ideal you" and "the real you." My capacity for self-deception is so great that I can start to believe the ideal me is the real me. It's not. "The real me" is the one who screamed at my wife and kids all the way to church and then appeared to everyone else as though I'm the model husband and father. The truth is when I pay attention to the real me, I come face to face with the reality that I don't have it altogether. There's a lot inside of me that needs improvement. Living with this awareness is a great motivator for me to give grace to others. It also dramatically reduces my tendency to play the finger pointing game.

Jesus once told a story to accentuate our tendency to play the finger pointing game. In the parable, a Pharisee and tax collector go to the temple to pray. The Pharisee prays, "God, thank you I'm not like those thieves and adulterers over there." He pauses, opens his eyes, and points in the direction of the tax collector. "And God, thank you I'm not like that scum bag over there." It was clear the Pharisee thought he was morally superior to everyone else. Then, it came time for the tax collector to pray. He wouldn't even look in the direction of heaven, not to mention at anyone else. He merely stared at his feet and suddenly started to beat his chest. It was as if he was pointing the finger at himself. He prayed a simple prayer, "God, have mercy on me. I'm a sinner."

After the religious experience was over, Jesus said the tax collector, not the Pharisee, was the one who found favor in God's sight. I find it fascinating the whole time the Pharisee was praying, he wasn't focused on his own spiritual condition. He was focused on everyone else's condition. "God, I'm glad I'm not like that tax collector over there." We know what the Pharisee thought about the tax collector. What we don't know is what the tax collector thought about the Pharisee. He never mentions him. You know why? He wasn't thinking about the Pharisee. While he was praying, he was thinking about his own broken condition. "God, have mercy on me, I see my depravity. I see my sin. I see the real me. And when I look at the real me, I know I'm in desperate need of your grace and mercy."

The Pharisee was blind to his own condition. He thought he was the epitome of spirituality, but Jesus didn't think so. He was oblivious to his own sin, especially the self-righteous, condemning spirit that was ruling his life. That's one thing about the Pharisee; he had a very narrow view of sin. For him, sin was avoiding the biggies like adultery and thievery.

Pharisees were serious about avoiding the biggies. People in the first century commonly referred to the Pharisees as "blind and bleeding Pharisees." They earned the title because whenever a woman came in view, they would immediately close their eyes because they didn't want to lust. Not exactly a smart thing to do when you're walking down Main Street. Because of this, they were continually falling off curbs and running into buildings. Thus, they were blind and bleeding Pharisees. They believed as long as they kept themselves from certain things, they could maintain the right kind of heart.

Jesus had a different perspective on sin. He took the wide view of sin, rather than the narrow view. Jesus said it's possible to avoid the act of sin but be guilty of a sinful attitude. Jesus said, "Maybe you've never committed the act of adultery, but let's talk about the sinful attitude that stands behind the act. Anyone who looks at a woman to lust after her has already committed adultery in his heart." Jesus said, "Maybe you've never committed the act of murder, but let's talk about the sinful attitude behind the act. Anybody who has a deep sense of hatred toward someone has already been guilty of murder." Jesus had a very wide view of sin. So should we. A wide view of sin does wonders for our humility. When I look at my own attitudes, which are often selfish, prideful, critical, and lustful, I see enough sin in my own life not to worry about the sin in everyone else's life.

No one can say Jesus didn't have a good sense of humor. Remember when He told us not to go after the speck in our brother's eye when we have a 2 x 4 in our own eye? When Jesus first made the remark, Peter, James, and John probably fell off their camels they were laughing so hard. When Jesus told jokes, He made people laugh, but He also taught them important lessons about life. He was a left shoe, right shoe kind of a guy. Jesus wanted the disciples to apply what He was teaching them. Jesus said, "First, remove the plank that's in your own eye, then you'll be able to see clearly so you can remove the speck from your brother's eye." God wants us to consider our own sin before we start to consider someone else's sin.

It's amazing how ugly my sin looks on someone else. Have you ever noticed the same about your own sin? Somehow I find a way to rationalize my thoughts, attitudes, and actions, but I condemn those same thoughts in others. I can spot sin in other people, but like the Pharisee, I have a rough time seeing my own. Perhaps you learned the Christian cliché like I did, "Love the sinner, hate the sin." That's our Christian duty, right? I'm not so sure about that. I don't think that's the best representation of what Jesus taught. Jesus didn't teach us to "Love the sinner and hate the sin." He taught us to "Love the sinner and hate our own sin." God wants us to spend more time thinking about our sin than everybody else's sin.

Here Comes A Jerk, Maybe He's Not In The Family

When my children misbehave, I'm responsible to correct them. I correct them so they will learn from their mistakes. When the kids next door mess up, do I go over and handle their misbehavior? No! Why not? They're not my kids. They're not in my family.

Contrary to what some Christians think, it's not our responsibility to get the culture to stop sinning. That's God's job. Neither is it our responsibility to hold unbelievers to the same standard we have. Here's a paradigm shifting thought: never expect an unbeliever to act like a believer until he becomes one. Unbelievers do what they do, say what they say, and have the values they have because they don't know the God who made them and loves them.

The Bible teaches it's not my business to judge people who are outside the church. 1 Corinthians 5:12 says, "For what have I to do with judging outsiders?" Paul goes on to say we are responsible to hold people accountable who are within the church but not those who are outside the church. We want to hold our spiritual family accountable, yet we should never expect unbelievers to act like believers. We judge unbelievers all the time. We complain, whine, and bemoan about the way they talk, their morals, and their deplorable behavior. But what should we expect? Sinners sin! That's what they do. They don't have the power to change until Christ changes them.

One Tuesday evening, my wife and I went to a Duke basketball game. If you've never been to a Duke game, it's a cross between a religious experience and a rock concert. While we were at the game, occasionally, during parts of the game, the whole student section started shouting curse words in unison. These four letter words were echoing throughout Cameron Indoor Stadium. You know what my reaction was? I didn't find my heart breaking saying, "Oh God, if these people only knew how much you loved them. If they only knew the extent Christ went to demonstrate His love for them. If they only knew the purpose and plan you have for their lives." I didn't find myself thinking, "Oh God, I could be in the same situation right now apart from your grace." You know what my reaction was? After we got home, I turned to Caryn and said, "Could you believe that? Could you believe all the cursing and godless behavior in the stadium? What losers!" Later on, God convicted me about my self-righteous attitude. In a quiet way, God said, "Clay, wouldn't these be the kind of people Jesus would be spending time with? Wouldn't these be the kind of folks Jesus would be demonstrating His love to?" I put my face in my hands, and said, "Oh God, forgive me, sometimes I can be so unlike your Son." Sometimes we judge unbelievers, holding them to our standard, when we need to be reaching out to them in love.

When I was pastoring outside of Charlotte, North Carolina, I was periodically invited to lead the invocation at the city council meetings. It was nice to find out that the city council wanted to open their meetings with prayer. After I attended the council meetings a few times, I quickly got a feel for the mayor of the city. He was interesting to say the least. During the meetings, He would frequently use colorful explicatives. The mayor was also a heavy drinker. One night, this was confirmed when he came to the city council meeting inebriated. He was stumbling all over himself. After a handful of these meetings with the mayor, I was totally turned off. Then, one day, I had another pastor in our community call and invite me to lunch.

Bob Gruver, the pastor, was very involved in the community. He was an affectionate man who was often referred to as "Hugging Bob." It makes sense now because the first time I met Bob for lunch, he gave me such a strong hug I thought I was going to pass out. He's wasn't exactly a "soft" guy either. He flew fighter planes during the Desert Storm conflict in Iraq.

While we were eating lunch, somehow the topic of conversation turned to the mayor. I was pretty much giving the mayor a verbal beating par excel lance. I said, "I can't believe the mayor of our city. I'm embarrassed that he's our mayor. We've got to get him out of office." I went on and on complaining about the character and conduct of our mayor. When I finally stopped swinging my verbal stick, Bob Gruver glanced up at me with what looked to be a tear in his eye. With gentleness and respect in his voice, he said, "Clay, maybe God will use you to the love the mayor all the way to Jesus. Maybe God brought you to our city to love the mayor into the Kingdom."

I knew I was busted. I knew Bob was right. I knew my attitude was childish. I wanted to crawl under the table. In my mind, I had written the mayor off because of his behavior. I didn't want to associate with him because his behavior made me feel uncomfortable. After Bob's gracious rebuke, I never looked at the mayor the same way. God used my lunch with Bob to give me a major attitude adjustment. The mayor became someone I wanted to spend time with.

We have to try to see people the way Jesus saw them. Jesus loved everyone before they were lovable. Jesus was more concerned about where they were headed than where they were when He found them. He saw people, not for what they were, but for what they could become if they were redeemed. You never know. If you treat the jerk in your life with the right attitude, you may help him take one more step in the direction of heaven.

Decision 7: Will I Live For What Matters Today?

CHAPTER 19

What To Think about Pigs and Priorities

SEVERAL YEARS AGO, I WAS having breakfast with a member of my church, a world-renowned cardiologist. He is known around the world for his medical inventions. As we sat down for breakfast, I found it somewhat fascinating that the doctor ordered bacon for breakfast.

For years, my father, who owns a health club, has been telling me, "Clay, every day, eat five servings of fruits and vegetables." Thus, we have public health campaigns called, *The Five a Day for Better Health* plan. So when I sat down to have breakfast with a world-renowned cardiologist, I was expecting an order of eggs and fruit. I was thoroughly surprised when the doctor ordered bacon.

At first, I thought, "Maybe the doc is splurging today, after all it's an occasion to celebrate— he's having breakfast with his pastor." I have to admit when this heart expert ordered a side dish of bacon, I became mesmerized. I took one of those pastoral risks that all great leaders have to take from time to time. I asked, "Did you just order bacon?" He said, "Yes." I took another risk. I said, "I've often heard that bacon isn't very good for us." He responded, "Actually, it's not that big of a deal in moderation." He went on to elaborate… "The scientific research seems to suggest we should be more worried about carbohydrates than a little bit of bacon."

Now, I was really confused. I had changed my diet 4 years earlier to tackle some major stomach problems. One of the things I eliminated was bacon. Now, one of the top cardiologists in the world tells me that a small portion of bacon is not as bad as a big mound of mashed potatoes. Herein lies the great dilemma. What should a man believe when it comes to diet? There's the Atkins diet which says you can have unlimited amounts of meat, butter, and eggs. There's the South Beach diet which says that certain meats are bad for you. Then, there's the Grapefruit Diet, Rice Diet, 17 Day Diet, and my favorite of all, the Cabbage Soup Diet. Each diet cites scientific research supporting the superior benefits of each diet. We're back to the million dollar question, "What should a man believe when it comes to diet?" With so many voices, the water can get murky.

Choosing our priorities can be just as confusing as deciding what we should or shouldn't eat. With so many things vying for our attention, it's easy to veer off course with misaligned priorities. One wrong move with our priorities could be far more costly than eating a side order of bacon. In fact, thanks to a little time with a world renowned cardiologist, my perception of bacon has changed some. Now I know that occasionally eating a country ham biscuit probably won't increase my mortality rate at an unprecedented speed. I can celebrate the pig after all. I'm glad the doctor cleared up my confusion.

That's my goal for this chapter—to clear up any confusion we may have about priorities. Let me state the obvious: it's impossible to be number one in every area of life. We're often told, "You can have it all, and all at one time." We're told we can be number one on the golf course, number one at the office, number one at home, and number one in the community. It's the myth of "having it all and all at one time." The truth is you can't have it all. You have to decide what part of the "all" really matters. You don't have time for everything. And everything is not of equal worth. The most important thing you will ever do is to decide where you want to be number one.

Speaking of world renowned doctors, one of the greatest events of medical history happened years ago by a man named Evan O'Neil Cane. Dr. Cane was a skilled surgeon who theorized that there were certain surgeries that could be done faster, quicker, and more effective with local anesthesia as opposed to general anesthesia. It was a great theory, but every time Dr. Cane asked for volunteers to test the theory, no one would volunteer.

One night, a patient showed up with extreme abdominal pain. The patient gave Dr. Cane permission to try a saddle block in the mid region area of the abdomen. This allowed Dr. Cane the opportunity to perform exploratory surgery. The saddle block was administered, and then he took his well-defined scalpel and started to cut. Dr. Cane discovered that the patient's appendix had ruptured, and gangrene had already started to set in. With his incredible hands, Dr. Cane took out the diseased organ and cleared out the gangrene. Then, as only a skilled surgeon could do, he sewed the patient's body back together. The surgery was done, and it was successful.

The most amazing thing about this surgery was not that the surgery had been performed with local anesthesia; it wasn't that the surgery was performed by a skilled surgeon at a reputable hospital; the most amazing thing about this surgery was that on this particular night, Dr. Cane was both the surgeon and the patient. Dr. Cane performed surgery on his own body. Today it still stands as one of the most amazing medical stories ever recorded.

Here lies a great secret to managing your priorities. You are the only one who can perform surgery on your own priorities. You are the doctor and the patient. No one can truly evaluate your priorities like you. Other people can give you feedback about what they perceive your priorities to be, but you are the only one who can take out the scalpel and remove things that shouldn't be there.

A good place to start is by looking at how you spend your time and how you spend your money. Your calendar and your checkbook reveal volumes about your priorities. If you followed me for one week and took scrupulous notes on how I spent my time and money, you would get a good idea about my priorities.

Choosing Between the Good and the Best

In Luke 10, we meet a woman whose life is a little lopsided; her priorities were out of line. One day Jesus came to visit Mary and Martha in their home. The Bible says, "Martha was distracted by her many tasks." The Bible doesn't say Martha was defiant; neither does it say she was rebellious, or guilty of egregious sin. The adjective used to describe her is straightforward— she's distracted.

Martha came to Jesus and asked, "Lord, don't you care that my sister has left me to do all the work by myself? Tell her to get in the kitchen and help me slave over this spaghetti." Earlier, Mary had gone and sat at the feet of Jesus. Undoubtedly, Martha was outraged that Mary left her to do all the grunt work in the kitchen. Jesus said, "Martha, only one thing is needed, and Mary has chosen what is best."

Let's give it to Martha. She was trying to be hospitable. She took the initiative in inviting Jesus into her home. She knew there were no Hampton Inns or Marriott's in the area. Martha had good intentions by opening her home to Jesus. When Jesus finally arrives, she immediately started slaving in the kitchen. She was determined to dazzle Jesus with a world class dish of spaghetti. Let's give credit where credit is due; she was at least trying to be a good hostess. Martha had good intentions, but Mary was the one who had the right priorities. When we set our priorities, we're usually not choosing between good and bad things; we're choosing between the good and the best. Martha was doing some good things, but Mary had chosen what was best.

I rarely meet people whose lives are fouled up, but I do regularly meet people who just aren't focused. It's not that they are living for wrong things; they're simply living for frivolous things. Like Martha, they're distracted. I remember one presidential race where two candidates continued to debate about family values. But they could never agree what family values are. I think there is a reason for that. There's no such thing as family values. There are only life values. The same values that make you a great husband are the same values that make you a great employee, a great citizen, and a great friend. Your life values determine your priorities. When your values are properly aligned, your priorities will fall in line as well.

This is what Bob Russell calls a "top button truth." When you're buttoning your shirt, if you get the top button right, all the other buttons will fall into place as well. If, however, you miss the top button, none of the other buttons will be in place. Your values serve as the top button for your life. Do you know what's really running your life? It's your values. This is why it's so important to determine your values in life. Your core values are going to drive your life.

When your core values are correct, your priorities will naturally fall into place.

The Core Value of Relationships

If you've ever worked in retail, you know that shoplifting is a big problem. The U.S. Department of Commerce estimates that 35 million people shoplift every year. They estimate that at least one in every fifty-two customers in the average American business will attempt to shoplift. Out of the 35 million shoplifters, only about 5 million are caught shoplifting.

Sometimes we complain about why things are priced so high. One reason is that business owners have to factor in a certain percentage just to cover their loss of merchandise. Since I grew up working in my father's sporting goods store, it didn't take me long to figure out that shoplifting was a big problem. Sometimes people who wanted to steal went about it in a more sophisticated way. One of the problems we had is that customers would come in and they would change the price tags on merchandise. This was before the day of bar codes, so it's a little harder to do today. The would-be thief would take the price tag off of a pair of socks that cost $7.00 and he would put the price tag on a shirt that was supposed to cost $17.00.

Given this problem, it was important for each clerk to have a good idea about the cost of the merchandise. Every clerk needed to know that the t-shirts were more valuable than the socks. Each employee needed to know the tennis shoes were more valuable than the t-shirts. If you didn't have an idea of what products were more valuable than other products, you could be ripped off and never know it.

In life, it's common for people to end up putting the wrong price tags on the wrong things. Some people put a higher price tag on their achievements than their relationships. But we know our relationships are far more important than our achievements. Failing to put the right value on the right things could translate into a long list of regrets.

If a doctor told you that you only had several days to live, at that very moment, the most important thing in your life wouldn't be your paycheck; it wouldn't be the size of your retirement fund; it wouldn't be the size of your company; it wouldn't be the initials to the right of your name. At a sobering moment like that, the one thing that would take a giant leap forward on your priority list would be your relationships. Nothing in life should have a higher price tag than our relationships.

As a pastor, I've been called to the bedside of a number of people who were in their final moments of life, and I have never heard anyone say, "Bring my diplomas. I want to look at them one more time." I've never heard anyone say, "Bring me my sales awards, or bring me my Rolex watch. Could you bring me the books that bear my name?" When life on earth is coming to an end, I've heard the same thing again and again, "Bring me the people I love the most. Bring me my friends; bring me my family." Don't wait until your deathbed to realize that relationships are the most valuable part of life. It will be too late then.

We say relationships are more important than anything else, but we constantly cheat relationships for the sake of work and money. Especially as men, we tend to overlook the importance of strong relationships. Did you know 80% of all suicides are committed by men? There are different theories as to why this is the case. One of the most prominent theories is that men don't have as many close relationships as women. Men tend to have fewer genuine friends than women, and they often think they can make sense out of life without great relationships. It's a false notion that has piercing consequences.

Some people fail to make relationships a priority because they don't make time for them. They seldom cultivate friendships because they are too busy achieving. They may have a long list of contacts on their i Phone, but not one single friend. If we want to have meaningful relationships and friendships, we have to start by making it a priority. It comes back to carving out time for what matters most in life. No one ever has deep friendships by chance. Friendships don't just happen. If you ever meet people who seem to have deep, long term friendships, it's not because they are lucky. It's has nothing to do with luck. It's a choice. We choose to develop relationships by making time for them.

The Core Value of Forgiveness

Maybe you've noticed a common denominator in all of humanity. We're imperfect. That also applies to followers of Christ. Everybody has flaws, quirks, idiosyncrasies, bad habits, junk and yes, plain old-fashioned sin. Given this fact about human nature, everyone around us needs grace from us.

When you are offended, how good are you at letting it go? Jesus said something interesting about offenses. In Matthew 18:7, Jesus said, "Woe to the world because of offenses. For offenses must come, but woe to that man by whom the offense comes." Jesus is telling us straight up that offenses will come.

People offend us by what they do. People offend us by what they don't do. People offend us without even knowing they offended us. Some offenses are accidental; others are intentional. Jesus said life is going to set up plenty of occasions where we're going to feel offended. This is why it is so important not to be easily offended. If you are easily offended by every little misstep or misspoken word, you will never be a happy person. Learn to shake off the offenses by giving the offender the benefit of the doubt. Accept them in their fallen condition. At some point, we have to let it go and decide to give people grace.

Who is it in your life that you still have on the hook? Who is it that you need to forgive? Maybe it's your spouse? Every time your spouse does something or says something you don't like, do you pull out something from the past and hang it over them? Do you use the failure as ammunition? Such a habit is a great way to kill a marriage. In marriage, if you never show mercy to your spouse, before long, your marriage will shrivel up and die.

In marriage, you see the best of someone and the worst of someone. You have a front row seat to their wonderful qualities and their irritating qualities. You have a front row seat to their selfishness, bad attitudes, and their failures. When the worst comes out of them, you have to decide you're not going to nail them to the wall each time. I believe 75% of all marriage conflicts could be resolved if we decided to show mercy to our spouses when they blow it. At some point, you have to decide to accept your spouse, including the good, the bad, and the ugly. It is a high watermark moment when you realize you will never be able to change your spouse. That's something only God can do.

Remember Pavlov's dog. Pavlov was the Russian scientist who would ring a bell before he fed his dogs. At first, the dogs would start salivating when they saw the food. Over time, though, the dogs associated the sound of the bell with food, and they started to salivate the moment they heard the bell. This response came to be called a "conditioned response." I know we have to be careful with animal analogies. You and I are not animals, but the exact same thing can happen in human beings. We can develop a conditioned response to offenses. When someone hurts our feelings, we can decide to nurse the offense. Deciding to nurse offenses can become our default mode for handling people who disappoint us. We can decide to hold a grudge but not without the grudge holding us. The grudge places us in a self-imposed prison.

When we're offended, it's possible to develop a conditioned response of forgiveness. Jesus taught us to pray in the Lord's Prayer, "Forgive us as we forgive our debtors." The little word "as" is perhaps one of the most important words in the whole Bible. In the prayer, we're asking God to forgive us in the same manner we forgive others. We want there to be a correlation on how much grace God gives us in direct proportion to the amount of grace we give others. The measuring rod we use toward others will be the measuring rod God uses toward us.

The Last 5 Minutes of Life

One of the saddest stories in the Bible is in 1 Kings. It's a tragic story about David when he was on his deathbed. Because of his declining health, David knows he is getting ready to die. David calls Solomon, his son, into his bedroom. It is the last time David has a one on one conversation with his son. David wants to give Solomon some advice before he leaves earth. For all practical purposes, this is his last will and testament. David looks at Solomon and speaks some surprising words, "Son, whatever you do, don't let Joab die without paying him back. Make sure before Joab goes to his grave that you pay him back for the pain he has caused me." David has been holding on to a grudge all these years; it dates back to years earlier when David felt Joab wronged him.

In the final hours of his life, David is determined to settle the score. I think about how David's life could have ended. David could have called Solomon to his bedside. He could have spoken different words, "Son, I'm getting ready to die. I'm going to meet my Maker. Son, I want you to know something. Remember Joab, the man who did me so much harm? Well, I've turned him over to God, and I have forgiven Him. Whatever you do, don't spend the rest of your life trying to pay him back." Imagine the impact that would have had on Solomon. Unfortunately, that's not the way David died.

Jonathan Edwards was a brilliant man. Some have said he had the greatest mind America has ever known. Jonathan Edwards was an accomplished theologian; at one point, he also served as the president at Princeton. Edwards developed what he called "Resolutions." The list contained pithy axioms and resolutions he was determined to live by. One of his resolutions went like this: "I am resolved not to say anything or do anything that I would not do if it were the last 5 minutes of my life." Let that sink in for a moment.

Talk about minimizing your life regrets. Jonathan Edwards didn't want to do anything that he would not do if it were the last 5 minutes of his life. If we were in the last 5 minutes of life, getting ready to face God, I know one thing none of us would do. We wouldn't withhold forgiveness from someone who needed it. Remember the "as." "Forgive us as we forgive our debtors." When I meet my Maker, I know I will need His grace and forgiveness. In a mysterious and unexplainable way, by withholding forgiveness from someone else, I could be limiting the amount of grace I receive when I really need it. Live with the "as" in mind.

The Core Value of Integrity

Have you ever had a piece of equipment where everything seemed to work with the exception of one little defect. Several years ago, my laptop had a letter on the keyboard that was on the blink. Everything was fine until I had to type words that contained the letter. My spell check was running in overdrive because I could barely compose half a sentence without misspelling a word. That one defective letter paralyzed my ability to write. That's how it works with our character. It only takes one small defect, one mistake, or one slip up, and our character is damaged.

Daniel was around sixteen years old when he was exiled to live in Babylon (modern day Iraq). The new King of Babylon, Darius, really liked Daniel. Daniel essentially became the teacher's pet, and Darius was considering promoting Daniel to the highest position in the Kingdom. This didn't go over so well with some of the others serving in the King's administration. Because they were jealous of Daniel, they tried to find a hole in Daniel's character and work, to no avail. In fact, Daniel is described in Scripture as man "in whom there was no defect."

Daniel's integrity and character were sparkling clean. Because they couldn't find a flaw in Daniel's character, his jealous co-workers tried to set a booby trap for him. They conned the King into establishing a decree that made everyone pray to the King for 30 days. It became law, and everyone knew breaking the King's law would have severe consequences. So what did Daniel do? He kept on praying to the God of Israel. He didn't compromise his convictions, even if it meant being thrown into a den of hungry lions. He refused to compromise his integrity.

Integrity is standing up for what's right, even when no one else does. When King Darius gave the decree that no one could pray to anyone but him, everybody stopped praying. There were a lot of other Jews who could have kept praying to the God of Israel. Daniel wasn't the only Jew in captivity. Yet, the Bible doesn't mention anyone who continued to pray to the one true God with the exception of Daniel. Daniel stood up for what was right when no one else did. Integrity means you don't look for a majority vote before you do what's right.

In the first century, the gladiatorial games were a part of Roman entertainment. The gladiatorial games were held in the Roman coliseum, where two gladiators would fight. The crowd watching the event would decide the winner. The loser of the games was literally at the mercy of the crowd. If the crowd gave the thumbs up sign, the loser retained his life, but if they gave the thumbs down sign, he lost his life. But then Telemachus came on the scene.

Telemachus was grieved over the violence and the inhuman nature of the gladiatorial games. One day, the people were gathered in the coliseum watching the gladiators fight. As usual, one of the gladiators prevailed. In trademark fashion, the crowd gave the thumbs down sign which meant they wanted the loser to die by the sword. The gladiator raised his sword to run through his opponent's body. Suddenly, Telemachus jumped out of the stands, ran down to the field, and stood between the two gladiators. He said, "In the name of Jesus Christ, stop!"

While Telemachus stood between the two gladiators, the audience became outraged that he was interfering with their bloody pastime. The people in the coliseum started to hurl stones in his direction. In the end, the stones crushed and pulverized his body. There, on the surface of the open coliseum, Telemachus died. The common observer may have thought Telemachus was the one who really lost that day. I would disagree. Telemachus didn't lose because there was God in heaven giving him the thumb's up sign. The crowds filed out of the coliseum that day, and they didn't know it at the time, but that would be the last time the gladiators would ever kill each other again. Honorius, bishop of Rome, was so impressed with his martyrdom that he issued a ban on all gladiator fights. When Telemachus took his stand for what was right, it spelled the death sentence for the gladiatorial games. By standing up for what is right, you may accomplish far more than you intended at the moment. Your one decision may create ripples that cascade throughout history.[56]

---

56   http://orthodoxwiki.org/Telemachus

CHAPTER 20

How To Get The Most Out Of Life

JESUS IS NOT A LIAR. That's why those red letters in your Bible are so important. When Jesus speaks, we should listen. I'm far more likely to mess up my life than Jesus is. Jesus tells me what's really important. In fact, the most important thing in life is to determine what's most important. Jesus helps us out here.

One afternoon, a scribe approached Jesus with a question. As Bible scholars, scribes were routinely giving out answers to questions about the Bible. But this time, the scribe has a question himself. He asked, "Jesus, of all the commandments in the Bible, which one is the most important?" Interestingly, Jesus answers the question. He didn't say, "There's not a commandment more important than the others." Neither did Jesus say, "I can't answer that because everything in the Bible is equally important."

Jesus went on to select a particular commandment He believed was more important than the other commandments. This is because though everything in the Bible is equally inspired, everything in the Bible is not equally important. Jesus said here's the commandment I consider the most important, "And you shall love the Lord your God with all your heart, and with all your soul and with all your mind, and with all your strength..." According to Jesus, this is the most important commandment in the Bible. This is what matters most in life—Loving God. If you get this commandment right, you'll get most of life right.

Don't speed by this deep truth. It's possible for you to love God. This is what distinguishes you from the animal kingdom, or from plant life. You can receive love from God, and you can express love to God.

In the very first chapter of the Bible, God is busy creating the world for six days. He created the sun, moon, and the stars. God made the plant life, and animal kingdom, and then He came to the crowning achievement of creation. God made man. In Genesis 1:26 God says, "Let us make man in our image, according to our likeness." This is what differentiates us, as homo sapiens, from plant life and animal life. We are made in the image of God.

This primarily means we were created so we can have a relationship with God. A plant or an animal can't have a relationship with God. God certainly designed plants and animals to accomplish His purposes while they are on earth, but they were never designed to relate to God. They don't have souls. But when God made you, He made you in His image, with a living soul. There is more to you than the flesh on your bones. You are not just a physical being; you are a spiritual being, and you have a physical dimension as well.

Jesus took out the guess work. When we're ordering our priorities, the one that is supposed to be in first place is the priority of loving God. Since we're supposed to structure life around loving God, we should probably have an idea of what loving God looks like. We're going to get there, but before we do, it's important to point out what loving God is not.

Loving God Is Not Being Religious

If you can't get along with Jesus, the problem is not with Jesus. In the New Testament, there's a group of people who are constantly colliding with Jesus, the infamous Pharisees. In their day, the Pharisees were highly respected because they were so religious, but ironically, Jesus was never impressed. Jesus saw through all their pomp and circumstance. He saw the true condition of their hearts.

Jesus had a special name He liked to call the Pharisees. We use it today, but it had more punch back when Jesus used it. Jesus often called them "hypocrites." The word was actually a theatrical word. In the first century, one person would play many parts in a performance. An actor would come out wearing one particular mask so he could play one part, then he would go back stage, put on another mask, and play an entirely different part. The person playing these different parts was called the hypocrite.

Jesus took this theatrical term and branded the Pharisees with it. Jesus was saying, "You're playing a part, wearing a mask, and striking a pose." Jesus saved His most scathing remarks for the Pharisees because their religion was a Broadway show.

Jesus wants us to know it's possible to be religious and not love God. In Luke 10, Jesus tells one of His most famous stories. We call it the story of The Good Samaritan. The story is about some not so good religious people.

In the famous story, a man is traveling from Jerusalem to Jericho on what was commonly called the Jericho Road. While he's traveling down the road, he is robbed, beaten, and left to die. While he is lying in the road, in desperate need of help, three different people walk by. A priest walks by. A Levite walks by. A Samaritan man walks by. But only the Samaritan man stops to help the injured man.

If the story was only intended to teach a lesson about compassion, Jesus didn't need the priest and Levite in the story. He could have told the story about the man who was robbed and beaten, and lo and behold, there came a Samaritan to save the day, but that's not all Jesus wanted us to know from the story. Therefore, He introduced two religious people who didn't stop to help the man.

The priest was the first person to pass the injured man. Perhaps he was walking down this same Jericho Road because he was on his way to an inductive Bible study. To stop and help the desperate man would mean he would have to miss his Bible study. What would the people around him think if he missed his weekly Bible study? He decides to walk on by.

Jesus introduces us to another man in the story, another religious man. The Levite was walking down the same Jericho Road, probably on his way back to Jerusalem. Perhaps he had a special committee meeting back at the temple, since Levites had responsibilities at the temple. Nonetheless, the Levite saw the man on the road, bleeding and dying, but he ignored the injured man, and he walked right on by.

Why would Jesus include the priest and Levite in the story? Jesus didn't need them in the story to drive home the message of compassion. He only needed the Samaritan who stopped and helped the wounded man. However, in the story, Jesus included the religious people who refused to stop and help the injured man. Jesus is giving us a tall truth in his short story. If we're not careful, religion can keep us from truly loving God. It can also keep us from truly loving other people, which is the ultimate expression of our love for God.

We can get so busy with Bible studies, retreats, and church activities that we walk right by the people God wants us to serve. We can become so sidetracked with religious activities we fail to do the one thing that matters most in life—loving God by loving other people. The Pharisees were deeply devoted. They prayed long and hard. They fasted every Monday and Wednesday. They tithed off of everything they received. They followed every ritual to the tenth degree. However, they never broke out of their system of religion so they could truly love God.

Loving God is Not Keeping Rules

The reason Jesus had such a tough time with the Pharisees is because they were legalists. They lived and died by their list of do's and don'ts. Legalism reduces faith down to a checklist.

The Pharisees went through the Old Testament and meticulously counted 613 commandments. Of these, 356 of them were negative commands, things they shouldn't do. The other 248 commands were positive commandments, things they should do. The Pharisees even categorized the commandments. The commandments were classified as being either heavy or light. The heavy ones were considered to be the most important to obey. The light commands were less important.

The Pharisees were notorious for taking a principle of Scripture and then adding a lot of rules to go along with it. For example, the Old Testament taught to "Remember the Sabbath day, to keep it holy," so the Pharisees took the Sabbath principle and developed a list of 1,521 things you could not do on the Sabbath. You couldn't rescue a drowning person on the Sabbath because you would have to work to get him out of the water. You couldn't cook on the Sabbath. Here's one for you you couldn't kill a mosquito on the Sabbath because it would require you to exert some energy, thus making it work.

Legalists in our day do exactly the same thing. They take a principle of Scripture, and then add a lot of rules to go along with it. I could cite plenty of examples, but I'll limit myself to one I encounter occasionally. For some strange reason, legalism tends to migrate toward a specific gender—females. I'm sorry; it just happens that way. Here's a passage that gets twisted into a list of do's and don'ts.

> *"Likewise, wives, be subject to your own husbands, so that even if some do not obey the word, they may be won without a word by the conduct of their wives, when they see your respectful and pure conduct. Do not let your adorning be external---the braiding of hair and the putting on of gold jewelry, or the clothing you wear"* (**1 Peter 3:1-3, ESV**).

There are several biblical principles in this text, but one of the dominant ones relates to modesty. Peter is encouraging Christian women to be modest in their outward appearance. Most everyone, including you ladies, would embrace this wholeheartedly. The general principle of modesty is not a problem, but here's where the problem comes in. The legalist comes along, takes this biblical principle, and makes some very specific applications with it. Applications go like this, "Women shouldn't wear make up"; "Women shouldn't wear pants"; "Women shouldn't wear shorts"; "Women shouldn't wear tank tops." Really? I keep reading this passage, but I can't find these rules. They are conspicuously absent from the text. The principle of modesty is present, but all these other rules are not spelled out.

Legalists also fall into the trap of applying the Bible selectively. In the words of Marilynne Robinson, "People who insist that the sacredness of Scripture depends on belief in creation in a literal six days seem never to insist on a literal reading of 'to him who asks, give,' or 'sell what you have and give the money to the poor.' "

Legalism doesn't come from the doctrines of the Bible; legalism comes from the application of those doctrines. What happens is that good truth is applied in the wrong way. When good truth is applied the wrong way, you get legalism. The problem with some Christians is they take the Bible farther than the Bible goes. Let's go as far as the Bible goes and no farther. You can find Christian colleges in our country that tell the students they can't hold hands with their boyfriend or girlfriend. If they do, they're written up. After enough times of holding your boyfriend's hand, you might just get expelled from school. I've never encountered such a commandment in the Bible.

Legalism leaves no latitude and room for gray areas. Legalism says every act, every habit, and every type of behavior is either white or black, right or wrong. Legalists classify things as being sinful or not sinful whether the Bible mentions them or not. There are no gray areas. There's also no room and no latitude to disagree on secondary doctrinal issues. You have to believe exactly just like the person next to you.

The truth is there is room for us to disagree about secondary doctrinal issues. We don't debate or negotiate about primary doctrine. The deity of Christ is not up for debate. The authority of Scripture is not up for debate. The substitutionary death of Christ for our sins is not up for negotiation. The bodily resurrection of Jesus is a non-debatable issue. The historic truths of our faith are fixed. Yet, the healthiest Christians down through the centuries have provided latitude to disagree with other believers about secondary doctrinal issues.

One of the church fathers said it best, "In the essentials, we have unity. In the nonessentials, we have liberty (the freedom to disagree), but in all things we have charity." When we draw battle lines over secondary doctrinal issues, it's confusing. From an outsider looking in, the whole thing can leave us scratching our heads. Let's start with denominational tags, which typically revolve around secondary doctrinal matters. Baptist, Methodist, Presbyterian, Pentecostal, Catholic, Assemblies of God, Non-denominational, and the beat goes on…Though I pastor a church affiliated with a denomination, I have to admit, the denominational labels can be puzzling, especially to the unchurched.

For several years, Shelley, a middle-aged woman, attended the church I pastor. After about a year, she became a Christ-follower. Though she had a Mormon background, she came to our worship services for a full year, and the whole time, Shelley was investigating the claims of Christ. The day came when Shelley stepped across the line for Christ. Just before her baptism, she sent me an e-mail. She said, "Pastor Clay, now that I'm following Christ, I've noticed Jesus said a lot about unity in the Bible. Can you explain the reasons why we have so many different kinds of Christian churches?" Of course, the differences typically revolve around secondary doctrinal issues. But I found myself somewhat embarrassed and uncomfortable that I even had to respond to the question. If it was confusing to Shelley, a new believer, just imagine how confusing this is to the average unchurched person.

Martin Luther said the church is often like a drunk man who is trying to ride a horse. After riding for a while, he falls off the left side of the horse. He gets back on the horse and goes a little further, then falls off the right side of horse. Luther said the church has this same tendency. We find it difficult to stay balanced. We either fall to an extreme left which is liberalism, or we fall to an extreme right which is legalism. Both extremes are dangerous. The healthiest believers I know can hold the great truths of Scripture in balance. Shortly after his conversion, C.S. Lewis wrote to a friend, "When all is said about divisions of Christendom, there remains, by God's mercy, an enormous common ground."[57]

Missing What Matters Most

I've heard countless people express regrets about life. They get to the end of their days only to express deep regrets about the way they've managed their priorities. Usually it comes out this way, "How could I miss the one thing in life that matters the most?" Yet it happens all the time.

----

57   *A Mind Awake: An Anthology of C.S. Lewis*, ed. Clyde Kilby (New York: Harcourt Brace Jovanovich, 1980), 128.

Ask the CEO Jesus once called a fool. When Jesus called someone a fool, it wasn't because he had a low IQ. It was because he was unwise, never thinking about where his decisions were taking him. This CEO was prospering so much he didn't know what to do with the all the extra grain he had. He decided to tear down his smaller barns, and build bigger and better barns. For some strange reason, he never thought about building someone else a barn. He kept everything for himself. God appears to him and tells him it's his last day on earth. His final number is being punched. God says, "You fool. You built your own little empire, but you never got around to what matters most. You were rich, but not rich toward God."

Epictetus, first century Greek philosopher, summed up our human condition. Epictetus said, "This is our predicament. Over and over again, we lose sight of what is important and what isn't." No one deliberately decides to miss out on what matters most in life. Perhaps God was even listed on the CEO's list of priorities. He probably thought, "When life slows down, I'll eventually get around to what matters most. I'll eventually devote myself to loving God." He probably had God somewhere on his list of priorities. He soon discovered it's a lot easier to list our priorities than it is to live our priorities. To make loving God our number one priority, it's important to build a few disciplines into the rhythm and structure of our lives.

Loving God by Applying Scripture

There is an enormous difference in reading the Bible for transformation and reading it for information. When the goal of the reading the Bible is simply to acquire information, we miss the whole point of the Bible. The Bible wasn't given for information; it was given for transformation. Romans 12:2 says, "Don't be conformed to this world, but be transformed by the renewing of your mind." When we come to the Bible with a sincere desire to apply it, it transforms us.

Biblical knowledge, doctrinal clarity, and theological understanding are very important. They're essential for us to be well-rounded believers. Our knowledge, though, has to go hand in hand with our desire to be changed by the Bible. If you want a picture of a changed life, don't always look for the Bible-answer person. Look for the person who has rearranged their attitudes, values, decisions, finances, and marriage around the Bible. Look for someone who applies the truth.

I used to be impressed by people who knew their Bibles like the back of their hands. If someone could quote one Scripture after another, I used to be razzled and dazzled by it. I used to equate knowledge with depth. Then I started to meet people who had a lot of Bible knowledge, but they were mean as snakes. They had bad attitudes. They were judgmental and critical of others, and at first, it was very confusing to me. I came to understand Bible knowledge doesn't automatically get translated into Christ-likeness.

When I was in seminary, one afternoon I parked my car in a certain lot on the campus. Parking was really tight; the cars were parked side by side, with very little distance between each car. I parked my car, attended my afternoon classes, and then returned to my car at the end of the day. When I arrived at my car, I found a note on my windshield from another seminary student. The note read, "If you ever park this close to my car again, I'll slash all 4 of your tires."

Keep in mind the note was left by a seminary student. Just think—he's someone's pastor today. This is a guy who had an incredible amount of knowledge about the Bible. Most likely, he knew Greek and Hebrew. He had classes in Systematic Theology, Church History, and Christian Ethics. Yet, something tells me he had a few things that needed to be settled in his heart.

It's possible to be filled with a head full of knowledge about the Bible but never be transformed by it. It takes applying Scripture to be changed by it. Jesus said, "You shall know the truth and the truth shall set you free" (John 8:32). The truth does set us free, but most of the time it makes us miserable first. The Word of God opens us up, exposes our motives, points out our faults, rebukes our sin, and shows us where we need to change.

To apply Scripture, we have to develop the discipline of reading the Bible regularly. The good news is we are all disciplined, just in different areas. You may be disciplined with your exercise program.

You wouldn't let anything get in the way between you and your treadmill. You could be disciplined in your career. You arrive promptly, work diligently, and know that giving 99% on the job is 1% short. What if you applied the same level of discipline toward applying God's Word?

Here's a simple suggestion as you start the process. Don't set a goal of how much you have to read in the Bible each day. If you set a goal of reading 5 chapters every day, you'll probably never stop and think about the things you are reading. Instead of the time being encouraging, it will become like the number of sits up you have to do. You'll find yourself trying to get the activity over with as soon as possible. Instead, carve out at least 15 minutes every day, and spend time reading. After every few verses, stop and think about what you're reading.

To stay consistent in the Scriptures, develop a regular reading plan. I've used the one chapter approach for years. You read one chapter a day, and then spend time thinking about what you have read. The next day, you come back and read the next chapter. You can work your way through a particular book, and then move on to another book when all the chapters have been read.

At the same time, there will be times when you need to break away from your regular plan. If you're struggling with something in your life, don't be a slave to your reading plan. Stop your plan, and spend some time thinking about passages that will help you manage your circumstances. The habit of daily Scripture reading is one of the most important disciplines you can develop in life.

Several years ago, I stayed up late one night to watch one of the best national championship games ever. In men's NCAA basketball, it was one for the books. Kansas beat Memphis in overtime. Memphis would have probably won the game if they would have made their free throws. They were ice cold at the line, unable to make their free throw shots. Memphis had trouble all year long with their free throws. The coach tried to convince the media and his players that even though they didn't make their free throws throughout the year, things would be different in the final game. Yet, when it was crunch time, they didn't make the shots. There's a great parallel in the game of life. The habits you establish when everything is going right will see you through when everything is going wrong. The habits you establish during the mundane, routine days of your life will see you through when it's crunch time. Never forget that. If you will make it a priority to read the Bible on good days, it will be natural for you to read the Bible on bad days.

A word of warning is due here. Some Christians equate loving God exclusively with reading their Bibles. Their path to spiritual growth is one dimensional. If they have a "quiet time," they feel like that is all that is needed. It is important to remember that for much of church history, most people didn't have Bibles. Even if they did have Bibles, they wouldn't have been able to read them. Christians didn't have a daily personal devotional life as we think of it. Most of their devotional life was in more of a communal setting. The reading of Scripture and prayers took place in community worship. Christians couldn't have their own Bibles because there were no printing presses. However, discipleship was fully alive back then as well. We can take a lesson from history. Sometimes the best way to apply Scripture is within the context of a local worship community.[58]

Loving God with Simple Obedience

Jesus said, "If you love me, keep my commandments" (Jh 14:15). Jesus said your obedience is the true test of your love for Him. Thomas A Kempis said, "At the Day of Judgment we shall not be asked what we have read but what we have done." It's what we do that ultimately reveals our love for God. Sometimes, people assume Christians obey God out of duty or out of fear. They think, "If Christians don't obey, God may peer over heaven with His machine gun and pull the trigger." They think God is a cosmic zapper who enjoys zapping His children if they get out of line. The opposite is true. We obey God, not out of duty, obligation, or fear. We obey God out of love. When God commands us to care for the poor, orphan, and the widow; when He commands us to forgive; when He

---

58   Bill Hull, *The Complete Book of Discipleship* (Colorado Springs: NavPress, 2006) 91.

commands us to support Kingdom work through tithing; when God commands us to keep our lives holy and pure, we obey principally for the purpose of expressing our love to Him.

We obey God because we believe He knows what is best for us. When you think of God, I don't know what comes to your mind. One image that comes to mind when I think of God is a doctor. Jesus seemed to allude to this image when He said, "People who are well don't need a doctor; people who are sick are the ones who need a doctor." I think having an image of God as a doctor is a fitting image. A good doctor has one primary goal-your health. Doctors take the Hippocratic Oath, pledging they will do you no harm. Because my doctor is looking out for my health, I gladly turn to him for guidance.

One Saturday, I spent the day playing outside with my sons. Later that same evening, I discovered a tick was attached to my leg. No big deal. Being an outdoorsman, I've pulled plenty of ticks off my body. Several days later, my leg started to swell where I was bitten by the tick. By this time, a brown ring started to make a circle on my leg. I had never seen these symptoms from other tick bites, so I decided to call my doctor. My doctor suggested I come in for an office visit so he could look at the bite. After examining my leg, the doctor said "Clay, I'm not totally sure about this, but it looks like the beginning sign of Lymes Disease." The doctor said, in no uncertain terms, "We're not going to play around with this. I'm going to go ahead and put you on an antibiotic for 14 days." Lymes Disease can be very serious if left untreated, but my doctor assured me the antibiotic would take care of the problem. Do you want to guess if I listened to my doctor or ignored his advice? I didn't want Lymes Disease. That's why I did exactly what the doctor told me to do. I didn't disregard His instructions because I knew he had my best interests in mind.

This is exactly the same reason why we obey God. God has our best interests in mind. Like a doctor, He knows some things I don't know. God can see further down the road than I can see. The reason we should obey God is not because God enjoys dropping His heavenly sledgehammer on us when we don't obey. We follow His instructions and obey Him because we know He wants the best for our lives. Ignoring God and His truth keeps us from experiencing His best plan.

Shortly after I became a Christ-follower, one day I remember asking myself a rhetorical question. It was during a season when I was struggling with sexual temptation. I asked myself this question: "Clay, are you more likely to mess up your life, or is God more likely to mess up your life?" After about a nano second, I came up with the answer—I was more likely to mess up my life. Upholding the sexual ethics of Scripture was suddenly cast in a whole new light for me. Obeying God is the only way to experience His best plan for us.

As a spiritual leader, I often challenge people to do great things for God, but do you know what pleases God more than anything else? It is not the big, audacious things but the small things. When you obey God in the simplest and smallest parts of your life, it pleases God more than anything else you could do. When you take out the trash to serve your wife, God is thrilled. When you visit someone in a nursing center, it puts a smile on the face of God. When you surf the Internet without clicking on sites that would damage your soul, God is pleased. When you treat the custodian in your office with the same dignity as the CEO of your company, God is delighted. The Bible says, "It's better to obey than to sacrifice." God is saying nothing we do will ever replace our obedience. Giving God our time is good; sharing our resources to advance His Kingdom is also smart; making personal sacrifices to help the underprivileged is commendable, but it will never replace your desire to obey God.

Your Own Personal Pathway

There's no magic pill we can take to make us love God. There's also no set formula that works the same for everybody. God made each of us unique, and we have to develop a growth plan that will be unique to us. This is the way it works in marriage. Every married couple needs to cultivate and work on their relationship. One couple may like to have breakfast together once a week. Another couple may like to schedule regular date nights so that they can go out to dinner. Another couple may prefer to spend their time together after the kids go down at night. Other couples may do periodic weekends away without the kids. What it takes to enrich your marriage will look different from couple to couple, but every couple needs to work at enriching their marriage. What we need to ask is, "What works for us?"

The same is true for our spiritual lives. We all need to grow spiritually, but what helps us grow can look different from person to person. In a book called *Sacred Pathways*, Gary Thomas points out that there are certain pathways that help us experience the presence of God. These pathways are different for each person. For example, one of my pathways is intellectual. I can find myself drawn to God by reading a book. However, that same book may put my wife to sleep. At the same time, my wife can write in her journal, and she can feel close to God as she's writing about what's happening in her life. I would rather watch grass grow than write in a journal.

Some people connect with God through nature. They feel the closest to God when they are in nature. Some people are activists; they feel most alive when their charging ahead with a righteous cause. Some people feel closest to God when they're having fellowship with friends. For others, it could be music. Music is their sacred pathway and it helps them experience God in their lives. Don't feel guilty if your pathway is different from someone else's pathway. You may also find your pathway changes as you journey through different seasons of life.[59] I've heard busy mothers say they could pursue spiritual growth better before their kids came on the scene. In their minds, loving God was equivalent with a having a "quiet time." Reading passages of Scripture counted as a spiritual growth practice, but serving two little children didn't count for some strange reason. We can become so compartmentalized in the way we see spiritual growth. There's a real possibility that loving those two little children with a spirit of servant-hood may do more for those mothers than memorizing the book of Ephesians. Find your pathway for this season of your life. Take every opportunity to love God, even in the mundane parts of your life. The best way to get the most out of life is to spend it loving God.

---

59   Gary Thomas, *Sacred Pathways:Discover Your Soul's Path to God* (Grand Rapids: Zondervan, 2009).

CHAPTER 21

I Get To Go To School On Fridays

I LOVE FRIDAYS. MOST PEOPLE do. But I don't know anyone who loves Fridays more than my two sons. Friday happens to be my day off, and this means I get to take my sons to school and pick them up at the end of the day.

Because of their condition, Graham and Lawson are both in special education classes. Believe me: it is a big deal that Daddy gets to take them to school on Fridays. In fact, because of their cognitive challenges, they haven't quite mastered knowing the days of the week. I'm asked regularly throughout the week, "Daddy, is it Friday? Is today the day you get to take me to school?" What started out as only a big deal for my sons has now become a big deal for Dad. Let me share a handful of lessons I've learned about priorities by taking my kids to school on Friday.

Simple Things Really Matter

It has happened Friday after Friday. While walking down the sidewalk to reach their classrooms, I've glanced out of the corner of my eye to see two big smiles beaming back at me. It's hard to believe that something this simple, a walk less than forty yards, could create so much joy, but their smiles speak volumes. As parents, it's easy to believe that spectacular events are what create lasting memories for our kids. Disney World, Barnum and Bailey Circus, an evening out at Chuck E Cheese's are often thought to be the events that create the greatest memories for our kids. I'm a pro-spectacular event guy. If you can take your kids to Disney and do some unique events together, go for it. However, I'm convinced it's the simple, less glamorous things we do that will leave lasting memories for our families. It's the simple walk every Friday to the classroom, the simple bedtime story, the simple game of catch in the backyard, or the simple prayer at night that will be forever planted in your child's memory. Lawson, my youngest son, is enamored by the simple act of eating Mexican food. Every Thursday night, we have a running family tradition of eating at our favorite Mexican restaurant. Lawson has been known to wake me up at 6 a.m. and ask, "Daddy is today the day we get to go eat Mexican?" It's the simple things you do on a routine basis that make a huge difference.

This is why it's so important to give large chunks of time to our children. Added together, the simple things are like compounding interest. They add up to produce emotionally healthy children. Yet, it takes time to do the simple things on a regular basis. Children spell love T-I-M-E. When a child has an uninvolved parent, the message they receive is blistering, "You and the things you do are not important." It's a big time blow to their self-image.

When We Cheat Our Families

Dr. Armand Nicholi, a professor at Harvard University, found that American parents spend less time with their children than parents in any other country except Great Britain.[60] In our minds, we have to decide we are not going to cheat our families. What does cheating our family look like? It's being absent at critical times. It's not being at the soccer game, piano recital, or the school play. Cheating our families means we make empty promises that we never intend on keeping. It's saying, "Son, we'll go fishing on Saturday." But when Saturday arrives, it's time to catch up on paper work.

Cheating our families means we're always getting home late from the office. Will you ever have to work late? Of course you will if you're going to be a hard worker, but when there is a perpetual, habitual pattern of always getting home late, we are cheating our families. You know what I'm discovering? I could work 24 hours day and I would never complete my job. Your job is probably no different from my job. There's always one more customer to call on, one more patient to see, one more phone call to return, one more

---

60   The Washington Post, July 21, 1993, p. E 13.

project to oversee, or one more conference to attend. If we're going to place our families at the top of our priority list, we have to quit work before all the work is done.

One week I was preparing to speak on the Golden Rule. In Matthew 7:12, Jesus said, "Do unto others as you would have them do unto you." This statement has been called the most influential statement in the history of the human race. That's why it's called the Golden Rule. While I was preparing the message, I decided I was going to challenge our congregation to live the next 7 days with Golden Rule eyes. Here's the idea. In every interaction they had with another human being, I asked them to see life from the other person's perspective. I challenged them to ask this fog cutting question, "What would I want if I were in the other person's shoes?"

During the week I was preparing the message, I had my own Golden Rule moment. One evening, I came in from a hard day at work. I was tired, and my mind was exhausted. I wasn't looking for a Golden Rule moment; all I wanted was a La-Z-Boy moment. I wanted to sink into my La-Z-Boy chair and veg out for a while. After I arrived home, I went upstairs to change clothes. Lawson, my youngest son, followed me up the stairs. He said, "Daddy, can I go out and ride my big wheel?" At first, I said, "No, Lawson, I want us just to stay inside for a while." He persisted, "Please, Daddy, I really want to ride my big wheel." Remember, I had been working on the Golden Rule all week. It was hardly something I could just brush off. Suddenly, it dawned on me, "See this moment from Lawson's perspective."

In about five minutes we were outside, and I was watching Lawson ride his big wheel. While I was standing there, watching Lawson ride his big wheel, I had a sudden flashback. I could see myself riding my own big wheel. It seemed like yesterday when I was a child in my driveway, riding my big wheel. As I stood there, I had vivid memories of what my big wheel looked like. It was blue with big black wheels. I recalled the unique clicking sound it made when I was making a turn around a corner. That day, it rained and it left some big mud puddles out in the cul-de-sac. Lawson was having the time of his life, driving his big wheel through all the mud puddles. I thought about how I used to love to drive through mud puddles on my big wheel. While I stood at the end of my driveway, watching Lawson, I thought about just how fast life races by. It was more than a big wheel moment for me—it was a Golden Rule moment. I saw life from Lawson's perspective, and as I laid down that night to go to sleep, I was so thankful I did. When we stop and see life from our child's perspective, it reinforces how precious our time with them can be.

Charles Adams, a political figure who lived in the 1800s, was a busy man. Even though he kept a hectic schedule, he never missed a day writing in his diary. One day he made this entry in his diary, "Went fishing with my son today—a wasted day." His son, Brook Adams, also kept a diary. It's still in existence today. On the same day his father wrote in his diary, Brook also made an entry in his diary. This is what he wrote, "Went fishing with my dad today--it was the greatest day of my life!" Nothing is as important as being there for our kids.

The Greatest Gift: A Strong Marriage

One of the most important ways you can build a winning family is by making your marriage a priority. A good marriage is also one of the greatest gifts you can give your children. It's not designer clothes, the latest gadget, a brand new car, or even an Ivy League education. The greatest thing a father can do for his children is to love their mother. And the greatest thing a mother can do for her children is to love their father. The health of your marriage determines the environment in which your kids grow up. More than anything else, our marriages set the temperature and atmosphere for the home. More than one couple has said to me, "Thank goodness our children don't know how unhappy we are." I have to restrain my response. In my mind, I'm thinking, "Dream on. Your kids live with you. They have front row seats. They know if you have a bad marriage."

There's not a good time to have a bad marriage, but the worst time to have a bad marriage is when we have children in the home. Children are going to follow our example. Do you know how your sons are going to treat their wives? In the same way you treat your wife. Do you know how your daughters are going to treat their husbands? For the most part, exactly the same way you treat your husband. When our kids are in the home, we are modeling how to do marriage and family.

When children come into the picture, we get really busy. Children take up an extraordinary amount of our time. Usually, we end up giving leftovers to our spouse. We think we are doing our children a favor when we give our attention exclusively to them. In reality, if we don't take time to work on our marriages, our children will suffer. Our marriage sets the temperature for the rest of our family relationships.

On Friday, after I take my boys to school, I spend the day with my wife. We have a standing breakfast each Friday where we can catch up about life. It's not that we always have deep conversations over breakfast, but we try to give each other undivided attention. After breakfast, we often take a walk at a park and hold hands while we're walking. It's our special time without the kids. I normally don't take my cell phone with me on Fridays. I don't want to be distracted with calls and emails. Some couples enjoy date nights, or weekends away. Each couple has to determine what works best for their family. Much like the simple things you do with your kids, it's the simple things you do with your spouse that will build a fulfilling marriage.

Begin the Day With Hugs and Kisses

For several years, Graham had a classmate named Tariq. The moment we walked through the door, Tariq, who has Down syndrome, was there to give both of my sons a hug. After the hug, Graham typically rubbed Tariq's bald head, and then he gave Tariq a big kiss on the cheek. It's a sight that would melt the hardest heart. I can never recall a Friday when Tariq failed to give out his big hug. I can never recall a Friday when Graham failed to kiss Tariq in return. And I can never recall a Friday, after watching this event take place, when dad didn't walk away without a lump in his throat. In their special education classrooms, the kids begin the day with hugs and kisses.

Psychological research tells us we should work hard on making the first five minutes of the day and the last five minutes of the day positive. How we interact with our children in the first minutes of the day will more than likely set the stage for the rest of the day. Likewise, how we interact with our kids in the last five minutes of the day, just before they go to bed, will probably be what stays on their minds throughout the night. Before marching off to school, try giving your children a hug. At the end of the day, do something affirming that will communicate love to your children. I started a bed time routine several years ago. I tuck each of my boys in bed, have prayer, and then I say, "Of all the little boys in the world, I wonder why God gave me the two best ones?" My goal is to make the last five minutes of the day special and affirming.

Special needs children often give out loads of love with their affection. Recently, we were eating out at our favorite Mexican restaurant on a Thursday night. As we were leaving the restaurant, my sons spotted one of their friends from school. Rosa, who has Down syndrome, was thrilled to see my sons. She was so excited she got up from her table and gave both of my boys a hug.

Each day when I arrive home from work, Graham is at the door, with a smile on his face, ready to give me a hug. Trust me— it's not the typical hug. Graham hugs like a linebacker. He puts a new meaning to the term "bear hug." This is his way of showing me he's glad I'm home for the night.

Sometimes, after I've been home for a while, I have to go back outside and get something I left in my car. Graham often forgets that he has already greeted me. He will stand at the door once again, with a glowing smile on his face. When I walk through the door, he gives me another one of his trademark linebacker hugs.

Family experts say that children who are hugged, held, touched, and caressed develop healthier emotional lives than those who go without any physical contact. Your skin and deeper tissues contain millions of touch receptors. The receptors communicate to your entire nervous system. Touch communicates feelings of well being. It communicates that you are important, loved, and valued. When a newborn baby or a small child is upset, sometimes the only thing that can bring comfort to the child is a mother's or father's touch.

I keep coming back again and again to one passage in the Bible which has revolutionized my life. It's the story of Jesus touching the leper. It was against the Jewish law to touch a leper. Can you imagine how long it had been since someone had last touched this man? This is why lepers had to shout "Unclean, Unclean" everywhere they went. It was supposed to keep everybody at a distance. Imagine how long it had been since he held his wife's hand? Imagine how long it had been since he was hugged by his children? His children couldn't come and take his hand and say, "Daddy, let's take a walk." It was against the law to touch their dad's hand; he was a leper.

Leprosy was physically painful, but the worst part about leprosy was the emotional pain inflicted on its victims. The isolation and loneliness left you feeling rejected and hopeless. Imagine the emotional state of this leper when Christ first encountered him? He hadn't been touched in years. Though it was against the law, Jesus did the unthinkable. Jesus stretched out His hand and touched the leper. Remember, Jesus didn't have to touch him in order to heal him. Jesus could have healed him by speaking a simple word. The New Testament records multiple occasions when Jesus spoke a single word and someone was healed. But that's not the route Jesus takes with the leper. He leaves everyone stunned by reaching out and touching him. It brings up an obvious question? If Jesus didn't have to touch him to heal him, why did He touch him? For one profound reason--touch communicates love. Jesus often touched people who no one else would touch. He wanted them to know they were loved. Touch communicates love, and that's especially true when you think about a parent's affection toward a child.

Based on the law of averages, I know what some of you are thinking, "I'm just not an affectionate person. I'm not the huggy, touchy type. I didn't grow up in a home where we hugged and touched each other a lot." I understand your home environment probably shaped how much affection you give out. Yet, if we want our children to be emotionally healthy and experience our love, we will have to break out of our comfort zones. We need to learn to practice appropriate affection. Everything from a kiss on the cheek, to a hug, an arm around the shoulder, a pat on the back, or even playful wrestling will communicate love to your kids.

I know showing affection becomes more complicated as children grow into their teenage years. I've known fathers who do a good job at showing affection to their daughters when they are young, but then puberty hits, and many dads pull away. They think, "My little girl is no longer little. She's starting to mature, so I better not show her any affection." Just about the time dad pulls away, guess who shows up at his doorstep? Hormone Harry. Hormone Harry is more than willing to give your daughter some affection. Your daughter will look for affection from someone. What's important is to make sure she gets it from you and not from some other boy.

I also know it's easier to give affection to younger children. When our children become teenagers, especially boys, they tend to resist affection. They think touching them will hijack their coolness, so we have to be creative. Arm wrestle with them. If you have to, come up behind them and pop them in the back of the head. Grab their biceps and say, "You don't have anything on your dad." We may have to get creative, but it is vitally important to touch our children.

Image Doesn't Matter

Once I get my sons in their classroom, I help Graham into a special chair which gives him added support. I also make sure his helmet is close by for his teachers to use. For several years now, Graham has had to wear a helmet at school to protect him from any potential falls. With an average of 3-4 seizures a day, the risk is too great for potential head injuries. When Graham had to start wearing a helmet to school, it really bothered me. I wondered how this would make him feel. Though it bothered me, it didn't bother Graham. Like most special needs children and adults, Graham isn't concerned about his image. He's not trying to impress anyone and is quite happy just being himself.

I have a confession to make. I used to be an image maniac. I was constantly practicing what I call "image management." When we manage our images, we're constantly thinking about how we appear to other people. When we're practicing image management, we're trying to control what other people think about us. We want everyone to think that we're really smart, clever, and successful so we manage our image to build ourselves up in their eyes. However, in my sons' classroom, no one is worried about their image. No one is striking a pose. This is why children with disabilities are often the happiest. They're not trying to impress anyone.

Managing your integrity is far more important than managing your image. This is why our number one responsibility as a parent is to teach our children character. Don't let anyone mislead you—it's a difficult job. Frankly, it's much easier to stay on the job, or out on the golf course than to go home and teach character. Teaching our kids character is something we should begin as soon as possible. When children are young, their curiosity is at an all time high. This is why they say "Why?" five thousand times in a day. They are eager to learn. At a young age, their memory is also great. Children are learning foreign languages when they're six and seven years old. When a child is young, the trust factor is also at its highest peak. They, by default, trust you to give them guidance.

Let me rattle off a few character traits. While you're reading the list, ask yourself, "Who is teaching these virtues to my son or daughter?" Here's the list: contentment, courage, courtesy, discernment, fairness, friendliness, generosity, gentleness, honesty, humility, kindness, obedience, patience, persistence, self-control, tactfulness, thankfulness, thriftiness, wisdom, and zeal. Where are your children going to learn these character traits from? When it comes to character development, God intended us to be their primary teacher.

The best way to teach character is by modeling it. Nothing can replace your personal example. Writer Dan Clark tells about the day he learned an important lesson about character from his father. When he was a small child, his dad took him to the circus. He and his dad were waiting in line to buy tickets to get in the circus. Standing in front of them was another family. The mom and dad were holding hands, and they had eight children standing in line with them. The kids were so excited about getting to go to the circus. You could tell it was going to be a real treat for the family. They were modestly dressed and probably didn't have a lot of money.

When the couple came up to the counter, the attendant asked how many tickets they needed. The father spoke up and said, "I'll need eight tickets for my children, and two adult tickets for my wife and me." When the attendant quoted the price back to him, he leaned forward and quietly said, "What did you say?" She quoted the price back to him again. His entire countenance changed. His head dropped. His eyes filled with tears. You could tell the father looked crushed. Obviously, he didn't have enough money to get into the circus.

Dan Clark says his dad was watching all of this happen in front of them. Suddenly, he watched his dad pull a $20.00 bill out of his wallet and drop it on the ground. He tapped the father in front him on the shoulder. "Sir, excuse me," he said, pointing to the $20.00 dollar bill lying on the ground, "I think you just dropped this out of your pocket." The father looked at him, knowing what Dan's father had just done for him. Wiping a tear off his face, he said, "Thank you sir, Thank you."

What happened next is what Dan remembers most about that day. Right after the family in front of them received their tickets, Dan and his father, got out of line, walked back to their car, and drove home. They drove home instead of going to the circus. They had no choice because after his father gave away his money, they didn't have enough money to buy tickets themselves. Dan Clark said it didn't matter. What he learned that day from his father was far better than anything that he could get from the circus.[61]

Be Real with Your Kids

What we model for our kids is far greater than what we tell them. What our kids really want to tell us sometimes is, "I can't hear what you're

61   Jack Canfield and Mark Victor Hansen, *A 2nd Helping of Chicken Soup for the Soul* (HCI, 1994).

saying because what you're doing is so loud." Sometimes our example drowns out what we're trying to teach them.

We forget our kids really are watching us. Several years ago, our family was riding in the car together, and a lady pulled out in front of me. I slammed on the brakes and blurted out, "Come on lady!" I know some of you are way too spiritual to have said something like that, but that's what I said. Several weeks later, we were riding along in the car and I had to slam on my brakes again. This time I didn't say anything, but suddenly from the back seat of the car I heard Lawson say, "Come on lady!" I couldn't believe it. I thought, "Where did he get that from?" Then I realized, "Oh, I know where he learned that from—his dad, the one who is always self-controlled."

Just because you are committed to be a consistent role model doesn't mean you will be perfect. Parents don't need to be perfect; we just need to be honest. When we are inconsistent, we have to be humble enough to say, "I blew it! I'm sorry." Remember our kids have box seats. They are on the front row. They know when we blow it. They know when we speak unloving to them and our spouses. They see our sour and selfish attitudes. Nothing will turn kids off faster, especially teenagers, than when mom and dad act as if they do everything perfectly.

One of the most misunderstood passages in the Bible comes from the book of Proverbs. Proverbs 22:6 says, "Train up a child in the way he should go and when he is old, he will not depart from it." Let me try to clear up some of the muddy water that surrounds this verse. First, this verse is not a guarantee your children are going to turn out just the way you want them to. The book of Proverbs is a book of wise sayings. The principles outlined in Proverbs are generally true, but they are not blanket promises to claim. As a general rule, parents who train up their kids using biblical principles see a positive effect on the character of their kids. However, this is not a guarantee that your children will follow your example.

I have known many fine Christian parents who lived Christ-honoring lives. They taught their kids the truth and gave them a biblical worldview. They provided a consistent model for their children to follow, but their kids grew up and rebelled. Some of them have abandoned the faith of their parents. I have watched some of these parents beat themselves up, and it usually revolves around this one verse from Proverbs. They reason, "Doesn't the Bible say if I train up my child in the Lord, my child won't depart from it? Undoubtedly, I didn't do a good job training them because they departed from the faith." This line of reasoning leads to false guilt.

Your success in parenting isn't measured by what your child does. Your success as a parent is defined by what you do. If you live out a consistent Christian life, upholding integrity, love, and a nourishing environment for your kids, you will be successful. The outcome of a child is not a reliable gauge of your job as a parent. Your children will eventually reach a time of accountability; they are accountable to God for their own decisions. Much like the prodigal son, many of these children return to the faith. After logging in some time in the pig pin, they realize God's plan is much better.

Fridays

Each week I can't wait until Friday arrives. It's a special day for me, a day I'm glad is on the calendar every week. As a pastor, I get a reprieve and have an opportunity to detox from my grinding schedule. I get to have breakfast with my wife, enjoy a walk in the park, and catch up with her about what's going on in our corner of the world. I usually get to enjoy sipping on a cup of coffee while reading one of my favorite books. But all of this pales in comparison to what I enjoy most. I get to go to school on Fridays.